Forgotten Casualties

World War II: The Global, Human, and Ethical Dimension

G. Kurt Piehler, *series editor*

Forgotten Casualties

Downed American Airmen and Axis Violence in World War II

Kevin T Hall

Fordham University Press | New York   2023

Copyright © 2023 Fordham University Press

All rights reserved. No part of this publication may be reproduced, stored in a retrieval system, or transmitted in any form or by any means—electronic, mechanical, photocopy, recording, or any other—except for brief quotations in printed reviews, without the prior permission of the publisher.

Fordham University Press has no responsibility for the persistence or accuracy of URLs for external or third-party Internet websites referred to in this publication and does not guarantee that any content on such websites is, or will remain, accurate or appropriate.

Fordham University Press also publishes its books in a variety of electronic formats. Some content that appears in print may not be available in electronic books.

Visit us online at www.fordhampress.com.

Library of Congress Cataloging-in-Publication Data available online at https://catalog.loc.gov.

Printed in the United States of America

25 24 23   5 4 3 2 1

First edition

I thank my family for their unwavering support. My wife, Lena; my mother, Lyn;
and my grandmother Elizabeth deserve special recognition
for their immeasurable encouragement and love.
I dedicate this book to them.

Contents

List of Abbreviations		ix
Introduction		1
1.	**Axis Policies to Combat Downed Enemy Flyers**	29
2.	**War Crimes Narratives: Pacific and Southeast Asia**	63
3.	**War Crimes Narratives: Europe**	104
4.	**US Postwar Flyer Trials**	129
	Conclusion	143
	Appendix: Index of Analyzed US Flyer Trials Held in the Pacific and Southeast Asia	151
	Acknowledgments	243
	Notes	245
	Bibliography	271
	Index	303

Abbreviations

AA	Auswärtiges Amt; Foreign Ministry
AGAS	US Navy and Air-Ground Aid Section
Alte Kämpfer	lit. "old fighter"; refers to the members of the Nazi Party who joined before 1930
Auswertestelle West	Evaluation Center West
BDM	Bund Deutscher Mädel; League of German Girls
BdS	Befehlshaber der Sicherheitspolizei und des SD
Blockleiter	block leader (Nazi Party political rank)
DAF	Deutsche Arbeitsfront; German Labor Front
DPAA	Defense Prisoner of War/Missing in Action Accounting Agency
DPMO	US Department of Defense Department's Prisoner of War Missing Personnel Office
Dulag Luft	Durchgangslager der Luftwaffe; transit camp for Air Force Personnel
E&E Reports	Escape and Evasion Reports
Einsatzgruppen	lit. "task forces"; SS paramilitary groups responsible for mass killings
Gauleiter	regional leader (Nazi Party political rank)
Gestapo	Geheime Staatspolizei; Secret State Police
HJ	Hitlerjugend; Hitler Youth
IMT	International Military Tribunal
IMTFE	International Military Tribunal Far East
JAG Corps	Judge Advocate General's Corps
Jagdkommandos	Search and Pursuit Units
J-PAC	Joint POW/MIA Account Command
KdS	Kommandeure der Sicherheitspolizei und des SD
Kempeitai	Japanese military police
KIA	killed in action
Kindermörder	child murderers
Kreisleiter	county leader (Nazi Party political rank)

x | Abbreviations

KriPo	Kriminalpolizei; Criminal Police
Landwacht	Rural Police
Luftbanditen	Bandits of the Sky
Luftwaffe	German Air Force
Lynchjustiz	Lynch Justice
MACR	Missing Air Crew Reports
Maquis	French Resistance
MI9	British military intelligence, Section 9
MIA	missing in action
Milice	Vichy French collaborators
MIS-X	Military Intelligence Service
Mitläuferfabrik	lit., "factory to produce followers"
NSDAP	Nationalsozialistische Deutsche Arbeitspartei; National Socialist German Workers' Party (Nazi Party)
NSKK	Nationalsozialistisches Kraftfahrkorps; National Socialist Motor Corps
NWCO	National War Crimes Office
OKL	Oberkommando der Luftwaffe; High Command of the Air Force
OKW	Oberkommando der Wehrmacht; High Command of the Armed Forces
ONI	Office of Naval Intelligence
OrPo	Ordnungspolizei; Order Police
Ortsgruppenleiter	group leader (Nazi Party political rank)
OSS	Office of Strategic Services
POW	prisoner of war
RAD	Reichsarbeitsdienst; Reich Labor Force
RAF	Royal Air Force
RSHA	Reichssicherheitshauptamt; Reich Main Security Office
SA	Sturmabteilungen; Storm Troopers
SACO	Sino-American Cooperative Organization
SD	Sicherheitsdienst; Security Service (of the SS)
Selbstjustiz	self-justice
SHAEF	Supreme Headquarters Allied Expedition Force
SiPo	Sicherheitspolizei; Security Police
SOE	Special Operations Executive
Sonderbehandlung	lit. "special treatment"; euphemism for mass murder used by Nazi functionaries and the SS

Abbreviations | xi

Sonderkommando	Special Unit of the SS
SS	Schutzstaffeln; lit., "protection squadron"
Stalag Luft	Stammlager der Luftwaffe; Prisoner of War Camp for Air Force Personnel
Terrorflieger	lit., "terror flyer" (also called: *Luftgangster* [gangsters of the sky] and *Kindermörder* [child murderers])
USAAF	United States Army Air Forces
Vergeltungswaffen	lit., "revenge weapons"
Volksgemeinschaft	lit., "people's community"
Volksjustiz	peoples' justice
Volkssturm	home guard
WCIT	War Crime Investigation Teams
Wehrkreis	Military district

Forgotten Casualties

Introduction

On August 8, 1945—two days after the atomic bomb was dropped on Hiroshima—the last B-29 Superfortress (44-87664) was shot down during World War II. Nicknamed "Thunderbird," the aircraft was hit by flak during a bombing raid against the Nakajima aircraft factory near Tokyo, Japan. Severely damaged, the aircraft became uncontrollable. It rolled upside down and a few moments later exploded in mid-air, killing instantly ten of the twelve crewmembers (figures 1 and 2). Two crewmen, M/Sgt Lester C. Morris and S/Sgt Serafino Morone, managed to bail out of the plummeting aircraft and parachute safely to the ground, landing near Tachikawa, located less than twenty-five miles west of Tokyo.

Morris and Morone were immediately captured and taken to the Tachikawa Kempeitai (military police) headquarters; however, upon their arrival, a large mob of civilians—reportedly numbering four to five hundred people—confronted them. The mob was enraged and sought retribution for the devastation wreaked by the air raids. Although guards displayed Morris and Morone before the crowd for roughly half an hour, the flyers were not mistreated and were eventually confined in a cell at the Kempeitai headquarters overnight. As Morris recounted after the war, the interrogations

> were anything but gentle. Despite the fact that I was already in bad shape when captured, they beat me during questioning so much that I lost consciousness three times. Each time they brought me back to consciousness with buckets of cold water and continued the treatment. I believe they must have done worse to Morone because of the secret radio codes he may have possessed.

For nearly two days after his capture, Morris was not fully conscious due to a head injury; however, this possibly saved his life.[1]

The following day, Maj Yajima Shichisaburo, head of the local Kempeitai, decided it would be best to put a flyer (Morone) on display since many people were curious to see the enemy. Yajima further explained that this would be

2 | Introduction

a way to bolster the spirit among the populace to continue the war. Kempeitai officials arranged to use the grounds of a nearby school, as it provided more room to accommodate the large crowd that was expected. Fully aware that this incident would result in the death of Morone, officials obtained prior permission from the city council to dispose of his remains in the public cemetery. Around 1:00 p.m. that afternoon, three guards escorted Morone to the schoolyard, followed by a large crowd that had been notified in advance of the opportunity for revenge. Morone was reportedly only wearing pants, which were torn below the knees, and he was blindfolded with his hands tied together.[2]

Figure 1. Crew of the "Thunderbird"
Front Row (left to right): M/Sgt Lester C. Morris, S/Sgt Serafino Morone, T/Sgt Harold P. Brennan, S/Sgt James F. Payne, S/Sgt Mark E. Miller, Cpl Raymond G. Cagle.
Back Row (left to right): Capt James L. Shumate, 1st Lt Thomas O. Marshall, 1st Lt Nicholas Poulos, 1st Lt Norman M. Jones, 1st Lt Henry Yassas. (Not pictured: Maj Bob Anthony—observer during this mission). "Serafino Morone," accessed December 18, 2020, https://www.findagrave.com/memorial/116119571/serafino-morone#.

Once at the schoolyard, guards tied Morone to a post with his back toward the crowd. The guards displayed a sign that read: "This flyer was one of the persons who bombed Tokyo, and because of the bombings, we have lost our loved ones, brothers and sisters, and you will wreak your revenge upon this person." A guard, W/O Seki Noboru, then addressed the crowd, stating, "Ladies and gentlemen, you will now be permitted to beat this B-29 flyer. However, each one will only strike the prisoner one time." Although several members of the crowd came prepared with large clubs, guards insisted they use a split bamboo stick, to prolong the torture and prevent immediate death.[3]

As the beating began, the crowd allegedly grew to well over one thousand people, several hundred of whom, including women, lined up to beat Morone. The public display lasted nearly two hours and was only stopped due to an air raid alarm. Clearly suffering in pain throughout the ordeal, witnesses reported that Morone was delirious and that guards gave him water now and then to revive him, only to continue the beating. As the crowd eventually dispersed, guards placed Morone on a stretcher, as he was far too weak to walk, and carried him to the cemetery, where his grave had already been dug. They placed Morone next to the grave and an officer approached, drew his sword, and decapitated him. Morone's body fell into the grave, which was quickly filled in. Afterward, Kempeitai officials requested that a doctor, Nakayama, fill out a death certificate that stated Morone died from injuries sustained in the crash of his aircraft and was burned completely. By the end of September, several weeks after the war ended, Seki ordered soldiers to disinter Morone's body and cremate his remains to cover up his murder. Following this, Morone's remains were placed in a box and reinterred in the same grave.[4] After the war, US war crimes investigators discovered Morone's remains and pieced together the circumstances surrounding his death. A US war crimes tribunal held Yajima accountable for his role in Morone's death and sentenced him to life imprisonment while Seki received twenty years' confinement. As for Morris, he was transferred (for unknown reasons) a short time after Morone's execution to the Kempeitai headquarters in Tokyo, where he experienced severe torture during interrogations before he was sent to Omori POW camp. He did, however, manage to survive the war.

A similar incident occurred roughly a year earlier in Gross-Gerau, Germany. The crew of a B-17 Flying Fortress (42-97946), nicknamed "Hard to Get," was shot down by flak during a bombing mission over Gelsenkirchen on August 26, 1944. Five crewmembers, 1st Lt Dean C. Allen, 2nd Lt Charles H. Evans Jr., S/Sgt James R. Carey, S/Sgt Richard C. Huebotter, and

Figure 2. Final moments of the "Thunderbird." "Serafino Morone," accessed December 18, 2020, https://www.findagrave.com/memorial/116119571/serafino-morone#.

T/Sgt Harvey J. Purkey, safely parachuted from their damaged aircraft and landed in the vicinity of Rheinberg—located roughly fifteen miles north of Duisburg (figure 3). The flyers were apprehended immediately and transported to a nearby Luftwaffe airfield, where they were held in custody overnight. The following day, guards transported the airmen by train to Dulag Luft (the main Luftwaffe interrogation center) in Oberursel for questioning. During their journey, both Evans and Purkey managed to escape from the train near the village of Trebur after the train had stopped at a small station and their guards were sleeping. They were, however, quickly captured, and guards escorted them to the nearby town of Gross-Gerau. This town is located four miles east of Trebur and roughly eight miles south of Rüsselsheim—the location where the most infamous case of *Lynchjustiz* (lynch justice) in Europe had occurred just three days prior.[5]

Witnesses reported that locals were in a "state of great excitement," as they had experienced a heavy air raid a few days prior that killed twenty-seven civilians—mostly women and children. Unfortunately for the flyers, the funeral for these individuals killed in the air raid was scheduled for this ill-fated day. The timing of the funeral with the airmen's presence, in addition to the Nazi regime's support, and often promotion, of German citizens desire to seek revenge, surely gave the flyers reason to worry for their safety.[6]

Figure 3. Crew of "Hard to Get"
Front Row (left to right): 1st Lt Dean Allen, 1st Lt Charles Rapp, Jr, 2nd Lt Charles Donahue (replaced by 2nd Lt Charles H. Evans, Jr.), 1st Lt Michael Vlahos
Back Row (left to right): T/Sgt Harvey Purkey, T/Sgt Robert Newsbigle, S/Sgt Eugene LeVeque, S/Sgt Richard Huebotter, S/Sgt Charles Reinartsen (not aboard for mission), S/Sgt James Carey SOURCE: "T/Sgt Harvey J. Purkey, Jr.," accessed March 17, 2022, https://www.findagrave.com/memorial/49302107/harvey-jenning-purkey.

The enraged mob of civilians quickly grew to several hundred people who savagely beat the airmen unconscious. Members of the mob punched and kicked the flyers and used boards, metal pipes, bricks, and virtually anything at hand. One woman admittedly used her shoe to beat an airman, directing the blows at his eyes. The spontaneity and the ferocity of the violence was alarming. A short time later, two police officers and the *Kreisleiter* arrived after word spread quickly throughout the town. The officials quickly agreed that the flyers "should be given to the people." Once the police chief arrived at the scene, he exclaimed to his two subordinates: "Why haven't they been beaten to death?!" The police chief then ordered the flyers to be taken to the courtyard of the city hall. All the while, irate civilians continued to mercilessly beat the helpless airmen. Upon arriving at the city hall, the police chief barred the mob from entering and ordered all windows and doors facing the courtyard to be closed. Preventing any onlookers from seeing the imminent and violent end to Purkey and Evans (figure 4), two men beat the flyers to death with iron bars. Their remains were then buried in the local cemetery.[7]

After the war, three war crimes trials convened and seven Germans were prosecuted for their role in mistreating and executing Purkey and Evans. The police chief and one of the men who wielded the iron bars were sentenced to death and executed on April 1, 1946. Four civilians, including two women, were tried for their participation in the mob violence. Three, including the two women, were sentenced to less than two years imprisonment while the fourth individual received a fifteen-year sentence. However, the

Figure 4. Memorial Plaque for Harvey J. Purkey and Charles H. Evans Jr. in Gross-Gerau. In August 2018, nearly seventy-five years after the murders, this memorial plaque was dedicated to Evans and Purkey in the local museum in Gross-Gerau. The plaque states: "We commemorate the American Air Force soldiers who died on August 29, 1944, here in the courtyard of the former town hall after an angry crowd had driven the US soldiers through the streets. We remember the occurrence with disgust. May the death of the American soldiers be a reminder for humanity, reconciliation, and peace." Courtesy of Cornelia Benz, Press- und Öffentlichkeitsarbeit, Kreisstadt Gross-Gerau.

latter verdict was eventually reduced, and the man was released by December 1952 after repeated appeals for review and clemency.

Thousands of instances such as these occurred throughout the duration and geographic scope of World War II; however, the mistreatment committed against downed airmen has been largely forgotten, overshadowed by the numerous Axis atrocities. The perpetrators were not solely fanatical soldiers or Nazi zealots but also included "ordinary" civilians. A combination of stimuli influenced and triggered the active involvement of the embattled populace, for example, the death and devastation inflicted by the war, the lack of security and despair caused by aerial attacks, the longing for retribution, extreme nationalism, as well as Axis propaganda (particularly in Nazi Germany) that approved *Lynchjustiz* (lynch justice) and encouraged citizens to take matters into their own hands. These experiences affected the perception of the enemy and the interpretation of (and response to) fighting tactics as well as the treatment of prisoners of war (POWs). As the war dragged on, the militarization of civilians, and especially Axis citizens' increased willingness to mistreat captured flyers, became an additional byproduct of this total war and represented a further example that pushed the moral and ethical boundaries to new extremes.

Dimensions of Axis Violence

Before the war ended the Allies initiated investigations into Axis war crimes, such as the mistreatment committed against downed airmen. The inquiries eventually supported the postwar trials held at Nuremberg, Tokyo, Dachau, Yokohama, and numerous other locations scattered throughout Europe and the Pacific. These trials offered an opportunity, albeit brief, for the world to examine the horrors and atrocities committed during the conflict; however, questionable actions committed by Allied troops, such as bombing urban centers, were largely suppressed or at the very least defended as an appropriate response to Axis brutality in the Allies' pursuit of safeguarding US President Franklin Delano Roosevelt's Four Freedoms: freedom of speech, freedom of religion, freedom from want, and freedom from fear.[8]

Especially for the countless families, whose sons, brothers, uncles, and fathers were killed during the war or who were still listed as missing, the postwar trials afforded an attempt to begin to find closure; however, families (and scholars) continue to try and comprehend the dimensions, stimuli, and justifications behind Axis violence. The unknown circumstances surrounding the grueling final moments of these young men's lives and the whereabouts of their remains caused the anguish of families to linger and had a lasting impact on generations thereafter.

8 | Introduction

The sheer scale of death and destruction of World War II reached extremes that remain hard to comprehend. In addition to the approximately six million Jewish victims of the Holocaust and the millions more who were persecuted based on their ethnicity, religion, political beliefs, or sexual orientation, millions of POWs (largely Soviets) died from starvation, exposure, disease, and execution. Estimates exceed twenty million military deaths for all sides during the conflict, and assessments of civilian deaths are more than twice as high. While the overwhelming majority of these casualties were victims of Axis armed forces, the Allied aerial offensives in both Europe and the Pacific resulted in approximately one million civilian deaths and a similar number of wounded. However, roughly 15 percent of these deaths belonged to the peoples being liberated, resulting, as Richard Overy explains, in "another layer of complexity to any legal or ethical judgments on the failure to respect civilian immunity."[9]

During the war, over 120,000 American airmen and a comparable number of Royal Air Force (RAF) flyers were shot down over Axis territory. While most of these men survived the often-horrible circumstances, a significant share failed to return home. Even for those lucky enough to survive, many returned home physically and mentally scarred. By the end of the war, roughly seventy-nine thousand US servicemen remained missing in action (MIA). Despite the determined effort of the US military and government to recover and identify these men, today over seventy-two thousand Americans are still unaccounted for from World War II. A large share of these is considered unrecoverable due in part, to their location, the uncertain circumstances surrounding death, or a lack of necessary evidence. Nevertheless, the US Defense POW/MIA Accounting Agency (DPAA) diligently continues to search, recover, identify, and repatriate missing servicemen and women lost during wartime conflicts.[10]

The crimes committed against Allied POWs withdrew relatively quickly from public discourse as the Cold War burgeoned and attention shifted to the next enemy (communism) and the new international conflict on the Korean Peninsula. Even today, the hearings of lower-level perpetrators and the crimes they committed generally remain overshadowed by the notorious Nuremberg and Tokyo trials of high-ranking Axis officials. Further, the European proceedings continue to dominate the overall discourse on postwar trials. Until now, very few studies have offered a comparison of the violence committed against downed airmen, the relationship between centralized authority and civilian action, and the overall assessment of downed flyers' experiences in the European, Mediterranean, Pacific, and Asian theaters of war. When scholars do offer a comparison, the increased mortality rate

Introduction | 9

among POWs held by the Japanese is generally the extent of the evaluation. For example, scholars estimate that up to 35 percent of the American POWs held by Japan died in captivity compared to roughly one percent of those held in German camps. This drastic disparity in deaths was due to a culmination of factors that included the use of POWs as forced laborers, often locating POW camps near military targets, the general displeasure of taking prisoners, transporting thousands of POWs on unmarked vessels (known as "Hell ships," many of which were mistakenly targeted by US submarines), and the widespread harsh conditions (shortage of food, clothing, and medical supplies) experienced, even among the Japanese, as the country was systematically destroyed.[11]

Studies focusing on captured airmen also often emphasize flyers' experiences in POW camps (and occasionally their attempts to evade and escape).[12] However, their experience during the transitional stage between being shot down and being confined in a POW camp, which could last mere minutes, months or even years—depending on weather and terrain, the ability to evade capture and receive assistance from locals, as well as the conviction of the captors—remains relatively overlooked.[13] This phase is significant, however, to understand the threats downed airmen faced, the ambiguity of prisoners' (especially airmen's) status, and the overall relationship between the air war and state-sponsored violence.

The latest investigations that focus on the mistreatment of flyers include Georg Hoffmann's innovative study, *Fliegerlynchjustiz* (flyer lynch justice), along with my own analysis, *Terror Flyers*, which concentrate on the violence committed against American airmen in Austria and Hungary as well as Nazi Germany, respectively. Combined, these studies reveal that thousands of Allied airmen were likely victims of Axis violence in Europe during World War II. In terms of the mistreatment committed against flyers shot down over the Japanese home islands and the surrounding ocean during the war, Fukubayashi Toru's examination concludes that roughly half of the nearly six hundred captured Allied flyers did not survive; they were either executed, poisoned, vivisected, or died from their wounds, diseases, or friendly fire (including the atomic bomb dropped on Hiroshima).[14] However, these figures are only preliminary indicators of Axis terror inflicted upon downed Allied airmen, as the dark figure is surely large.

Legal Shortcomings in Curbing Violence

The escalation of mistreating downed flyers had roots in experiences gained and tactics implemented during prior conflicts, for example, World War I (1914–1919), the Russian Civil War (1918–1921), RAF's so-called "aerial

10 | Introduction

policing" tactics during the Iraqi revolt of 1920, Japan's violent conquest of China during the 1920s–1930s, the Second Italo-Ethiopian War (1935–1937), and the Spanish Civil War (1936–1939). What can be viewed as testing grounds for World War II, these intensifying conflicts, especially during the interwar years, resulted in the increased militarization of societies as well as the development and implementation of new weapons and tactics—the most innovative of which was strategic aerial bombardment. Nations expected not only a greater involvement of their own population but also increasingly confronted enemy citizens (both combatant and noncombatant) in violent new ways.[15]

While the mistreatment of captured flyers reached unparalleled extremes in World War II, violence inflicted on downed airmen was not a new phenomenon. In fact, one of the earliest known instances occurred in October 1927 when two US Marine aviators, 2nd Lt Earl A. Thomas and Sgt Frank E. Dowdell, were tried before a Sandinista kangaroo court in Nicaragua and executed during part of the so-called "Banana Wars" (figure 5). As the Nicaraguan rebellion leader Augusto C. Sandino wrote in a letter recounting the event a few days later,

> Once more the cowardly punitives [,] who [. . .] have the advantage that in the airplanes they pilot they assassinate cravenly our peaceful countrymen, have suffered a defeat today. [. . .] [A]fter a strong bombardment with machine guns and bombs [. . .] the captured aviators [. . .] were judged by a Council of War and shot summarily, applying to them the same law that [. . .] [Major General Logan] Feland wanted to apply [. . .] [to me].[16]

The incident infuriated the US government, which claimed the executions were against the 1907 Hague Convention, specifically Article 23 (c). In retaliation, the US military no longer applied the laws of war to the Sandinista guerrilla fighters, and the conflict quickly devolved into a brutal war without quarter, which subsequently violated Article 23 (d) of the Convention. The claims of illegitimate aerial attacks, escalating hatred for the enemy, desire for revenge, and the growing disregard to adhere to international law highlighted the looming complexity of mechanized aerial warfare and the uncertainty of how downed airmen would be treated.

Despite the international attempts to establish laws of war, for example, the Hague and Geneva Conventions, flyers' status remained ambiguous during World War II and arguably persisted during the global and regional conflicts that followed. The first Geneva Convention of 1864, influenced greatly by the Lieber Code (1863) during the US Civil War, forbid the killing

Figure 5. US Marine, 2nd Lt Earl A. Thomas, hanged after a Sandinista court-martial sentenced him to death in Nicaragua in October 1927. Neill Macaulay, *The Sandino Affair* (Durham: Duke University Press, 1985), 93; Augusto C. Sandino, Communique, October 3, 1927, and photograph of the body of Lt Thomas with comments by Maj Ross E. Rowell, US Marine Corps Historical Archives (MCHA), Nicaragua: Box 10, Folder 2; Photo courtesy of Michael Schroeder, "The Sandino Rebellion, 1927–1934: October 12, 1927, O'Shea, Engagement at Sapotillal," accessed March 17, 2021, http://www.sandinorebellion.com/pcdocs/1927/PC271012-OShea.html.

12 | Introduction

of surrendered enemy combatants; however, this did not necessarily stop such atrocities from occurring. Subsequent international agreements were revised to better suit the changing battlefield technologies and tactics. For example, the Hague Convention of 1899 (Article IV) prohibited the bombardment of undefended towns and forbid signatories from using explosive-laden balloons. While the Convention of 1899 covered the laws of land warfare and the Hague Convention of 1907 incorporated the laws of naval warfare, aviation was still in its infancy and nations closely observed the progress in aerial technology and anticipated its potential advantages in future conflicts. This induced many nations, such as Germany, Japan, Italy, and Russia, to withhold signing or ratifying associated articles of the 1907 Convention.

Following the outbreak of the Great War, aerial attacks were used to bombard enemy supply networks, troop concentrations, and even urban centers. Technological improvements in aviation and explosives further developed aerial military strategies, which also pushed the boundaries of international law. For example, the bombing of cities, intended to destroy the enemy's morale, was introduced by Germany with the bombing of Liege, Belgium, in August 1914, shortly after the war began. Eventually, Germany's Zeppelin raids terrorized cities in England and France, and both the Central and Allied powers resorted to retaliatory aerial attacks. The disastrous bombing accuracy as well as the development of effective defensive measures to attack the large, slow, and highly flammable airships resulted in airplanes becoming more dominant by 1917. By the end of the war, most capital cities of the major European belligerents had been targeted through strategic bombing.[17] However, the attacks resulted in an overestimation of the material and psychological effects of bombing cities and greatly influenced well-known air war theorists, such as Guilio Douhet (Italy), Billy Mitchell (USA), Hugh Trenchard (Britain), and Walther Wever (Germany), during the interwar era.[18] In combination with the developments in aircraft technology, most people believed during the interwar years that "the bomber will always get through," as British Prime Minister Stanley Baldwin declared in a 1932 speech.[19] Ultimately, these dogmas combined to guide the tactics of World War II and resulted in widespread use of strategic and carpet bombing as well as instituting around-the-clock attacks, all of which further pushed the moral and ethical boundaries of acceptability.

To try and minimize the death and devastation in future conflicts, the United States, Great Britain, France, Italy, Japan, and the Netherlands sent military and legal experts to The Hague in 1922–23 to discuss how (in)adequately the laws of war covered the developing weapons and tactics in aerial warfare; however, the commission was merely established to debate the topic and was not actually tasked with adopting an international treaty. Following the Great War, many military and legal officials from around the world increasingly believed that making war more humane might also make it more probable. Despite the skepticism, the commissions' members maintained the importance of adapting international law to expand the rights of (non)combatants and restrict the use of developing technology (e.g., submarines, aircraft, poisonous gases) in combat. Known as the Hague Rules of Air Warfare, the drafted parameters called for the prevention of attacking parachutists from disabled aircraft (Article 20), the prohibition of terror bombing (Article 23) and indiscriminate attacks, especially against undefended places (Article 24), and ensurance that captured enemy airmen are considered POWs (Article 36). In the end, however, no agreement was ratified. For most countries, the provisions governing the use of aircraft were too strict, as many leaders and military strategists recognized the airplane as a promising weapon. While the commission did attempt to moderate the escalation of combat with these rules, glaring limitations were quickly evident, especially the lack of prohibiting indiscriminate bombing of noncombatants in defended places, which was greatly exacerbated by aerial bombardment during World War II. In fact, many limitations continue to create controversy today, for example, clearly differentiating between combat and noncombat zones, defining indiscriminate bombing, and determining the precise criteria for combatant status. Despite the failure of the Hague Rules of Air Warfare to result in a signed international agreement, it was influential in framing nations' individual policies of aerial warfare, and it supported transnational collaboration.[20]

In 1929, nations gathered again to discuss and define the proper treatment of combatants who laid down their arms. Known as the Geneva Convention on Prisoners of War, the treaty protected POWs from "outrages upon personal dignity, in particular humiliating and degrading treatment."[21] While both Germany and Japan were signatories among several other nations, Japan refused to ratify the convention. With the increased control of militarists in Japan during the 1920s and 1930s, many military and government officials feared that the treaty would make it harder to deter aerial bombing. Despite Japan's relatively isolated location, the technological advancements in airpower indicated that the surrounding seas would not provide enough protection in the future. For the militarists, Article 1 of the 1929 Geneva Convention incentivized enemy airmen to bomb countries such as Japan without concern about falling into the hands of the enemy, as positive treatment was secured.[22]

14 | Introduction

Further, while Japan complied with international standards for treating POWs during the Great War, the protracted guerrilla warfare during the Siberian Intervention (1918–1922) "encouraged indifference for human life" among Japanese militarists, according to Sarah Kovner, as officers increasingly associated being taken prisoner as dishonorable—a sentiment that similarly spread throughout Japanese society and would greatly influence the treatment of POWs during the Japanese occupation of China, Southeast Asia, and throughout the Pacific during World War II.[23]

Despite the attempts to reduce the death and destruction in battle through international conventions, military and government officials (even among the signatory nations) continued to find ways in which they could circumvent these regulations. In fact, many of the legal protections were already violated during the numerous armed conflicts of the 1930s: for example, German and Italian aircraft bombed cities during the Spanish Civil War (most famously when the German Condor Legion bombed Guernica in 1937); Japanese aircraft attacked Chinese cities (e.g., Nanking); Italy and Japan unleashed poison gas in their invasions of Ethiopia and China, correspondingly; and Japanese soldiers wildly executed Chinese POWs. Despite various attempts to pass legal resolutions that would regulate the use of aerial attacks by providing a more specific definition of what constituted "undefended cities" and overall safeguards for civilians as well as protection for airmen as POWs, no international body—whether the League of Nations or the Hague or Geneva Conventions—was successful in ratifying new restrictions nor establishing an international governing body to investigate and punish violations by the time the next global war broke out.[24]

From the outset of World War II in Europe, German Luftwaffe units attacked cities such as Wieluń, Warsaw, Rotterdam, and countless Soviet cities and eventually carried out the Blitz against Great Britain in 1940–1941. After enduring the surprise attack on Pearl Harbor on December 7, 1941, the United States retaliated by bombing strategic targets in Japan on April 18, 1942. While the attack, commonly known as the Doolittle Raid, shocked Japan, it was more of a victory for US propaganda than a strategic military success. When it was publicly revealed in October 1942 that the Japanese had captured eight Raiders and executed three of them (1st Lt William G. Farrow, 1st Lt Dean E. Hallmark, and Sgt Harold A. Spatz) after a kangaroo court found them guilty of indiscriminate bombing, the United States and its Allies were shocked and appalled. Many Allied citizens demanded revenge and an intensification of aerial attacks. Japan, and eventually Nazi Germany and Fascist Italy, threatened to continue trying captured flyers, whom they argued were responsible for targeting civilians and nonmilitary objectives.

In addition to the execution of the Doolittle Raiders, the Japanese Army launched punitive attacks in China. It razed the villages that aided the raiders' evasion and slaughtered hundreds of thousands of men, women, and children.[25] Ultimately, the violence foreshadowed the Axis retaliation that awaited downed Allied flyers and anyone who offered them assistance. Backed by the "Arsenal of Democracy," the Allies remained steadfast and intensified the air war, including attacks against urban centers, in hopes of expediting the end of the war by weakening Axis citizens' will to fight. Consequently, the Axis regimes increasingly detained airmen as criminals, spies, saboteurs, or terrorists (as opposed to POWs) in an attempt to skirt the international safeguards and seek their sworn revenge. A similar tactic was employed by the German military in occupied territories in Europe and by the Japanese military in China, where insurgents, partisans, and Soviet and Chinese POWs were often designated as bandits, thieves, or terrorists to emphasize their criminal status and to avoid legal barriers interfering with their execution. Even the several hundred thousand Italian soldiers taken prisoner by Germany after Italy surrendered in September 1943 experienced the suffering and vulnerability of not being properly classified upon capture. Deported to the Reich as "military internees," in order to bypass the protection afforded to POWs by the 1929 Geneva Convention, many were used as forced laborers, resulting in tens of thousands dying in captivity.[26]

For enemy prisoners detained as criminals, Axis investigations often used torture to determine, for example, whether aviators had participated in indiscriminate attacks against nonmilitary targets, or until the captors determined what treatment they (often subjectively) deemed appropriate. Varying factors, such as an airman's race, religion, and attitude, significantly influenced his (mis)treatment; even his association with the Allied air forces could be reason enough for a perpetrator to result to violence. In addition to the various forms of pressure by military superiors and government authorities, the death and destruction experienced during the war were further "catalysts of radical stimulation," as Nicholas Stargardt confirmed, that could result in (both spontaneous and organized) violence—even among "ordinary" civilians.[27]

Although the Allied nations were more likely to adhere to international laws regarding the treatment of POWs in World War II, they, unfortunately, were not immune to strong nationalistic (and even racist) propensities, and Allied soldiers even committed illicit acts of their own.[28] Famed aviation pioneer, Charles A. Lindbergh, recalled such incidents during his time in the Pacific Theater as a civilian engineering consultant. He recorded in his journal on June 11, 1944:

16 | Introduction

A long line of incidents parades before my mind: the story of our Marines firing on unarmed Japanese survivors who swam ashore on the beach at Midway; the accounts of our machine-gunning prisoners on a Hollandia airstrip; [. . .] of the shinbones cut, for letter openers and pen trays, from newly killed Japanese bodies on Noemfoor [New Guinea]; of the young pilot who was "going to cream that Jap hospital one of these days"; of American soldiers poking through the mouths of Japanese corpses for gold-filled teeth [. . .]; of Jap heads buried in anthills "to get them clean for souvenirs"; [. . .] of pictures of Mussolini and his mistress hung by the feet in an Italian city, to the approval of thousands of Americans who claim to stand for high, civilized ideals. As far back as one can go in history, these atrocities have been going on, not only in Germany with its Dachaus and its Buchenwalds and its Camp Doras, but in Russia, in the Pacific, in the rioting and lynchings at home, in the less-publicized uprisings in Central and South America, the cruelties of China, a few years ago in Spain, in pogroms of the past, the burning of witches in New England, tearing people apart on the English racks, burnings at the stake for the benefit of Christ and God. [. . .] This, I realize, is not a thing confined to any nation or to any people.[29]

While Lindbergh's questionable stance toward Nazi Germany and his outspoken anti-Semitic comments tarnished his legacy, his experiences as a pilot in the Pacific Theater offer an interesting perspective of what it was like to fly sorties. Despite his isolationist beliefs, Lindbergh flew fifty missions, mostly over Papua New Guinea, and took part in bombing and strafing raids against Japanese positions. He is even credited with shooting down one Japanese Zero. This, despite his main duties, which involved the evaluation of US aircraft, particularly the F4U Corsair and the P-38 Lightening, during combat conditions.[30]

Lindbergh acknowledged the questionable tactics of aerial attacks, especially feeling detached from the irrevocable death and destruction that aviators wreaked at the pull of the trigger; however, even he admitted to getting caught up in the moment during missions.[31] Military officials repeatedly warned and advised Lindbergh not to take part in bombing and strafing missions but rather observe, as he would likely be shot if he was forced down and was captured by the Japanese. Further, being such a high-profile individual also meant that he would have been a valuable hostage for Japanese propaganda. However, as he wrote in his journal, "I didn't see it made much difference what status you were on if you were forced down on Jap territory, because according to reports they shot you anyway. The Marine camps are full of stories about the torture and beheading of American pilots captured

Introduction | 17

by the Japanese."[32] While such stories were frequently embellished among GIs and airmen, and surely similar rumors circulated among Axis soldiers as well, the brutal torture and reciprocal violence carried out against enemy prisoners was extensive throughout the global conflict. Compared to all other modern armed conflicts, World War II exhibited the most widespread and ruthless violence committed against POWs.

The following account, entitled "Blood Carnival," is taken from the diary of an unidentified member of the Imperial Japanese Navy. It details the brutal and violent end that not only American flyers faced, but all downed Allied airmen:

March 29, 1943 — [. . .] Unit Commander Komai [. . .] told us personally that, in accordance with the compassionate sentiments of Japanese Bushido, he was going to kill the prisoner himself with his favorite sword. So, we gathered to observe this. [. . .]

The prisoner, who is at the side of the guard house, is given his last drink of water. [. . .] The time has come, so the prisoner, with his arms bound and his hair now cropped very close, totters forward. He probably suspects what is afoot; but he is put on the truck, and we set out for our destination. [. . .]

To the pleasant rumble of the engine, we run swiftly along the road in the growing twilight. The glowing sun has set behind the western hills, gigantic clouds rise before us, and the dusk is falling all around. It will not be long now. As I picture the scene we are about to witness, my heart beats faster.

I glance at the prisoner; he has probably resigned himself to his fate. As though saying farewell to the world as he sits in the truck he looks about at the hills, at the sea, and seems deep in thought. I feel a surge of pity and turn my eyes away. [. . .]

The truck runs along the sea shore. We have left the Navy guard sector behind us and now come into the Army guard sector. Here and there we see sentries in the grassy fields, and I thank them in my heart for their toil as we drive on. They must have got it in the bombing the night before last—there are great holes by the side of the road, full of water from the rain. In a little over twenty minutes, we arrive at our destination, and all get off.

Unit Commander Komai stands up and says to the prisoner, "We are now going to kill you." When he tells the prisoner that in accordance with Japanese bushido he would be killed with a Japanese sword, and that he would have two or three minutes grace, he listens with bowed head. The Flight Lieutenant says a few words in a low voice. Apparently he wants to be killed with one stroke of the sword. I hear him say the word "One." The Unit Commander becomes tense and his face stiffens as he replies, "Yes."

18 | Introduction

Now the time has come, and the prisoner is made to kneel on the bank of a bomb crater filled with water. He is apparently resigned; the precaution is taken of surrounding him with guards with fixed bayonets, but he remains calm. He even stretches out his neck, and is very brave. When I put myself in the prisoner's place, and think that in one more minute it will be goodbye to this world, although the daily bombings have filled me with hate, ordinary human feelings make me pity him.

The Unit Commander has drawn his favorite sword. [. . .] It glitters in the light and sends a cold shiver down my spine. He taps the prisoner's neck lightly with the back of the blade, then raises it above his head with both arms, and brings it down with a sweep. I had been standing with my muscles tensed, but in that moment I closed my eyes. [. . .]

All is over. The head is dead white, like a doll. The savageness which I felt only a little while ago is gone, and now I feel nothing but the true compassion of Japanese bushido. A senior corporal laughs loudly, "Well, he will enter Nirvana now." Then, a superior seaman of the medical unit takes the Chief Medical Officer's Japanese sword and, intent on paying off old scores, turns the headless body over on its back, and cuts the abdomen open with one clean stroke. "They are thick-skinned, these Keto ('Hairy foreigner'— common term of opprobrium for a white man)—even the skin of their bellies is thick." [. . .] It is pushed over into the crater at once and buried.

Now the wind blows mournfully and I see the scene again in my mind's eye. We get on to the truck again and start back. It is dark now. [. . .] This will be something to remember all my life. If ever I get back alive it will make a good story to tell, so I have written it down.[33]

Scattered amid the scores of grotesque brutalities and massacres that have come to symbolize Axis terror and exemplify the totality of the war, sources such as this provide a rare insight into not only the largely forgotten violence committed against downed airmen but also the emotions and justification of perpetrators.

Toward the end of the war in the Pacific, as the Allies progressed from "island hopping" to an all-out attack against the Japanese home islands, Australian forces took control over Papua New Guinea and discovered that the atrocity depicted in the diary entry had been committed at Salamaua. Investigators determined that the flyer executed on March 29 was most likely Flight Lieutenant William E. Newton of the Royal Australian Air Force's 22 Squadron. Newton and his crew (Flight Sergeant John Lyon and Sgt Basil Gilbert Eastwood) were shot down during a bombing mission over Salamaua after their aircraft, DB-7B Boston/A28-3, was disabled by

Introduction | 19

anti-aircraft fire. Newton and Lyon managed to bail out of the damaged aircraft; however, Eastwood was unable to escape and died after the plane crashed into the sea. Japanese soldiers then captured Newton and Lyon and held them at Salamaua. A week before Newton was beheaded, Lyon was executed on March 20, 1943. So far, however, no evidence indicates that anyone was held accountable for their deaths.

The similarly rigid hierarchy structure and pledge of utmost obedience to the symbolic figurehead in each nation, whether to the Japanese Emperor, Nazi *Führer*, or Fascist Italian *Duce*, established an environment in which the minds of the larger populace could be molded to carry out the desires of the supreme leaders. While the varying cultures and customs of each nation surely had some influence on the actions of the populace, the most impactful aspect was the Nazi government's public approval and promotion of civilians to commit mob justice against captured enemy airmen. The desire for a similar response likely existed among a significant portion of the population in Japan as well; however, the Japanese military most often dealt with captured flyers directly or directed civilians' involvement, as the initial example involving S/Sgt Serafino Morone illustrated.

Nevertheless, numerous personal accounts of airmen consistently report that they were mistreated by angry civilian mobs who acted on their own initiative. One such example involved 2nd Lt Fiske Hanley, who was shot down during a raid near the Shimonoseki Straits on March 27, 1945. In his memoirs, Hanley describes descending near the small village of Ueki, where a large crowd of forty to fifty angry and armed farmers immediately sur-rounded him after he landed in a rice paddy. As Hanley recalls,

One of the Japanese men, holding a bamboo spear, charged at me from my right front. His spear was leveled at my head. At his signal, the others joined in his charge. [. . .] I reached out and deflected his spear over my head. He lunged passed me! Then the excited horde was upon me. They were like a pack of crazed and starved animals after raw meat. They were so close that they couldn't use their larger weapons. They became a mass of jammed hu-manity as they milled around me. I was hit with fists and clubs. They hit me from every direction. Their main target seemed to be my head, and they didn't miss. My flak suit and survival gear gave me some protection and probably saved my vitals from severe wounds. Lack of a helmet made my head fair game. I tried to parry the vicious jabs at my eyes. Fortunately, no one had a knife. The women were especially vicious. [. . .]

There was no reprieve from the attack. I was being clubbed and beaten to death. These savages had no thought of allowing me to surrender. Capture

20 | Introduction

was not in their minds. They were out to kill me! The mob was in a frenzy and out of control. No one seemed to be in charge. Their shouting increased in tempo as they—men, women, and children—fought to get in lethal blows. I used my bloody hands and arms to protect my head, which was already burned from my bailout from the flaming airplane. I was bleeding profusely, my shirt soaked with blood. My instinct to live was foremost in my mind, but I was losing that battle. [. . .]

A figure several rows back in the mob managed to severely poke my face on the right cheekbone with an implement shaft of some kind. An inch above and it would have put out an eye. [. . .] I was knocked down countless times and each time struggled to my feet. I never lost consciousness during the beating. [. . .] This was a horrible way to die! By now, I was believing I had made the wrong decision. I should have shot myself. I kept yelling "I surrender!" and prayed. [. . .]

Suddenly, a tall, impressive-looking, black-uniformed figure waded through the mob toward me. [. . .] He was big and powerful and towered above the small peasant figures. He fought his way through the crazed savages and reached my side. Then he shouted some guttural [. . .] orders to the mob. They ignored his interference. He grabbed me and began pushing me from the center of this mayhem. The mob continued their murderous attack as we squeezed our way out of the milling mass. They were now beating both of us. He was knocked down several times. [. . .]

He finally dragged me free of the attackers. He barked curt orders to the mob. They began to move back. [. . .]

My rescuer pulled my arms behind my back and snapped handcuffs on my wrists. [. . .] The policemen produced a length of rope and tied it around my neck. He directed me to walk toward the road adjoining the rice paddy where I had landed. The screaming peasants formed a corridor along our path. A few of the more agitated attackers couldn't restrain themselves and hit my head with their clubs as we passed by. [. . .] I was in such a state of deep shock that these last mob actions were not even felt. [. . .][34]

While Hanley managed to survive his run-in with an angry civilian mob, thanks to the efforts of a police officer, Kempeitai officials quickly took Hanley into custody and held him at their headquarters in Tokyo. While there, he, along with over one hundred identified American flyers, were interrogated, severely tortured, and mistreated. Roughly 25 percent of the known airmen held there were killed or perished due to their injuries and lack of proper food and medical treatment. Hanley reflected on his experiences after the war and recorded two thought-provoking questions in his

Introduction | 21

memoirs: "What would an American mob have done if a Japanese airmen parachuted in their midst right after Pearl Harbor? What would I have done if people near and dear to me had been killed by the enemy?" No doubt, similar mobs of angry American citizens would have lashed out at an enemy that inflicted disastrous destruction and loss of life on US soil. After all, in the history of the United States, similar hostile mobs have needed much less cause or justification to commit vicious acts (e.g., lynchings) against their fellow citizens.

Flyers not only faced death in their aircraft during missions and on the ground by angry mobs but were also potential targets as they helplessly descended in their parachutes. While there were some debates among Allied and Axis officials regarding the appropriateness of shooting parachuting enemy flyers, for example, whether it made a difference if the airmen were over their own country or enemy territory, aviators generally avoided engaging enemy flyers after they bailed out of their aircraft. This was influenced by the traditions of pilots from World War I, who viewed themselves as chivalrous knights of the air. While there was no international law prohibiting such acts—until the 1977 Protocol 1 (Article 42) amendment to the 1949 Geneva Conventions—US General Dwight D. Eisenhower forbid such actions.[35] Nevertheless, several instances did occur, especially as the war escalated during the final year. Not only did Axis and Allied airmen attack parachuting pilots, but ground troops also targeted flyers as they descended. The US Office of Censorship, for example, intercepted a letter in the fall of 1944 from a Danish woman (Elly Vedel) living in Sweden. The letter described Vedel's shock about the latest circumstances involving Allied flyers. She wrote:

> They shoot all flyers now. Lately a plane crashed over Korsor [southwestern Sweden] the three flyers bailed out with their parachutes. They [the Nazis] shot the two while they were still hanging in the air. The third landed in the water. A fisherman went out with his boat to pick him up, but he was shot from a warship, which was controlling the water. This boat then sailed back and forth where the flyer went down to show that *they* killed him in this manner. The civilian population down there are permitted to kill all flyers who crash.[36]

Such occurrences largely remained an exception, though, as pilots were often far more occupied with making sure they themselves did not get shot down. Still, while shooting down enemy aircraft represented the main goal for flyers, some soldiers and civilians often construed that their duty

22 | Introduction

was to eliminate the airman as a future threat. In the Pacific Theater, Allied airmen reported that Japanese pilots had a bad reputation for shooting flyers dangling in their parachutes, as they viewed being captured and surrendering as dishonorable. While it remains difficult to uncover such incidents, they undoubtedly were committed by both sides during the heat of battle.[37]

The failure to acknowledge POW status exposed additional limitations of the prior international agreements. Most Axis authorities agreed that Allied flyers had committed crimes by attacking civilians and targets that had no military significance. While the accuracy and tactics of the Allied air war were at times questionable, captured flyers still warranted POW status under international law, as they were legitimate combatants, and reprisals were specifically banned under Article 2 of the 1929 Geneva Convention. Even if POWs were suspected of committing illegal acts, they still had to be treated humanely and in case of a court-martial receive a fair and impartial trial. Yet, as the war proceeded so too did the radicalization of combat, as the line dividing legality and criminality became more obscured. As S. P. MacKenzie confirmed, Axis leaders "proved alarmingly eager to ignore or downplay the danger of retaliation by attempting to exact revenge for what were seen as unacceptable actions." Ultimately, the fact that the detaining power determined the legitimacy of captives' status resulted in considerable uncertainty for downed airmen.[38]

Frequently located far behind enemy lines, either in the Axis home front or in occupied territories, captured flyers found themselves in direct contact with enraged, radicalized, and often armed citizens. The presence of an individual whom they could hold responsible for the death and destruction inflicted by the traumatic air war often triggered civilians to commit impulsive acts of violence. As Mackenzie concludes, "POWs were at best a disposable resource and at worst part of the unfinished business of the battlefield."[39] Often influenced and conditioned by propaganda, these encounters represented a "new 'front' in the heart of the Axis," as Laura C. Counts recognized.[40] As a result, "civilian immunity," according to Overy, "was compromised by the imperatives of total war, not only because civilians could be considered a full part of the enemy war effort, but because in many cases civilians chose to confront an occupying force with their own violence."[41]

Ultimately, allied commands justified the large number of civilian deaths as a military necessity. Flying over enemy territory, American airmen did not believe they were engaging in crimes by bombing urban and industrial areas. They instead focused on doing their part in ending the war as soon as possible and, of course, staying alive. The physical and psychological

Introduction | 23

distance that the air war offered flyers made it easier to displace their individual agency in the devastating attacks. Conversely, this inability to confront the enemy and uncertainty of when and where attacks would occur weighed heavily on the minds and bodies of Axis citizens, especially civilians. Ultimately, as Overy confirms, "the frictions of total war made crime inevitable."[42]

Potential Aid

During the transitional phase between flying over enemy territory and being captured, downed airmen occasionally received aid and assistance from the heroic resistance groups, underground networks, and even individual civilians. The most well-known networks were established throughout France and the Benelux countries and provided essential help for evading downed flyers and escaped POWs as well as European civilians fleeing Nazi persecution,[43] although escape and evasion were not without great danger and difficulty for both the individuals on the run and their helpers. Many factors, such as the terrain, weather, lack of proper clothing and training, cultural differences, language barriers, racial preconceptions, health, and composure, as well as sheer misfortune, often hindered downed airmen on their journey to freedom. Over two thousand individuals (including both flyers and persecuted civilians) successfully escaped via the numerous escape lines in western Europe. In addition, numerous airmen were rescued in France and Holland during secret missions carried out by Allied intelligence organizations (e.g., MI9, SOE, and OSS).[44] Similarly, the OSS rescued over 2,500 Allied flyers in eastern Europe, primarily in the Balkans, by the fall of 1944.[45]

Compared to Europe, the factors that influenced escape and evasions were intensified and often more complex in the Pacific and Southeast Asian theaters. Young and impressionable, many airmen were influenced by racialized prejudices and stereotypes of Asians upon their arrival in China and Southeast Asia. Despite the rather well-known opportunities for POWs to return to Allied hands in Europe, downed flyers in the Pacific and Asian theaters could rely on similar, yet often overlooked, forms of assistance that helped transform some evader's convictions.[46] If shot down over Japan, flyers had little chance of successfully escaping or evading capture; however, in Japanese-occupied territory local civilians and guerrilla fighters offered pilots the best chance of "walking-out." Nevertheless, not all civilians were helpful, as some worked (largely out of fear or for monetary reward) for the Japanese.

Similar to the underground networks in Western Europe, the US Navy and Air-Ground Aid Section (AGAS)-China, MIS-X, and other Allied intelligence groups sent individuals behind enemy lines throughout China and Southeast Asia to survey the terrain and secure the support of brave locals (whether Chinese nationalists or communists, guerrilla fighters, or local civilians) in assisting downed pilots' safe return to Allied hands. As Daniel Jackson revealed in his intriguing study of the fate of downed American flyers in China, "while underground organizations delivered less than twenty-five percent of airmen in Europe back to Allied control, more than ninety percent of those who survived in China returned to friendly territory." Jackson reasoned that "in western Europe the Germans found many more ideological converts than did the Japanese in China."[47]

In addition, members of the Sino-American Cooperative Organization (SACO), part of the US Naval Group China, were stationed throughout Southeast Asia and China to help train Chinese guerrillas, for example, in

Figure 6. Meeting of SACO Members at Camp Giggins in Kunming, China around August 1945. Courtesy of Richard I. Terpstra (pictured sitting third from left, wearing a hat).

demolition, sabotage, combat techniques, operating radios, and surveillance, as well as aircraft and ship recognition (figure 6).[48]

As a forerunner to the US Navy SEALS, these "frogmen" also relayed weather conditions along with Japanese troop and ship movements to the US Navy as well as assisting downed flyers. According to an Office of Naval Intelligence (ONI) report on escape and evasion in China, locals also received instructions on how to handle downed flyers and "the results of these field trips were compiled into surveys [that] were disseminated throughout operating units. The result was that the individual pilot [. . .] took a detailed study course of the area over which he was destined to fly. He knew the location of the principal 'stations,' carried a 'prepaid ticket' and had his 'accommodations reserved in advance' on the underground railroad."[49] As war correspondent Clarence Alton Beliel (commonly known as Don Bell), who survived over two years of imprisonment in a Japanese internment camp in the Philippines only to be shot down in March 1945 as an observer during a mission over Amoy Harbor in China, described his "walk-out" with 16 other US naval airmen:

> I want to express my personal admiration for [. . .] the way the Navy has organized its share of a China Coast Rescue Service that makes it 99 chances out of 100 that, if you drop in on China unexpectedly, you'll be taken care of and brought back to civilization. Why, they make a drop [. . .] turn out to be one of the finest vacations you've ever had.[50]

While the expansive underground network in China and Southeast Asia was indeed helpful and successfully brought well over seven hundred flyers out from behind Japanese lines, the dangers were far more extreme in practice than either the Navy intelligence report or Bell portrays.[51]

For flyers shot down at sea, the US Navy's long-range air-sea rescue aircraft and submarines offered potential assistance. These so-called "Dumbo" missions could pick up survivors (if the aircraft were capable) or drop emergency supplies and radio the coordinates to the nearest submarine or ship (figure 7). Although these missions (in addition to the successful evasion of airmen) offered a boost to flyers' morale when flying missions over the remote ocean and unforgiving jungles, they were severely limited by the weather, proximity of Japanese forces, and often the inability to quickly locate the downed airmen in the vast expanse of the Pacific Ocean and jungles of Asia. Nevertheless, these missions saved the lives of hundreds of flyers.[52]

Figure 7. Survivors of a bomber that crashed into the sea are helped into the rescue plane of the 13th Air Force, accessed November 16, 2021, https://www.fold3.com/image/55702041, NARA, RG 342, Series FH, Roll 3A45218-3A46062.

Outline and Comparative Perspectives

Using evidence presented at postwar courts-martial of lower-level perpetrators (largely held at Dachau and Yokohama, but also conducted at lesser-known locations in former Axis-occupied nations), the following analysis expands upon my previous study, *Terror Flyers*, by examining the extent and parallels of Axis violence inflicted upon downed airmen. While the US flyer trials analyzed in this study surely do not describe every instance relating to the mistreatment of downed airmen, they provide an opportunity to advance the relatively limited discourse on the mistreatment committed against flyers in World War II. Moreover, the comparison of the US flyer trials in Europe, Asia, and the Pacific offers an opportunity to expand upon the limited historiography and has the potential to assist in resolving unanswered questions regarding the circumstances surrounding the death of missing US servicemen.

Introduction | 27

Supplemented by examples of American airmen mistreated in Europe and the Pacific Theaters (including comparisons of Luftwaffe flyers shot down during the Battle of Britain and a Japanese pilot during the attack on Pearl Harbor), chapter 1 traces the development of Axis policies to combat downed flyers. As the war developed, Axis mistreatment of captured flyers intensified, reflecting the amplified brutality of combat, increased desire for revenge, and relaxed moral boundaries. The US retaliatory attack on Japan on April 18, 1942, commonly known as the Doolittle Raid, along with the Japanese response and the subsequent Allied bombing campaigns, which inflicted severe civilian losses, further induced the mistreatment of downed Allied airmen throughout the rest of the war in the Pacific and in Europe. Nazi Germany and Fascist Italy keenly monitored the mistreatment of the Doolittle Raiders as the air war intensified over Europe and the regime sought ways to combat Allied flyers. Both German and Italian officials publicly supported Japan's methods and threatened that similar treatment would occur in Europe.

The second and third chapters offer narratives of American flyers who fell victim to Axis violence in the Pacific, Southeast Asian, European, and Mediterranean Theaters. Accounts such as postwar trial testimonies by witnesses, perpetrators, and occasionally victims themselves, along with Missing Air Crew Reports (MACR) and Escape and Evasion reports, piece together the circumstances leading up to, during, and after an airman's mistreatment. Further, these narratives include perpetrators' explanations and justifications for their actions. Supplemented by photographs of victims, when possible, chapter 2 explores ten cases that span the vast geographic expanse of the Pacific and Southeast Asian Theaters while chapter 3 depicts eleven cases that occurred throughout Europe.

Chapter 4 provides a comparative quantitative analysis of the US postwar flyer trials held in Europe and the Pacific to assist in profiling the perpetrators held accountable for the violence committed against American airmen. While the hearings largely focused on convicting members of illegal organizations (e.g., the Nazi Party, especially *Alte Kämpfer*, and members of the SS, SA, SD, and Gestapo) along with Japanese military officers, they nevertheless provide an opportunity to explore the individuals (often civilians) who escaped justice. The relatively extensive judicial sources include investigative files and witness, perpetrator, and occasionally victim statements, a large catalog of Axis documents, transcripts of court proceedings, autopsy reports, appeals for clemency, and justifications for verdicts. As the best-known collection of sources that document the violence committed against downed

28 | Introduction

airmen, analyzing these postwar flyer trials provides an improved opportunity to comprehend the broader extent and parallels of Axis violence that traversed military campaigns and fronts during the global conflict. Further, the sources reveal the complex relationship among the air war, propaganda, the role of civilians, and state-sponsored terror during the radicalized conflict.

Whether spontaneous or premeditated, the mistreatment inflicted upon downed flyers represented an increasing response to the intense and devastating aerial attacks during the total war. The home front no longer afforded civilians safety from the effects of war, as death reached the doorsteps of Axis citizens. Downed airmen were the only enemies that Axis civilians encountered directly (through bombings) and could punish directly (through lynching). These encounters provided individuals, especially civilians, who were angered, vulnerable, and encouraged to seek revenge, with an unprecedented opportunity for personal retribution that simultaneously relieved the Axis regimes' inability to deter the air war and combat Allied flyers.

1   Axis Policies to Combat Downed Enemy Flyers

So live, that when thy summons comes to join
The innumerable caravan, which moves
To that mysterious realm, where each shall take
His chamber in the silent halls of death,
Thou go not, like the quarry-slave at night,
Scourged to his dungeon, but, sustained and soothed
By an unfaltering trust, approach thy grave,
Like one who wraps the drapery of his couch
About him, and lies down to pleasant dreams.
> —William Cullen Bryant, "Thanatopsis"

Pearl Harbor

The early morning attack of Pearl Harbor on December 7, 1941, took the world by surprise and launched the United States into a global conflict of unparalleled death and destruction. The intense struggle to defend Pearl Harbor on that infamous day has been captured and recounted by scholars, veterans, survivors, witnesses, and film directors ever since; however, a little known, yet significant, incident also occurred on that fateful day on the westernmost Hawaiian island of Niihau. Both incidents fulfilled a prophecy by the "father of the US Air Force," Major General William "Billy" Mitchell, who predicted decades earlier that not only was a war between the United States and Japan inevitable but that Niihau Island would be a strategic location for an attack on Pearl Harbor.[1]

Located roughly two hundred miles northwest of Pearl Harbor, the Japanese Navy designated the privately owned island as a potential emergency landing site for pilots during the December 7 attack. Yoshino Haruo, a Japanese pilot involved in the Pearl Harbor attack, recounted after the war, "We were told that if we had trouble, to land on the southern shoreline [of Niihau] so the rescue sub could see the plane on the beach and come in.

There was a submarine, waiting off the coast of Niihau, waiting to pick up any aviators whose planes were damaged."[2] However, this option was apparently "only for those of lesser rank [. . .] as they would have less information to give to the enemy." The remaining pilots were "ordered to find an American target and dive into it."[3]

During his attack on Bellows Field, located along Oahu's eastern shore, Lt Nishikaichi Shigenori's A6M2 Zero received small arms fire that punctured his fuel tank, which prevented him from returning to the aircraft carrier *Hiryu* (figure 1.1). Forced to either find a target and sacrifice himself or head for Niihau Island, Nishikaichi chose the latter.[4] Once he reached the island, he searched for the best possible area to land as well as scanned the ocean for the rescue submarine. Nishikaichi's hopes for an easy landing were dashed, however, as locals had plowed ditches throughout the dried lakebed. Convinced by Billy Mitchell's prophecy, the island owner, Aylmer Robinson, had locals laboriously dig furrows to prevent the island from being used as a potential site to launch aerial attacks against the US fleet anchored at Pearl Harbor. Although a beach landing would have been his best option, Nishikaichi's aircraft ran out of fuel before he could fully survey the area. He quickly decided to put the aircraft down on a small level area near a house owned by Hawila "Howell" Kaleohano.

Figure 1.1. Lt Nishikaichi Shigenori, accessed June 22, 2021, https://en.wikipedia.org/wiki/Niihau_incident#/media/File:Shigenori_Nishikaichi,_The_Niihau_Incident.jpg.

Axis Policies to Combat Downed Enemy Flyers | 31

The Zero hit the rocky terrain hard, shearing off the landing gear and drop tank as it skidded to a stop a short distance away from Kaleohano's house (figure 1.2). Shocked, Kaleohano ran to the aircraft, which was consumed by a cloud of red volcanic dust. As he reached the aircraft, he pulled the stunned flyer from the wreckage and secured his pistol and papers, which included a map and documents concerning the attack on Oahu. The language barrier made it difficult to converse with the dazed pilot; however, Kaleohano escorted Nishikaichi to his home, where his wife rendered first aid and prepared a meal. The attack on Pearl Harbor remained unknown to Kaleohano and the other locals at the time, as they had no direct contact with other islands; however, they were aware of the tense relations between the two nations.

Curious about the incident, the locals gathered at the crash site and at Kaleohano's home to see the foreign pilot. Three individuals of Japanese ancestry living on the island (Harada Yoshio, his wife Harada Umeno "Irene," and Ishimatsu Shintani) were asked to act as interpreters and explain to the local Hawaiians what was going on. Shintani arrived first but, after a brief conversation with the pilot, quickly left without conveying any information to the locals. As Syd Jones explained, Shintani's "traditional deference to a member of Japan's respected military class conflicted with loyalties to

Figure 1.2. Wreckage of Nishikaichi's Zero on Niihau Island, accessed June 22, 2021, https://en.wikipedia.org/wiki/Niihau_incident#/media/File:Nishikaichi's _Zero_BII-120.jpg.

32 | Axis Policies to Combat Downed Enemy Flyers

Aylmer, the Niihau community and his Hawaiian wife and their half-Hawaiian children."[5] The Haradas were then asked to interpret, and Nishikaichi revealed the attack on Oahu and insisted they help him retrieve his pistol and papers. Initially, the Haradas chose not to disclose the details of what the pilot said, contemplating if and how they could help him.[6]

Following Hawaiian tradition, the locals held a luau for their guest despite their suspicion. Throughout the following week, the locals attempted to send Nishikaichi to the neighboring island of Kauai via boat; however, following the attack on Pearl Harbor, the US military banned travel between the islands, and the owner, Robinson, was unable to make his trip scheduled for the day after the attack. Meanwhile, Shintani attempted to retrieve the flyer's papers from Kaleohano, even bribing him with money; however, this was unsuccessful, and he refused to help the pilot. Nishikaichi then convinced the Haradas to assist him in retrieving his papers. They resorted to using force and even took several locals hostage. The pilot threatened to kill everyone on the island unless he received his papers. Shocked by the situation, several local men escaped in a boat and set out for Kauai to get help. After reportedly paddling fifteen hours, they reached the neighboring island, located roughly seventeen miles away.[7]

Nishikaichi returned to the wreckage of his aircraft and attempted to make radio contact with Japanese forces; however, he was unsuccessful. After he removed a machine gun and the ammunition from the wreckage, he set it afire. Afraid that the pilot and his accomplices would kill the locals, two residents—Benehakaka "Benny" Kanahele and his wife, Ella—seized an opportunity during the morning of December 13 and disarmed Nishikaichi. Despite being shot three times during the struggle, Kanahele overpowered the flyer and threw him to the ground, headfirst into a rock. Weeks after the incident newspapers reported that Ella delivered the coup de grace by beating Nishikaichi in the head with a stone; however, only Benny ever received official credit. Harada Yoshio then shot himself and died a short time later.[8]

When US soldiers arrived from Kauai the following afternoon, George C. Larsen, who remained on the ship and manned the radio after they arrived, recalled in his memoirs that the soldiers reported

> the pilot was dead. That he was killed by a Hawaiian, who started to grapple with the pilot. [. . .] They end the story by telling us that his wife took out a knife and cut both of the pilot's ears off. We then got to inspect all the items they brought back with them. First, there was the synchronized machine gun from the fighter plane, then the fish skin waterproof wrapping that the pilot had wrapped around his waist containing things like a high school student

body card from a local Oahu High School, local maps, money and things necessary if he had to bail out over Oahu.⁹

Satisfied that there was no longer a threat on the island, the soldiers departed with Shintani and Harada for Kauai. US officials suspected Irene, an American citizen, of being a Japanese spy; however, she adamantly denied this and refused to accept any responsibility for what occurred on Niihau. Shintani was interned on the US mainland during the war and Irene was interned on Oahu until the summer of 1944. The American Legion awarded Benny and Howell with heroism medals for their actions and President FDR sent letters commending their bravery.¹⁰ Benny also received the Purple Heart for the wounds he suffered (figure 1.3). The incident received widespread attention in the United States, although it had no effect

Figure 1.3. Benehakaka "Benny" Kanahele, recognized for his actions on Niihau Island *SOURCE*: "Niihau Incident—Benehakaka Kanahele—WWII, Medal for Merit," accessed June 22, 2021, http://www.hawaiireporter.com/niihau-incident-benehakaka-ben-kanahele-wwii-medal-for-merit-purple-heart-1891-1962/.

34 | Axis Policies to Combat Downed Enemy Flyers

on appeasing the existing suspicion of Asian-Americans' loyalty to the United States.[11]

Pacific Theater

In the weeks after the attack on Pearl Harbor and the US declaration of war on Japan that followed, US Secretary of State Cordell Hull sent a message to the Japanese government via the American Legation in Bern, Switzerland, writing,

> Although the Japanese government is a signatory of the [Geneva and Red Cross] conventions [of 1929], it is understood not to have ratified the Geneva Prisoner of War Convention. The government of the United States nevertheless hopes that the Japanese government will apply the provisions of both conventions reciprocally in the above sense.[12]

The Japanese government responded by the end of January 1942 via the Swiss Minister in Tokyo and replied that "Japan is strictly observing Geneva Red Cross Convention as a signatory state. Although not bound by the Convention relative [to the] treatment [of] prisoners of war, Japan will apply *Mutatis mutandis* [all things being equal] provisions of that convention to American prisoners of war in its power."[13] While the US assumed this meant that Japan would commit to the Geneva Conventions of 1929, Japan actually intended to adapt their policies to the changing circumstances of war, that is, seeking reprisals (or the threat thereof) to combat (or deter) what they deemed were illegal acts committed by the Allies. The first attack on the Japanese mainland on April 18, 1942, commonly referred to as the Doolittle Raid, foreshadowed the fateful retaliation that awaited downed flyers in Japan. In the wake of these attacks, the Japanese responded by escalating their methods of mistreating POWs, especially downed Allied flyers, to seek retribution for their losses and as an attempt to intimidate the Allies from continuing the relentless attacks, particularly on urban communities. As legal scholar Michel Paradis explained, "Treating the Raiders as prisoners of war would [have] defeat[ed] the whole purpose of not having ratified the Geneva Convention in the first place."[14]

Although more of a victory for US propaganda than a strategic military success, the Doolittle Raid caused great shock, fear, and hatred among Japanese society. It demonstrated that Japan's remoteness no longer offered an impenetrable defense—surely invoking similar feelings felt in the US following the surprise attack on Pearl Harbor. Although the retaliatory attack was directed at military targets in Tokyo, Nagoya, Kobe, and Yokohama, dozens of civilians were killed, and hundreds wounded. As a result, Japan considered this attack to be contrary to international law, and military and government officials, along with the broader Japanese public, demanded revenge. For example, an article in *Photo Weekly Magazine* chastised the "guerrilla-type air raids" and the "cowardice acts" of the American flyers, who "focused their attacks on innocent people and ordinary city streets. [...] The fact that the enemy has gone so far as to strafe our schools and fire upon helpless children particularly reveals his true but diabolical character." During the nation's most trying moment of national security in generations, the press focused on portraying the Americans, as Paradis confirmed, "as the newest Mongol horde, drunk on the blood of innocent Japanese schoolchildren." Further, the Japanese government sought to reassure the public that the attack had been trivial, asserting that "there is no country which has been defeated only by air raids, regardless of how many it sustained."[15] As Tojo Hideki, General of the Imperial Japanese Army and Prime Minister of Japan for most of the war, later revealed in a postwar interrogation, Japan desired revenge and sought to intimidate the Allies, especially the air crews, and to prevent future aerial assaults by inflicting extreme punishment on the captured American flyers.[16] In fact, one article in *Nichi Nichi* proposed that "all enemy aviators who fall in our hands, after defacing this blessed land of ours, should be beheaded without discrimination."[17]

Of the sixteen B-25 bombers that participated in the Doolittle Raid, fifteen managed to land in China after completing their attack on Japan (figures 1.4–1.7). The sixteenth aircraft landed in Vladivostok (Soviet Union), and its crew was interned for over a year.[18] Out of the 80 crewmembers who participated in the raid, seventy-seven survived the mission, eight of whom were captured by Japanese forces in Eastern China (1st Lt Dean E. Hallmark, 1st Lt Robert J. Meder, 1st Lt Chase Nielsen, 1st Lt William G. Farrow, 1st Lt Robert L. Hite, 2nd Lt George Barr, Sgt Harold A. Spatz, and Sgt Jacob DeShazer).[19] After bailing out of their bomber off the coast and swimming ashore near Juexi, China, Nielson, Hallmark, and Meder were sheltered in the house of the mayor, Yang Shimiao. Locals reported, however, that the Japanese had massacred villagers, including the mayor, for assisting, or at least being friendly to, the flyers (figures 1.8–1.9).[20]

Over the next four months, the eight captured airmen endured intense interrogations at the hands of Japanese Army and Kempeitai officials (military police—similar to the Gestapo in Nazi Germany). The Kempeitai, as Paradis revealed, was "long a dumping ground for delinquent soldiers [... and] answerable only to itself in occupied foreign cities. [...]. That meant that being in the Kempeitai was a license to torture, kill, and steal."

Figure 1.4. Lt Col Doolittle sitting by the wing of his wrecked B-25 in China after he led the daring US air raid on Japan, accessed November 16, 2021, https://www.fold3.com/image/29022797, NARA, RG 342, Series FH, Roll: 3A02459-3A03299, Reference Number 3A02985-B25758AC.

Figure 1.5. Some of Doolittle's men grouped outside an air raid shelter carved into the mountainside in China, accessed November 16, 2021, https://www.fold3.com/image/29022793, NARA RG 342, Series FH, Roll 3A02459-3A03299, Reference Number 3A02984-C25758AC.

Figure 1.6. Four Doolittle Raiders (Left to Right: Lt Clayton J. Campbell, Sgt Adam R. Williams, Lt Edgar E. McElroy, and Sgt Robert C. Bourgeois) with Chinese soldiers, accessed November 16, 2021, https://www.fold3.com/image/29022815, NARA RG 342, Series FH, Roll 3A02459-3A03299, Reference Number 3A02987-A25759AC.

Figure 1.7. Four Doolittle Raiders in China. Left to Right: Lt James H. Macia, Jr., Lt Jack A. Sims, S/Sgt Jacob J. Eirman, and Maj Jack A. Hilger, accessed November 16, 2021, https://www.fold3.com/image/29022807, NARA RG 342, Series, FH, Roll 3A02459-3A03299, Reference Number 3A02986-25759AC.

38 | Axis Policies to Combat Downed Enemy Flyers

Figure 1.8. Example of a US propaganda leaflet dropped on Taiwan in March 1944. It explains in Chinese that the island must be bombed to expel the "Jap monkeys," accessed November 16, 2021, https://www.fold3.com/image/29019486, NARA RG 342, Series FH, Roll 3A02459-3A03299, Reference Number 3A02892A-27838AC.

Figure 1.9. Example of US propaganda leaflet dropped on the Japanese mainland warning civilians of looming attacks on cities if the Japanese continue to resist. "War for Civilians: 1945 Propaganda Leaflet," Pritzker Military Museum and Library, accessed November 16, 2021, https://www.pritzkermilitary.org/explore/museum/permanent-current-upcoming-exhibits/allied-race-victory-air-land-and-sea-ca/warning-civilians.

Interrogators demanded information concerning the flyers' roles in the air raid, especially their departure location, as well as broader intelligence on US military strategy and technology. After weeks of mistreatment that included beatings, waterboarding, use of a rack, electrocution, and deprivation of food and medical treatment, several flyers, surely exhausted and in agony, signed documents that admitted they had indiscriminately attacked nonmilitary targets. In doing so, the flyers ultimately signed their own death warrants.[21]

In July 1942, the Japanese Ministry of War issued a directive, identified as Army Secret Order No. 2190, which determined that enemy airmen who acted against these rules of war (i.e., participated in indiscriminate bombing) would be tried before special courts-martial and harshly disposed of (*genjushobun*) as war criminals. Building upon this ex post facto order, the Japanese government circulated Military Order No. 4 (also known as the "Enemy Airmen's Act") on August 13, 1942, which approved the execution, life imprisonment, or incarceration for a minimum of ten years for any enemy flyer who attacked civilians, their property, and any other nonmilitary targets on Japanese soil (including its occupied territories). This mandate set the

40 | Axis Policies to Combat Downed Enemy Flyers

precedent for Japan to retroactively prosecute the eight Doolittle Raiders and provided a model to deal with enemy flyers in the future.[22]

Two weeks later, on August 28, 1942, the eight Doolittle Raiders were put on trial for bombing civilians. The eight flyers had no knowledge they were even being prosecuted when they were assembled in a room before several Japanese officers. Only later did they learn that they were charged with having committed a war crime. During their hearing in a kangaroo court, the flyers did not receive the opportunity to appeal their charges; neither they nor witnesses were not allowed to testify at the proceedings; they were forbidden to give a defense and were not represented by counsel. No attempt was made at the trial to verify or prove that the signed confessions were genuine and under what circumstances they were made. The proceedings did not last long—roughly an hour—as the verdict had largely been agreed upon prior to the commencement of the hearing. Based on the signed confessions and the Kempeitai interrogation reports, the judges sentenced all eight flyers to death. Following the advice of Prime Minister Tojo, Emperor Hirohito eventually commuted the judgments of five flyers to life imprisonment. The death sentences for the three remaining airmen (Hallmark, Farrow, and Spatz) were, however, approved, as military and government officials alleged that they had killed children during their bombing attack. As a result, on October 14, 1942, Hallmark, Farrow, and Spatz were taken to a cemetery near Shanghai to be executed. Blindfolded and forced to kneel, guards tied the airmen to wooden crosses and a firing squad executed them. Afterwards, their bodies were cremated, and their ashes were placed in unmarked urns that were ultimately discovered by US investigators after the war.[23]

Despite perpetrators and their accomplices destroying countless documents in an attempt to conceal the details of the executions, investigators recovered letters written by Hallmark, Farrow, and Spatz to their family and friends. The young men found it difficult to comprehend the situation, but bravely encouraged their loved ones not to worry about them and to live a full and rich life. In the closing line to his mother, Farrow poignantly wrote, "Read 'Thanatopsis' by Bryant if you want to know how I am taking this. My faith in God is complete, so I am unafraid." Referring to the poem by American poet William Cullen Bryant, the epigraph for this chapter is the closing section of Bryant's poem.[24]

When it was finally made public in the United States in mid-October 1942 that Japanese forces had captured eight Doolittle Raiders and put them on trial as war criminals, the American public (and even the world) was in shock, as the US government had not previously revealed that there were any casualties among the eighty flyers. Headlines across the country read "Nation's Anger Rises at Jap Murders"; "Public Aroused by Cold Blooded Executions of American Fliers"; "Demands for New Offensives against Japanese."[25] The *New York Times* even criticized the US War Department for withholding this significant information, writing, "Surely it would have been better to announce these facts before Japan forced an announcement or at least refrained from statements encouraging a mistaken impression. The practices of withholding bad news or of making good news sound better than it is [causes...] a loss of public confidence."[26] It was not until April 1943 that the US government confirmed and revealed publicly the fate of Hallmark, Farrow, and Spatz (figure 1.10) The airmen's executions caused massive public outrage and prompted renewed calls for swift and just retribution against Japan, as had similarly followed the attack on Pearl Harbor. While President Franklin Delano Roosevelt (FDR) and a majority of the US Congress agreed during the war that a stern and just retribution must be authorized, they reasoned that the best justice was to prosecute the perpetrators after the war within the international standards that the Allies were fighting to preserve.

Japan did, however, receive support from the Axis powers in Europe, which were closely following the incident, especially given the gradually

Figure 1.10. Sgt Harold Spatz, Lt Dean Hallmark, and Lt William G. Farrow. *SOURCE*: "Execution of 3 Yank Flyers by Japs Revealed," *Washington Star*, September 26, 1945, accessed December 29, 2020, https://imtfe.law.virginia.edu/collections/phelps/1/1/execution-3-yank-flyers-japs-revealed-news-article.

42 | Axis Policies to Combat Downed Enemy Flyers

intensifying air war over Europe. By October 1942, Berlin radio broadcasts reportedly claimed that the German High Command was "contemplating severer measures against all war prisoners accused of employing 'gangster methods' including airmen who intentionally attack civilian objectives and civilians."[27] Once the fate of Hallmark, Farrow, and Spatz was made public in April 1943, Berlin radio broadcasts reportedly "applauded the execution of US airmen who raided Tokyo. The German people will approve of the Japanese precedent in the execution of airmen who deliberately bombed non-military objectives. [. . .] It was the proper answer to that form of aerial warfare, which the British and Americans have made their standard pattern, in the belief that it will wear down the Axis homefront."[28]

As the war progressed, fighting and tactics became more ruthless, as nations became more determined and desperate to succeed. Imperial Japan, Nazi Germany, and Fascist Italy not only publicized increased threats of severe punishment against downed American airmen but also reported their willingness to carry out further executions of captured flyers.[29] While deeply concerned, journalists in the United States rationalized,

> If it is an introduction to the vindictive maltreatment or execution of pris-
> oners [. . .] there is nothing to do about it immediately except speed up the
> end [of the war]. America cannot enter a contest of reprisal against helpless
> persons with Japan because it would almost immediately be on a sub-human
> level. If this country's punishment of Japan is going to mean hell for pris-
> oners, the only thing to do is to step up the pace and shorten the agony of
> the victims.[30]

Generally, when Japanese soldiers captured enemy flyers, they were sent to local army headquarters, where they were confined and questioned for information regarding past and future air raid targets, aircraft equipment, technology, capabilities, crew members, and mission tactics, although it was not out of the ordinary for flyers to be beaten, even killed, by civilian mobs before Japanese soldiers or police officers could take them into custody. The Japanese Army was ultimately responsible for captured flyers; however, the Kempeitai often conducted investigations, which involved brutal interroga-tions, to determine whether the airmen had participated in indiscriminate bombing. It was often impossible to determine which aircraft dropped bombs that inflicted damage on certain areas, especially when bombing formations could comprise hundreds of aircraft; yet, it was only a matter of time before the young men gave in to brutal torture, even if it meant falsely confessing to indiscriminate attacks.[31] However, if the gun camera in fighter aircraft was salvaged, the images could be used to verify whether or not the pilots targeted nonmilitary targets. If the flyers were not suspected of having participated in indiscriminate bombing, then they generally were sent to a POW camp, where mistreatment, malnourishment, lack of medical treatment, and forced labor remained common.

The treatment of captured flyers was based on multiple factors, including the personal and combat experiences of Japanese citizens as well as their varying dispositions regarding prisoners, the air war, and their xenophobic mindset regarding foreigners. Nevertheless, simply being an enemy prisoner, especially a flyer, was often cause enough for soldiers or civilians to resort to extreme violence. Occasionally, kangaroo courts were held; however, beginning in February 1944 with Army Secret Order No. 1289, permission first had to be secured from central authorities in Tokyo. Nevertheless, a guilty verdict was often agreed upon before a trial began. The rulings resulted mostly in the death penalty, and very few airmen managed to escape their sentences, as the Japanese swiftly carried out the punishment.

The vast geographic expanse of the Pacific Theater resulted in varying methods in which Japanese soldiers treated downed airmen. Generally, once Japanese forces captured an enemy flyer, they reported the case to military headquarters in Tokyo and waited for orders regarding further action. Numerous instances from remote Pacific islands and occupied territories reveal, however, that local Japanese officers often dealt with the circumstances on their own with "on-the-spot punishment" (*genchi-shobun*).[32] A rather common method used by the Japanese in China, Japanese soldiers resorted to such violent measures due to the intense combat, desire for revenge, the lack of prompt communication with Tokyo officials, or simply because they did not want to care for an enemy prisoner when it was difficult enough to provide food and water for their own soldiers. In fact, on more than one occasion Japanese officers permitted cannibalism among their soldiers as captured prisoners (including American flyers) and even their own dead comrades allegedly offered the only source of nourishment.[33]

In September 1944, as the war and the mistreatment of POWs continued to intensify, Japan approved Army Secret Order No. 9087, which prohibited any information regarding the capture of enemy airmen and the severe punishment imposed upon them to be made public. This was an attempt to conceal the increasing number of executions carried out on captured flyers and to prevent outrage of the Allied nations, which would surely increase the scale and frequency of the devastating bombing raids. The Japanese government and military also sought to prevent any potential internal division within Japanese society. While a significant portion of the Japanese

44 | Axis Policies to Combat Downed Enemy Flyers

public supported the revenge taken against captured enemy airmen, the ways and means by which the flyers were executed might have shocked Japanese civilians as being dishonorable and immoral.[34] Moreover, the Japanese government needed to prevent any potential discontent felt by the public toward the regime and its inability to hinder the Allied air raids.[35]

Following the conclusion of the war in Europe in May 1945, aerial bombing escalated in the Pacific to finally bring the global war to an end. As a result, public opinion and domestic stability in Japan became more critical, and the number of flyers executed peaked. Staff Headquarters in Tokyo dispatched orders to all armies that it was no longer necessary to send flyers to Tokyo unless they thought the airmen had some worthwhile information. Instead, the Army should conduct simple and speedy trials to deal with downed flyers. However, the Legal Bureau of the War Ministry intervened, reporting that it would be necessary to obtain approval from the War Ministry for the execution of airmen found guilty by a court-martial.[36]

There was a growing divide between the Japanese military and government (and even within the government itself) throughout the war, but especially during the final months of the conflict. Since the Doolittle Raid, flyers were considered a problem of an international nature, and government officials sought to avoid international complications, especially following the repeated protests from the United States. However, the devastation inflicted by the bombing raids aroused public opinion in Japan, and the government sought to take an immediate stance against those individuals they could hold responsible for the aerial attacks—downed Allied airmen. Thus, while government officials wanted to avoid the responsibility for ordering executions because they were allegedly worried their actions could provoke reprisals against the thousands of Japanese interned in the United States, Japanese military officials felt urged to take action.[37]

In June and July 1945, an emergency procedure was devised that permitted the execution of captured flyers. The Kempeitai Headquarters in Tokyo sent an unofficial message to the various Army headquarters, indicating that the process of court-martialing captured flyers was taking too long and that the War Ministry and General Staff Headquarters recommended that the Army "appropriately dispose" (*tekito ni shochi*) of flyers in their custody without trial. The "very secret" communiqué ordered that the document be burned after reading; however, recipients of the message interpreted it in two conflicting ways—either to forward captured flyers to a POW camp or to execute the flyers. Examples of both interpretations occurred; however, if captured enemy flyers were meant to be sent to a

Axis Policies to Combat Downed Enemy Flyers | 45

POW camp, there would not have been a need to keep the message secret and to destroy it.[38]

The Japanese government knew that international complications would arise following the punishment of flyers, and if America did protest, the government could say that no order or regulations to execute flyers without trial had been issued. Further, they could place blame on the commanding generals of the Army and Kempeitai officials, who voluntarily carried out the executions. For national defense and survival, it was necessary to prevent further incendiary bombings of cities, which were becoming insufferable. For this reason, the government indirectly agreed to execute the flyers.

As commanding general of both the Sixteenth Area Army and the Western District Army, Yokoyama Isamu decided to obey the intentions of the central government and immediately wrote an order to his subordinate officers, Ito Shoshin and Sato Yoshinao, stating that

> the Allied forces will probably burn all the cities in Japan by incendiary bombs; we must defend Kyushu; I have decided to go along with the new policy of the central government, that is, to omit the trial provided for in the Enemy Airmen Act; Ito and Sato are to conduct executions in accordance with the policy of the central government and conduct investigations as to the guilt of the flyers accurately.[39]

Yokoyama concluded his order, writing, "I have decided to concern myself only with the decisive battle and hereafter do not bother me with the problem of flyers." This resulted in local army officials believing that the central government gave them free rein regarding captured airmen.[40]

Maj Yanase Takahashi, from the Western District Kempeitai Headquarters, testified during a postwar crimes trial that the letter he received from the Kempeitai Headquarters in Tokyo stated that the Imperial Palace and Ise Shrine, which were the most sacred institutions of the Japanese people, had recently been subjected to bombings; that thereafter the air raids would become more intense and as a result the number of captured flyers would probably increase. Therefore, the letter suggested that each district Kempeitai Headquarters should contact the respective Army Headquarters in that area as soon as possible and to properly dispose of the airmen in their custody. No request was made for a report of the results, indicating the fear that the secret might leak out and the urgency of resolving the flyer problem. Thus, in view of all this information, Yanase concluded that the lower headquarters were to execute the flyers without trial. The following case narrative further demonstrates the result this secret message had on the treatment of captured flyers and the chaos that ensued in the final months of the war.[41]

On the night of June 19, 1945, Fukuoka was severely bombed, destroying a considerable portion of the city. At the time, eight US airmen were in custody under investigation for indiscriminate bombing. Following the air raid, Capt Wako Yusei inquired whether they should execute the airmen and make it appear that they had died in the bombing. Initially, Wako secured Yokoyama's permission to execute four flyers. He then ordered guards to dig a pit in a corner of the headquarters area. Meanwhile, officials decided to execute the remaining four flyers in custody as well. Each flyer was led to the pit, and each was subsequently beheaded before a crowd of numerous onlookers (figures 1.11–1.15). One of the executioners, Toji Kentaro (a member

Figure 1.11. Crew of B-29 44-69887. Back row (left to right): Capt Bernard L. McCaskill*, 1st Lt Buell T. Higgins*, 1st Lt Carl R. Gustavson, 1st Lt Joseph A. Ptaszkowski, M/Sgt Robert J. Aspinall. Front row (left to right): Sgt Dorsey L. Riddlemoser, Sgt Marvin L. Binger, Sgt Julius R. Rivss, Sgt Leon L. Melesky*, Sgt John C. Edwards, S/Sgt Galen J. Westmoreland. *On this fateful mission, the following three men replaced the designated crewmembers: 1st Lt Richard A. Gray, 1st Edger A. Grempler, and 2nd Lt Matt C. Myers. Courtesy of Hiroyuki Fukao.

Axis Policies to Combat Downed Enemy Flyers | 47

Figure 1.12. Monument for the crew of B-29 44-69887 in Japan. Courtesy of Hiroyuki Fukao.

Figure 1.13. Crew of B-29 42-63549. The crew included: 1st Lt James W. McKillip, 2nd Lt John Y. Lambert, Jr., 2nd Lt Norman S. Siegel, 2nd Lt Harley Hammerman, T/Sgt Edgar L. McElfresh, S/Sgt Albert A. Yokubonis, S/Sgt Lewis C. Balser, Jr., T/Sgt Vernon L. Galyardt, Sgt Ralph S. Romines, Sgt Otto W. Baumgarten, and Sgt William E. Beckman. Courtesy of Hiroyuki Fukao.

Figure 1.14. Monument for the crew of B-29 42-63549 "Empire Express." Courtesy of Hiroyuki Fukao.

Figure 1.15. Monument for the crew of B-29 42-63549 "Empire Express." Courtesy of Hiroyuki Fukao.

of the Air Intelligence Section of the Western Army), was building a coffin for his mother, who had been killed in the air raid the previous day, when he noticed that the executions of American airmen were about to take place. He eagerly volunteered along with numerous other men.[42]

The same Japanese officials who ordered and participated in the executions of the eight flyers on June 20, 1945, also ordered the brutal slayings of an additional twelve American airmen on about August 10 and 15, 1945. A guerrilla unit was ordered to carry out the executions to train the young men in guerrilla tactics for the expected Allied invasion of Japan. Officials anticipated that there might be a shortage of weapons, so the men were trained in using bows and arrows and karate.[43]

On August 10, a truck transported eight American flyers to the Aburayama crematorium in Fukuoka; all were blindfolded with their hands bound and unaware of the horrific fate that awaited them (figures 1.16–1.18). Witnesses reported that there were around thirty to forty onlookers, including civilians.

Figure 1.16. Crew of the B-29 42-93953. Back row (left to right): 1st Lt Ralph E. Miller, 1st Lt Clyde M Roush, 2nd Lt Charles C. Winder, 2nd Lt Joseph H. Finkelstein, *2nd Lt Jack M. Berry*. Front row (left to right): T/Sgt William H. Chapman, Sgt Albert R. Howard, *Sgt Jack V. Dengler, Cpl Irving A. Corliss*, Cpl Clark B. Bassett, Jr., *Pvt Merlin R. Calvin*. Italicized names indicate those who are known to have been executed. "Merlin R. Calvin," accessed February 3, 2021, https://www.findagrave.com/memorial/56117066/merlin-r.-calvin.

Figure 1.17. Back row (left to right): *1st Lt James E. Hewitt,* F/O Gerald E. Boleyn, *F/O Charles S.* Appleby, 1st Lt John W. Gothie, 2nd Lt Wayne A. Whitely. Front row (left to right): *S/SGT Ben Thornton,* T/Sgt William N. Andrews, Cpl Robert J. Zancker, Cpl Martin W. O'Brien, *Cpl Frederick A. Stearns,* Cpl Robert R. Sawdye. Italicized names indicate those who are known to have been executed. "Frederick Allen Stearns," accessed February 5, 2021, https://www.camptakodah.org/about/history/memorial-lodge/lost-takodians-world-war-ii/frederick-allen-stearns/; http://macrj.net/b24-42-94098/.

Everyone present was warned to keep the incident a secret. Many men volunteered to participate in the executions, and four were selected. The first five flyers were beheaded. However, Itezono Tatsuo suggested that karate be used to kill the sixth victim. A guard held the flyer by his left arm while another man, Noda Hidehiko, prepared himself. He stripped down to his undershirt, backed up three or four steps, assumed a crouched position, ran toward the prisoner, stopped just before reaching him and, in a boxer's stance, struck the flyer once in the diaphragm. The flyer moaned and slumped forward, whereupon the guard pulled him up straight. Noda repeated this a few more times. Enatsu Tokuji told Noda that he was not using proper technique and illustrated the proper way. Noda again punched the

Figure 1.18. Back row (left to right): 1st Lt Robert G. Neal and 1st Lt Louis J. Winiecki, Jr. Front row (left to right): 1st Lt Richard S. Lane, S/Sgt Robert W. Goulet, S/Sgt William Cohen. "Robert G. Neal Crew," accessed February 5, 2021, https://pacificwrecks.com/aircraft/b-25/44-31300/b25j-neal-pose.html.

flyer two or three times in the diaphragm. The flyer continued to moan in pain, doubling over in agony, but he refused to collapse. Annoyed with Noda's inability to kill the flyer, an officer took the American to the edge of the pit and executed him.[44]

Karate was attempted again on the next flyer; however, the blows continued to prove ineffective in killing the prisoner. Frustrated, one of the guards kicked the flyer twice between his legs, which caused him to fall forward in severe pain. Immediately, others began to strike the flyer. Dazed and in agony, the flyer was dragged to the pit and executed. For the next victim, Itezono ordered a guard to try *Kesagiri*, which involved cutting through the flyer's shoulder down through his lungs. Despite ruthlessly suffering from his wounds, the flyer remained alive. Itezono then ordered the guard to thrust his sword into his heart. The flyer's body was then thrown in the pit, and the guard was given a drink of whiskey as a token of approval.

For the final prisoner executed this day, officials wanted to try using a bow and arrow. The flyer was made to sit by a corner of the pit, facing the

52 | Axis Policies to Combat Downed Enemy Flyers

crowd as a guard, Otsuki Takahashi, kneeled about ten feet away. Otsuki fired an arrow that struck the flyer in his head, just above his left eye. The next arrow missed, and before he could shoot a third, Itezono stopped him, and the flyer was executed. After the executions, four Japanese soldiers rearranged the bodies in the pit, covered them in a straw mat and filled the pit with dirt. Before concluding the incident, Tomomori Kiyoharu, a subordinate of Itezono, addressed everyone present, stating that the men executed were enemies and not POWs. A few days later, on August 15, 1945, after listening to the emperor's radio broadcast in which he announced Japan's acceptance of the Potsdam Declaration (though he failed to use the word "surrender"), the same perpetrators executed seventeen additional American flyers at the Aburayama Cemetery in Fukuoka. Only after the war did US war crimes investigators discover that similar incidents had occurred throughout Japan after the secret letter from the Kempeitai Headquarters was dispersed in June 1945. Those that are known so far include twenty-seven flyers killed in the Tokai military district, forty-three executed in the Central military district, and twenty-four killed at Fukuoka.[45]

The United States apprehended and prosecuted four Japanese officers, Sawada Shigeru, Wako Yusei, Okada Ryuhei, and Tatsuta Sotojiro, who were involved in the 1942 show trial of the Doolittle Raiders and, after a seventeen-day trial in 1946, sentenced them to from five to nine years imprisonment. The verdict shocked everyone at the trial and the broader public as well. Americans and Japanese (both military and civilians alike) felt certain that the accused would be sentenced to death. Newspapers throughout the United States ran scornful articles criticizing the US military trial and demanding a new trial. The mothers of Dean Hallmark and William Farrow told reporters that the Japanese "deserve the death penalty. Nothing the Americans could do to them would be equal to what they did to my son and the other fliers." Yet, Harold Spatz's father responded that, while unfortunate, "It is all a part of war, we must take it as it comes."[46] Upon review of the verdict, Colonel Edward H. Young, Army Judge Advocate for US forces in China, concluded that "such extremely lenient and inadequate penalties committed a serious error of judgement. However, [. . .] with few recorded precedents available [. . .,] if an error in judgement was made, then contrary to the Japanese ideas of justice and humanity, the commission favored the accused with all the benefits thereof."[47] In the end, Sawada, Okada, and Tatsuta were released from prison by January 1950. The fourth convicted perpetrator, Wako, was tried again (in 1948) for having committed similar crimes against American flyers in Fukuoka and ultimately sentenced to death; however, this was suspended after Jacob DeShazer—a surviving raider who became a missionary in Japan—wrote a letter opposing Wako's death sentence. "By executing criminals," DeShazer wrote, "we are putting ourselves, in the eyes of God and the other nations of the world, on the same cruel level as the butchering Nazi and Japanese governments." He continued, "Wako was once an enemy who had some obscure job of punishing his enemies, myself, and some of my friends, but [. . .] I now earnestly forgive him." Wako was ultimately released from prison with all remaining Japanese war criminals in December 1958.[48]

European Theater

In Europe, the mistreatment of downed airmen became an escalating problem after the fall of 1942, as the Allied air raids increased in frequency and degree of devastation. As previously cited, the international press quoted radio broadcasts from Berlin that not only applauded the Japanese murders of the Doolittle Raiders but also indicated that Nazi Germany was "contemplating severer measures" against prisoners who employed "gangster methods."[49] The treatment of captured flyers was, however, a concern in Germany from the early stages of the war. In May 1940, following the invasion of France, reports of downed German airmen mistreated by French civilians and soldiers resulted in Berlin radio broadcasts announcing that "every time the murder of a German airman is reported, 25 captured French airmen will be shot. If German airmen are attacked while parachuting for their lives, 50 French prisoners will be shot."[50] While it remains to be determined if these statements were purely propaganda, they do express the mounting escalation of the war, particularly the increased desire among the enemy population (both military and civilian) to seek revenge against downed enemy flyers.

As the war persisted, the intensity of combat was drastically amplified. Aerial attacks became an augmented characteristic of the war during the Battle of Britain as the Luftwaffe and the RAF fought for air superiority over Great Britain, though, much to the chagrin of the Germans, the Blitz not only failed to conquer the skies over the United Kingdom but also failed to demoralize the citizens—despite killing over forty thousand—or seriously hinder war production efforts.[51] While Great Britain managed to successfully defend against the Luftwaffe attacks, its citizens continued to endure aerial attacks throughout the war. The "revenge weapons" (*Vergeltungswaffen*) particularly wreaked death and destruction on London and other cities in southern England (as well as in Belgium and the Netherlands); however, they were far less destructive than the Blitz.

54 | Axis Policies to Combat Downed Enemy Flyers

Of the hundreds of German flyers shot down over Great Britain during the war, few are known to have been mistreated; however, one documented incident resulted in the court-martial of British Brigadier General Guy Percy Lumsden Drake-Brookman. On September 17, 1940, British spitfires shot down a German Ju-88 (#3188) before it could bomb the Warrington Propellor factory—situated between Liverpool and Manchester. The pilot, Maj Heinz Cramer, crashed near Imber, just outside of Warminster in southern England. One crewmember, Lt Otto Heinrich, died due to wounds sustained in the attack, and the three remaining men aboard the aircraft (Maj Cramer, Sgt Paul Stützel, and Sgt Friedrich Schultz) survived with minor wounds.[52]

British soldiers took the flyers into custody and transported them to a nearby army camp where they were guarded outside an orderly room. A crowd of curious civilians and soldiers gathered to finally see the enemy firsthand. Shortly thereafter, Drake-Brookman arrived and approached the flyers. To humiliate the German crew, he ordered them to remove their overalls, coats, and boots, and then removed his knife and slit their trousers, which fell to their ankles. He then assaulted the prisoners with a stick, hitting them in the groin and head, and reportedly yelled: "You buggers bombed London! You bastards have killed my mother!" By this point, several members of the crowd voiced their disapproval of the treatment, but the officer continued. Before the incident became too serious, guards removed the flyers and placed them in separate cells in the guard house for protection.[53]

A fellow British officer, Maj R.M. Millar, testified during a hearing in October 1940 that Drake-Brookman told him, "Let's go and brass up those prisoners again." However, he responded that they had to be held for the RAF interrogation officer and should not be interfered with. Annoyed and angered by his response, Drake-Brookman returned to where the flyers were being held and forced his way into their cells. He cut several badges from the airmen's coats and pushed them, reciting "You bombed London!" several more times. When he approached Cramer, he asked if he spoke English, and when he received no reply said to him, "I'm going to shoot you." However, the incident did not escalate to that point.[54]

As a result of his actions and the countless witnesses, a court-martial was convened to investigate the incident. The prosecutor referred to Drake-Brookman's conduct as "scandalous" and said that he showed complete disregard for "what might happen as a result of his behavior to British prisoners who might fall into German hands or who might be already in German hands." The defense argued that this was a rather harmless incident and that local shepherds had alleged the flyers came down with its guns firing at them. Further, he explained that the accused was under great duress after losing his home and possessions in the aerial bombings and that his mother had a mental breakdown because of her experiences during the air raids. The latter, according to Drake-Brookman, was worse than if she had been killed.[55]

Ultimately, the court found Drake-Brookman guilty of conduct prejudicial of good order and military discipline and for committing a civil offence (common assault) while in uniform. After serving twenty-six years in the British Army, he was dismissed from the military for his actions; however, eager to continue fighting against Nazi Germany, he subsequently enlisted in the Canadian Army. Although this incident occurred relatively early in the war, and it was not particularly vicious, especially when compared to the known Axis violence committed against Allied flyers, it provides an initial comparison to the complex relationship between "the bombers and the bombed."[56] While the British population naturally desired (to an extent) to seek retribution and revenge against German flyers, the British government disapproved of such malevolent violence, and there was relatively limited contact between British citizens and German flyers during the war, unlike in Nazi Germany. Further, the amplified scale of death and destruction inflicted upon Germany through the air war surely had a psychological impact on the population as well. Combined, these factors help explain why atrocities were more likely to be committed against downed Allied flyers.[57]

With the United States entering the war at the end of 1941, the air war became increasing deadly as air supremacy was vital to securing victory. On October 18, 1942, four days after the execution of the Doolittle Raiders, Hitler's Commando Order instructed that "from now on, all enemy soldiers [. . .] in battle or attempting to escape are to be killed to the last man regardless of whether they are seamen, airmen, or paratroopers. Secret agents and saboteurs [. . .] are to be given over to the SD."[58] This initiated the precedent for the verbal orders to "exterminate terror [flyers] and sabotage troops."[59] While scholars have largely understood this order to exclude downed airmen, Axis civilians and soldiers often considered Allied flyers as terrorists and "terror flyers" (*Terrorflieger*). It was difficult for many individuals to differentiate between sabotage troops and downed airmen, even when they honestly desired. Further complicating the distinction between downed flyers and sabotage troops or spies, underground and resistance fighters often gave airmen civilian clothes to help disguise their identity; however, if captured in civilian clothes, Germans commonly regarded such flyers as enemy agents and sought to dispose of them accordingly.

56 | Axis Policies to Combat Downed Enemy Flyers

Beginning in the summer of 1943, the Combined Bomber Offensive attacked Axis targets day and night. Air-to-ground combat raised profound ethical, not to mention legal, issues as aerial attacks killed large numbers of civilians. As a result, Axis citizens encountered an increasing number of downed Allied flyers. Similar to soldiers on the front, the Hague and Geneva Conventions were furthest from their minds as local, party, and military officials increasingly exhibited little restraint of civilians or soldiers from mistreating downed flyers.[60] Heinrich Himmler instructed police officials in August 1943 that "it is not the job of the police to interfere between the German folk and downed English and American terror flyers."[61] Roughly a year later, as the air war engulfed most of Europe, Joseph Goebbels published his well-known article in May 1944, deploring Allied aerial attacks on non-military targets. He even approved and urged Germans to take action as they saw fit and to seek revenge.[62] The Nazi regime's propaganda targeted the "savageness" of Allied airmen, and the media campaign drastically developed following Goebbels's call to arms (figure 1.19). As the plenipotentiary for total war measures, Goebbels sought to increase the responsibility of "ordinary" Germans in the defense of the nation, including the lynching of captured flyers. Although the regime tried to strengthen the *Volksgemeinschaft*, Jürgen Förster and others have demonstrated that the government was incapable of exerting complete control over the population.[63] Using the propaganda to help develop the desired image of enemy flyers, the regime conditioned citizens to act on behalf, and in the defense, of the nation, but also afforded them the validation to act on their own accord. The call for summary justice and lynching by civilians indicated that the regime was desperate to combat the bombings by any means necessary, even if that meant delegating such "justice" to civilians.

In the spring of 1944, Goebbels sought to institute hearings in kangaroo courts for captured Allied airmen to intimidate flyers from attacking the Reich. It was also a direct response to the Soviet military trial held in Kharkov (present-day Ukraine) in December 1943. As the first time German soldiers were tried for war crimes committed during World War II, the tribunal charged three German officers—members of the Wehrmacht Secret Field Police (*Geheime Feldpolizei*), Auxiliary Police, and SD *Sonderkommando*—in participating in the execution of tens of thousands of Soviet citizens (Jews, Communists, Soviet POWs, and other civilians) during the German occupation of Kharkov from October 1941 until August 1943.[64] After Soviet troops discovered mass graves of men, women and children, the German defendants admitted their role in committing the crimes, even describing in detail their

Axis Policies to Combat Downed Enemy Flyers | 57

Figure 1.19. Entitled "'Scientific' Bombing." FDR states to American flyers: "So, boys—pay attention. All the churches and national sanctuaries are marked in red on the map." *Kladderadatsch*, August 15, 1943, page 2, http://digi.ub.uni-heidelberg.de/diglit/kla1943/0443.

58 | Axis Policies to Combat Downed Enemy Flyers

methods, for example using gas vans, mass shootings, beatings, hangings, and burnings. While they argued that they had simply followed orders and, therefore, should not be held responsible, the Soviet tribunal convicted and executed the Germans. This, and the fact that details of the Nazi system of mass extermination were gradually being publicly revealed, enraged Goebbels. He immediately tried to whitewash the accounts of German atrocities in the international press and demanded retribution; however, German military officials protested holding hearings of downed flyers in kangaroo courts, similar to the ones conducted by Japan, because they were concerned about the fate of German POWs as well as how the trials would affect the "increasing public feeling against Allied airmen, many of whom have been murdered by infuriated civilians [. . .] in German territory after raids on German cities."[65]

Throughout June 1944, the process of finalizing the classification of a *Terrorflieger* took place. The desired treatment of enemy flyers was also established as well as how to implement the topic in propaganda. After the initial meeting on June 6, 1944, the specifics were set by June 14, with the Reich Foreign Ministry (Auswärtiges Amt) agreeing to them by June 20. The latter did, however, have "objections founded on international law."[66] Nevertheless, the regime proceeded. Clearly influenced by Japan's Enemy Airmen's Act from August 1942, Germany established four criteria that constituted acts of terror for which airmen could be executed. These included: 1) attacking civilians, 2) firing at German aircrews as they descended in their parachutes, 3) attacking passenger trains in public service, and 4) attacking military and civilian hospitals and hospital trains, which are clearly marked with the Red Cross. This information was distributed by the High Command of the Armed Forces (Oberkommando der Wehrmacht [OKW]) to the High Command of the Air Force (Oberkommando der Luftwaffe [OKL]), the Reich Foreign Ministry, and the chiefs of the Security Police (Sicherheitspolizei [SiPo]) and Security Service of the SS (Sicherheitsdienst [SD]), and was used to "justify the transfer of POW enemy airmen from the Oberursel flyer processing camp [Dulag Luft] to the SD for *Sonderbehandlung*."[67]

Since Germany was a signatory of the Geneva Convention, the main issue that the Reich Foreign Ministry had to solve was the redesignation of POWs to "legally" impose "special treatment" (*Sonderbehandlung*). According to the Reich Foreign Ministry, "When an enemy airman has been captured by the armed forces or by the police and has been delivered to Dulag Luft at Oberursel, he thereby has already acquired the legal status of a prisoner of war."[68] Thus, officials maintained that an emergency solution would be to prevent suspected airmen from ever attaining a legal prisoner of war status; that is, that immediately upon seizure they be told that they are regarded not as prisoners of war, but as criminals, and that they will be delivered not to [. . .] a prisoner of war camp, but to the authorities [. . .] for the prosecution of criminal acts. If interrogations during those proceedings should reveal circumstances which show that *Sonderbehandlung* is not applicable to the particular case, then the airman concerned might [. . .] be subsequently transferred to the legal status of prisoners of war by being sent to the reception camp at Oberursel. Naturally even this expedient would not prevent Germany from being accused of violating existing treaties [. . .] but at least this [. . .] would make it possible to follow a clear line; thus, relieving us of the necessity of openly renouncing the present agreements, or, upon publication of each individual case, using excuses which no one will believe.[69]

While *Sonderbehandlung* is a notorious Nazi euphemism used to indicate execution, for example, of Jews, Sinti, Roma, the handicapped, and others designated as "undesirable" during the regime's campaign of mass murder and genocide, the term also signified a potential treatment with which captured flyers could be confronted. The inclusion of Allied airmen in the group of potential victims of this violence reveals the Nazi regime's deep hatred for enemy flyers and the severe impact the air war had on Axis violence.

Although the Luftwaffe was ultimately responsible for downed Allied airmen, there remained confusion among German military forces and frustration among the various police units regarding jurisdiction. Such irritation is evident in a memo from the head of the SiPo and SD in Rhein/Westmark to the Gestapo, KriPo, and SD within the region in October 1944: "The Wehrmacht often prevents the suitable procedure by the [German] population against the downed *Tiefflieger* by arresting and guarding them. In the future, all related cases are to be immediately and thoroughly documented and reported, detailing the individuals and the incidents."[70]

A December 1944 order from Lieutenant General Schmidt reiterated this issue, referring to Goebbels's newspaper article from May of that same year. Schmidt wrote that

recently, soldiers have actively protected Anglo-American *Terrorflieger* from the civilian population, thus causing justified resentment. You will take immediate steps to ensure by oral instruction of all subordinate units and

60 | Axis Policies to Combat Downed Enemy Flyers

authorities that soldiers do not oppose the civilian population in such cases by demanding that the enemy flyers be handed over to them as prisoners, and by protecting, and thus ostensibly siding with, the enemy *Terrorflieger*.[71]

Like the orders in Japan, once these instructions were verbally distributed to lower-level officials, all correspondence relating to the mistreatment of *Terrorflieger* was to be destroyed. Although the verbal transmission of orders was to conceal the perpetrators' actions and prevent any potential future reprisal by Allied forces, it also resulted in confusion between and within the government, military, and police forces regarding the proper and desired treatment of captured flyers.

As Germany's defeat became evident to its citizens, Berlin issued a general order in March 1945 to Kreisleiter and Ortsgruppenleiter throughout the Reich, demanding that captured enemy flyers be killed. During a postwar US investigation that implicated the Kreisleiter of Berchtesgaden, Bernhard Stredele, and Ortsgruppenleiter in Berchtesgaden County (August Kobus and others) in the mistreatment of downed American airmen, witnesses revealed that Stredele verbally circulated the directions from Berlin, ordering that "all American pilots who bombed German cities and villages are not soldiers, but should be considered criminals," and "whenever any of them land they should be done away with."[72]

A few weeks after this meeting, on April 16, 1945—just three weeks before the war ended in Europe—an American flyer, Captain Chester E. Coggeshall Jr. was shot down near the small village of Sillersdorf, located a few miles northwest of Freilassing, across the border from Salzburg, Austria (figure 1.20). During a strafing mission, a mechanical issue forced Coggeshall to belly land his P-51 Mustang, nicknamed "Cape Cod Express," in an open field. His wingmen reported that his aircraft's right wing dug into the ground, going at a high rate of speed, and then the aircraft cartwheeled into a small farm building along the edge of the field; however, Coggeshall was only slightly wounded and managed to climb out of the wreckage. Members of the local Gendarmerie and military personnel immediately surrounded Coggeshall and escorted him to the courthouse in Freilassing.[73]

The Ortsgruppenleiter and mayor of Freilassing, August Kobus, allegedly refused to execute the flyer; however, after discussing the situation on the telephone with his superior, Stredele, who scolded Kobus and threatened that he would "make an example out of him if he did not take advantage of the opportunity given to him," Kobus conceded. Kobus and two soldiers

Figure 1.20. Capt Chester E. Coggeshall, Jr. "Chester E. Coggeshall, Jr.," accessed June 22, 2021, https://www.findagrave.com/memorial/2639236/chester-e-coggeshall.

(Karl Boehm and Rudige von Massow) escorted Coggeshall to a secluded woods outside of town where Kobus shot him twice in the head. The flyer's remains were buried in the local cemetery and eventually discovered by US military after the war.[74] A US war crimes tribunal found Kobus guilty of killing Coggeshall and sentenced him to death, and he was executed on March 15, 1946. As for Kreisleiter Stredele, he was tried and sentenced to death as well in March 1946; however, this ruling was reduced to life imprisonment by a review board. He was eventually paroled in April 1957 after serving just twelve years in prison.[75]

The similarities of Axis methods to deal with downed flyers represented a combination of both calculated and spontaneous responses to the intense and devastating aerial attacks that razed cities and killed hundreds of thousands of Axis civilians. As a result of the escalating conflict, the Axis home front no longer afforded civilians safety from the effects of war. Despite increased technological advancements and the growing reliance on aircraft to support combat operations, aerial attacks were often far from precise, and strategic bombing sought to attack centers of industry and cities to hinder future military production and cripple the enemy's will to fight. The air war brought death to the doorsteps of Axis citizens, as industrial targets were often located near urban centers. Subsequently, the conflict deteriorated at times into an all-out, retaliatory melee and resulted in recurring intrusions on the boundaries of moral acceptability.

2 War Crimes Narratives: Pacific and Southeast Asia

The following ten case narratives were chosen to provide an overall example of the mistreatment downed American flyers faced in the Pacific and Southeast Asia. When known, they identify the victims and perpetrators, describe perpetrators' justifications for mistreating airmen, and portray how the violence transpired. These cases span the vast geographic expanse of the theaters and focus primarily on incidents that occurred in the final year of the war, as they generally offer the most evidence and sources. Using postwar trial testimonies by witnesses, perpetrators, and occasionally victims themselves, in addition to Missing Air Crew Reports (MACR), these examples supplement the statistical analysis of the flyer trials (chapter 4 of this volume) by portraying the personal experiences of mistreated flyers.

December 16, 1944—Hankow (Wuhan), China

On November 21, 1944, Captain Richard G. McMillan and his crew aboard their B-29 Superfortress (42-93848) were returning to Piardoba Airfield in India following a bombing raid over the city of Omura, Japan. The tail gunner, S/Sgt Anthony Tomczak, recalled, "We were attacked by an enemy fighter plane between 1200 and 1300 hours over occupied China. The enemy succeeded in setting number 2 engine afire. [. . .] All efforts were unsuccessful in putting out the fire, and we were losing altitude."[1] Shortly thereafter, McMillan gave the order to bail out, and five crewmembers (T/Sgt Benjamin J. Lisowski, S/Sgt William McMahan, S/Sgt Anthony Tomczak, and Sgt Frank S. Sommer) exited the rear of the aircraft.[2] By this time, however, two of the four engines were knocked out, and the fire spread to the fuselage. The damage made it impossible to lower the landing gear and prevented the crew from bailing out the front escape hatch. They were trapped in the fiery wreckage and had no option but to make a forced landing.

According to the copilot, 1st Lt Vernon Douglas Schaefer, "When we were about 1,500 feet from the ground, we picked up light ground fire and I was hit in the head with a rifle bullet." This rendered Schaefer unconscious, but

64 | War Crimes Narratives: Pacific and Southeast Asia

the wound was not fatal. McMillan belly-landed the aircraft in a rice paddy about 150 miles north of Hankow (present-day Wuhan), China. Once Schaefer regained consciousness, he found himself in a Japanese guard post with three members of his crew—2nd Lt Lester R. White, Sgt Henry W. Wheaton, and Sgt James E. Forbes Jr.—all of whom survived the forced landing. Schaefer attempted to ask them about the whereabouts of the remaining crew but was quickly prevented by a Japanese guard who repeatedly struck him, knocking him unconscious for a second time. Unknown to Schaefer and even to the US military until after the war, Captain Richard G. McMillan (pilot), 2nd Lt Horace R. Brown (navigator), and 2nd Lt James E. Brewer (bombardier) died in the crash. After the war, their remains were discovered in a grave near the crash site.

When Schaefer regained consciousness for a second time, he was alone, and his crewmembers were gone. A Japanese medic arrived a short time later to provide Schaefer with first aid and told him that guards took his crew to Hankow and that he would soon follow. However, this was the final time Schaefer would see White, Wheaton, and Forbes. Roughly a week went by before guards escorted Schaefer to Hankow, where he arrived on December 11 after a long riverboat ride. Held there roughly one month, he was kept isolated for the first three weeks in a makeshift cell and repeatedly interrogated about his crew, their aircraft, and missions. During his final week in Hankow, he was moved to a jail where he reported seeing other POWs, but there remained no sign of White, Wheaton, or Forbes.

Around mid-December Schaefer was transferred to a POW camp near Shanghai following a four-day river boat ride, where he was held roughly until May 1945. He, along with other POWs, were then moved to Peking by train, where he remained for roughly a month. The POWs were then transferred to Shimonnoseki, Japan, via Mukden, Manchuria, and Fusan, Korea. From there, they traveled by train north to Sapporo, where they remained until liberation on September 12, 1945.

As for White, Wheaton, and Forbes, however, they remained in Hankow. Instead of transferring them to a POW camp, as had happened with Schaefer, Chief of Staff of the Japanese 34th Army, Kaburagi Masataka, ordered the three flyers to be confined in the military prison in Hankow (figures 2.1–2.3). During a meeting between Japanese military, gendarmerie, and consulate officials at the residence of Consul General Manabe Ryoichi on December 8, 1944, which happened to be the three-year anniversary of the war between the United States and Japan, the members decided to make an example out of these flyers. As the aerial bombardment of Hankow was wreaking havoc on the city and its inhabitants, Japanese officials saw these airmen as an opportunity to seek revenge as well as a chance to further solidify their influence over the locals. Witnesses at the meeting testified that Lt Gen Sano urged for action, reportedly stating, "The bombing of Hankow has gradually increased in intensity, and if we do not do anything about the situation, damage to the populace will greatly increase. I believe that the situation certainly warrants it, so let us carry out a parade of the American POWs through the streets."[3] While a postwar tribunal was unable to determine Sano's role, due to his death by the end of the war, it was clear that perpetrators sought to place blame on their superiors and deceased comrades.

Similar incidents committed against American flyers were described at the meeting to have occurred elsewhere in the Pacific and that the results had favorably affected civilian morale. Thus, offering the captured flyers to the local populace provided the Japanese with a way to relieve locals' growing discontent caused by the aerial bombardments. Further, it assisted in strengthening Japanese support among the local Chinese and reinforced Japanese authority, as well as providing an ultimate method to deal with captured airmen.

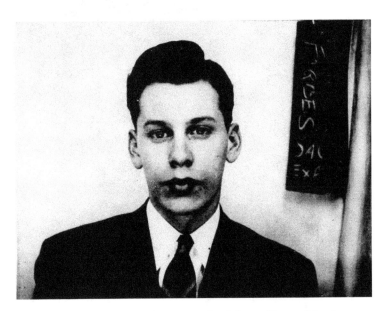

Figure 2.1. Sgt James E. Forbes, Jr. Trial Exhibit C, Photo of Sgt James E. Forbes, Jr. provided by his family, US vs Masataka Kaburagi, et al., Shanghai, China, February 14, 1946, https://www.legal-tools.org/doc/ob3a09/pdf.

Figure 2.2. Sgt Henry W. Wheaton. Trial Exhibit A, Photo of Sgt Henry W. Wheaton provided by his family, US vs Masataka Kaburagi, et al., Shanghai, China, February 14, 1946, https://www.legal-tools.org/doc/0b3a09/pdf.

Figure 2.3. 2nd Lt Lester R. White. Trial Exhibit B, Photo of 2nd Lt Lester R. White provided by his family, US vs Masataka Kaburagi, et al., Shanghai, China, February 14, 1946, https://www.legal-tools.org/doc/0b3a09/pdf.

Chinese civilians, especially the youth, were the primary target of the propaganda and were invited to attend the roughly two-hour-long parade. Fully aware of the illegality of these actions, 1st Lt Izuma relayed his orders to the local Youth Corps for them to take charge of the parade in order to avoid the appearance of the Japanese Army's direct role. A few Army officials had voiced concern that mistreating POWs could have a negative effect on their compatriots in America.[4] Therefore, every attempt was made to evoke a favorable impression upon the public that the event was carried

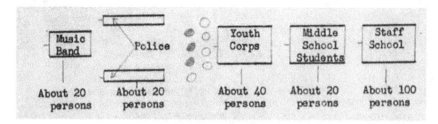

Figure 2.4. Exhibit D—Diagram of the parade layout. The three shaded in circles represent the American flyers and the remaining circles indicate the positions of the Japanese gendarme, wearing Chinese clothes. Exhibit D, Diagram of the parade layout, in US vs Masataka Kaburagi, et al., February 14, 1946, https://www.legal-tools.org/doc/0b3a09/pdf.

out solely by the Chinese. In addition to nearly one hundred Chinese youth from the local middle school, Youth Corps and Youth Cadet School, Izuma even made sure that a band was organized to march in front of the flyers in the parade (figure 2.4).[5]

Shortly before 11:00 a.m. on December 16, gendarme guards bound the arms of White, Wheaton, and Forbes, placed them in the back of a covered truck, and drove them to the Youth Corps school. The flyers had to be held in an office at the school until the parade began around 2:00 p.m., as the guards were unable to handle the large crowd of public on-lookers who came to see the Americans. According to the head of the Japanese gendarmerie, Colonel Kameji Kumuoto, the Army Information Section, sent a report that said, "The parade [. . .] will be a Chinese affair, so the duty of the gendarmes will be to prevent the Japanese people from participating in mob violence and to act as security against escape of the prisoners." Because of this, the five Japanese guards wore Chinese civilian clothes. Kameji further stated in his postwar testimony that,

> from the moment the parade left the school, mob violence against the prisoners broke out. The prisoners were beaten in the parade with a stick by Sgt Takeuchi and with fists by Sgt Fujii and Tsukada. The prisoners were beaten by the crowd [. . .] with their fists, sticks, poles. [. . .] At Hunan Road Tsukada was pushed by someone [in the crowd] and blood from a prisoner's nose stained his overcoat. The parade stopped at [. . . five] places, during which speeches were made by participants of the parade and propaganda leaflets were distributed. No one suggested that the parade be stopped. [. . .] Gendarme Captain Yumoto [. . .] saw that the prisoners' faces were bloody. The Americans were then assaulted in front of the gendarme headquarters. [. . .] The parade

ended at the Youth Corps [school. . .] where the prisoners rested on the lawn. They were so fatigued that they were leaning on each other's shoulders, and practically sleeping with their faces uplifted to the skies.[6]

By the end of the parade, Izumi reportedly told the head of the gendarme guards to prevent any further beating of the prisoners as it had "reached an atrocious stage." While it remains in question whether Izumi actually desired to prevent the mistreatment of the flyers at the end of the parade, as was claimed during the postwar trial, the hostility of the crowd is evident. The conclusion of the parade surely offered the flyers a brief reprieve from the pain and suffering inflicted upon them during the nearly four-mile-long gauntlet of violence; however, the brutality had only just begun.

Roughly an hour after the parade ended, a truck picked up the airmen and brought them to the gendarmerie headquarters. In the meantime, the sun had set; instead of returning the prisoners to their cells, at least five additional gendarme guards boarded the truck, and they departed the jail. Colonel Kameji later described how "arrangements had been made at 9 [p.m.] by the gendarmerie with the crematorium." The Chinese caretaker testified during the postwar crime trial that he was preparing the ovens when the flyers arrived at the crematorium. They were unloaded from the truck and dragged to the waiting room (figure 2.5).[7] Each was given a cigarette as they

Figure 2.5. Crematorium in Hankow, China. Exhibit 17, US vs Masataka Kaburagi, et al., Shanghai, China, February 14, 1946, https://www.legal-tools.org/doc/ob3a09/pdf.

sat next to each other on a long bench with their hands still tied together. The airmen were extremely exhausted due to their prolonged beating during the parade; they could not stand by themselves and were covered in bruises. One at a time, each flyer was led outside to the terrace of the crematorium, beaten with wooden sticks, and forced to lie face up on the ground. From inside the crematorium, Chinese workers reported hearing the flyers' groans and the Japanese soldiers' laughter.[8]

As gendarme Sgt Maj Masui Shozo described during the postwar trial, the guards untied the airman's' hands and put the "rope around the neck of the prisoner and two persons held either end of the rope and pulled and somebody else held the legs and arms of the prisoner." He stated that after several minutes the airman was dead, and they carried his body into the crematorium and placed it in the ovens. This was repeated for the two remaining prisoners, both of whom surely could hear the grim fate that awaited them.[9]

The following morning, Chinese workers arrived and saw the blood on the terrace where the prisoners were beaten and executed. A Japanese gendarme instructed them to throw the ashes into a nearby pond; however, the Chinese workers collected the remains in a dustpan and buried them in a shallow grave beside the crematorium.[10] Izumi told his staff that "whatever you saw or heard last night, you must never tell anyone else and [if necessary, say. . .] that the prisoners were sent to Shanghai." Further, he wrote a report of the incident in which he depicted to his superiors how the "Youth Corps took charge of parading of the American airmen [. . . and that] during the parade, the citizens, especially the women, who had suffered damages and losses because of the bombings, threw themselves at the chests of the American moaning and lamenting. A situation arose in which the populace began to assault the POWs[,] and the gendarmes who were there as security [. . .] were also beaten."[11] While the Japanese officials achieved their desired outcome, even Kaburagi, head of the gendarmerie, mentioned that "the people were more violent than had been expected."[12]

The following evening, on December 17, the city of Hankow was heavily bombed by the US Air Force. While rumors circulated throughout the town that it was retaliation for beating the flyers during the parade, Japanese military and government officials did not believe that the US could have possibly learned so quickly about the beatings during the parade and the execution of the flyers.[13] The air raid not only inflicted renewed physical and psychological damage in Hankow but also likely affected the impact that the propaganda parade had on the local populace the day before.

Following the war, a US war crimes investigation tried eighteen perpetrators, mostly members of the Japanese 34th Army and gendarmerie, for their involvement in committing cruel, inhumane, and brutal atrocities against White, Wheaton, and Forbes. Typical in such war crimes trials, the perpetrators sought to defend their actions by describing their need to strictly follow superior orders; however, the court quickly dismissed these arguments. The offenders similarly sought to place most of the responsibility on Izumi and Sano, who had died by the time of the postwar trial.

The court ultimately sentenced five perpetrators to death, and they were executed in April 1946. One perpetrator received life imprisonment, eleven received sentences ranging from eighteen months to twenty years, and one was acquitted for insufficient evidence. At the end of the trial, when asked whether he thought his participation in killing the flyers was wrong, Masui replied that "once something has been decided by the superiors, we cannot question the right or wrong of the orders."[14] Despite not feeling any regret for participating in the execution of the flyers, Shirakawa (one of the gendarme guards who executed the flyers that night at the crematorium) stated during the trial: "At that time I did not think about [. . .] whether it was right or wrong. [. . .] However, I felt sorry that they had to be killed."[15]

February 1945—Samarinda, Borneo, Indonesia

In the early morning hours of January 12, 1945, 2nd Lt Gordon E. Bruns and his crew departed from Pitu Airfield on the island of Moratai in their B-24 (44-41078) to target Sanga Sanga Oil Fields on the island of Borneo. At around 6:30 a.m., after flying for roughly four and a half hours, 2nd Lt John Workman reported that he contacted Bruns via radio at the initial waypoint as they continued on their course to the target. Upon arriving at the target area a few hours later, the radar operator of Workman's crew reported that he detected Bruns' aircraft "following about seven miles behind" the main formation. Workman recounted afterward that

> I climbed to 8,000 feet to bomb the secondary target. [. . .] Then I tried to contact Lt Bruns but received no answer. [. . .] I bombed the secondary target at 9:30 a.m. then turned to head home. [. . .] We sighted Lt Bruns heading into the target area. [. . .] We passed each other about three miles apart. [. . .] Fifteen minutes after sighting Lt Bruns I started calling him on VHF but received no answer. I tried to contact him all the way back.[16]

72 | War Crimes Narratives: Pacific and Southeast Asia

After the war, the Australian military re-occupied this area and discovered that three men of Bruns' crew (2nd Lt Leslie W. Jacobs, Sgt James W. Hagerty, and Cpl Frank J. Molinari) managed to survive the mission (figures 2.6 and 2.7). They most likely parachuted from their damaged aircraft; however, Japanese soldiers executed the flyers a short time later in February 1945 at Samarinda. The Australians initially investigated the incident before the US military took over, interviewing witnesses and collecting significant evidence that assisted the US military in convicting the perpetrators. With this information, a US Graves Registration Unit discovered the crash site of Lt Bruns aircraft in the Mahakam Delta near Samarinda in December 1945. The aircraft had disintegrated on contact with the trees and came to rest in a swamp. The wreckage was spread over a large area and the engines were completely submerged in mud, indicating the aircraft was traveling at a high rate of speed. The only evidence of the remaining crew was a uniform patch and eleven bone fragments, which were later interred at the Balikpapan War Cemetery.[17]

During the postwar trial, Hong Lo Sioe, a Chinese civilian forced to work as a house boy for the Japanese Kempeitai in Samarinda, testified that he

saw two Europeans brought to the wharf at Samarinda opposite the office of the special police. One was wounded and his right arm was in splints. There were bandages on his left arm and around both legs. They were dressed in shirts, long trousers and suede boots, all of a drab color. The wounded one was wearing a Japanese type shirt. They were blindfolded and led to the cells at the rear of the office where they were chained together at the wrists. [. . .] About four days later I saw another European arrive. [. . .] [He] was blindfolded, his hands tied behind his back, and he was put into another cell. [. . .] Every day I took food to the three men and accompanied them when they went to the lavatory. They tried to speak to me, but I could not understand what they said. [. . .] By signs they indicated they wanted food. When I gave them anything, they used to say, "Thank you." [. . .] One night the wounded man was taken to another room. [. . .] Soon afterwards I heard the sound of someone moaning in the room. About an hour later I was ordered to take some water into the room. [. . .] He had a long bamboo stick in his hand. I gave the water to the European and he said, "Thank you." His eyes were red, and his face was swollen with mosquito bites. He appeared to have been crying. When I left the room [. . .] I could hear them questioning the wounded man. The next day a Japanese doctor came and treated the

War Crimes Narratives: Pacific and Southeast Asia | 73

Figure 2.6. Exhibit C. Believed to be Sgt James W. Hagerty (left) and Cpl Frank J. Molinari (right). Exhibit C, US vs Sentaro Yamaguchi et al., vol. I, September 5, 1946, Manila, Philippines, page 77, https://www.legal-tools.org/doc/e4538a/pdf.

Figure 2.7. Exhibit B. Believed to be the Navigator, 2nd Lt Leslie W. Jacobs with Japanese guard. Exhibit B, US vs Sentaro Yamaguchi et al., vol. I, September 5, 1946, Manila, Philippines, page 76, https://www.legal-tools.org/doc/e4538a/pdf.

74 | War Crimes Narratives: Pacific and Southeast Asia

man's wounds. [. . .] When the bandages were removed, I saw marks and bruises around the wound on his arm, and also on his shoulders as if he had been beaten with a stick. [. . .]

One day Nagata told me that the three men were Americans. [. . .] He said the wounded man was the gunner [Hagerty], the man who arrived with him was the mechanic [Molinari] and the third man the navigator [Jacobs]. The mechanic had a tattoo on his right upper arm and all three wore plain gold band rings. [. . .]

The men were kept in the cells for approximately one month. One night about 8:00 p.m. the Japanese told me to go to my room. I looked through a hole in the door and [. . .] I saw the Japanese blindfold the airmen and tie their hands behind their backs. [. . .] After they had left, I asked Nagata where the Americans were, and he said they had gone to be killed. He told me not to say anything about it. About an hour later the Japanese returned [. . .] carrying two pairs of . . . the American boots [. . .] two hoes, a spade [. . .] and swords. [. . .] The next day Sugawara [Isaburo] and Nashida gave me their clothes to wash. There was a lot of blood on the bottom of their trousers and some spots on the front of their jackets.[18]

On October 14, 1945, Sgt H. Brokenshire (Australian military) testified that on September 21, 1945, he entered the cells where the flyers were kept in Samarinda. He stated that

each cell was approximately six feet by four feet and ten feet high. There were no windows. [. . .] In one cell I saw scratches on the wall the following letters: *868 Bomb Sqn—Cpl FJM, Sgt JWH, Lt LWJ*. There were other marks scratched but they were very faint, and I could not decipher them. In the third cell [. . .] I saw scratched on the wall [. . .] *FJM—USA*. [. . .] Lo Hong [a Chinese witness] then took me to a spot about 500 yards from the cells [. . .] and showed me where the earth had been disturbed. About 1400 hours that day I went [. . .] to this spot and was present when a working party of Japanese uncovered what appeared to me to be human remains about two feet below the surface of the ground. The earth was removed from around the spot and revealed what appeared to be three human bodies, partly decomposed. The heads of two were completely severed and placed on top of the bodies. The third head was not quite severed and still on the body. All three heads had blindfold bandages around the eyes. [. . .] The clothing on the remains was so decayed that I could not say whether it was American issue. [. . .] The three bodies were re-interred in the same grave and a Christian burial service read by Chaplain Maddack.[19]

The US tribunal charged three perpetrators, all members of the Japanese Navy, with unlawfully killing Jacobs, Hagerty, and Molinari. The criminals claimed that the flyers had escaped and were later caught about three hundred yards away from the jail. Because of the fear that they might organize native resistance against the Japanese should they escape again, the perpetrators allegedly received instructions the following day to execute the airmen.[20] Although there were more perpetrators involved, as confirmed by witness statements, the war crimes tribunal found the three accused guilty and sentenced them to death by hanging. They were subsequently executed in April 1947.

April 15, 1945—Ishigaki Island (Okinawa)

Assigned to the US naval carrier USS Makassar Strait, Lt Vernon L. Tebo and his crew (Warren H. Lloyd ARM 1/c and Robert Tuggle, Jr. ARM 1/c) boarded their TBM Avenger (68767) on the morning of April 15, 1945, for a bombing mission over the island of Ishigaki, Japan (figure 2.8). It was just six days before Lt Tebo's twenty-eighth birthday. During the mission severe damage to the aircraft forced the crew to bail out over Ohama Beach. Braving the unknown perils that awaited them, the flyers parachuted into the sea. Members of the Ishigaki naval defense guards rescued all three airmen, as they struggled to stay afloat. Being saved from the perilous ocean surely offered an initial sense of relief for the flyers; however, as they reached the Japanese headquarters their luck quickly turned.

After arriving at the headquarters, under the command of Naval officer Inoue Otochiko, members of the Kempeitai and Navy interrogated the flyers for roughly two hours. Inoue told the flyers that if they answered the questions honestly, they would be treated properly as POWs. The guards stood near the flyers with fixed bayonets during the questioning, which concerned the crew's personal information, their fleet and aircraft data, along with Allied operations and targets in the region.

Later that evening Inoue received a response from Kempeitai officials regarding what to do with the flyers. The Kempeitai allegedly had no available means to transport the flyers to Formosa and subsequently to a POW camp; however, witnesses testified during the postwar trial that transportation by aircraft would have been possible. Not wanting to deal with the prisoners, Inoue and several other officers decided at dinner that evening that the flyers should be executed. The idea was so widely supported that Inoue decided to execute the flyers that night. Witnesses

Figure 2.8. Left to right: Robert Tuggle, Jr. AOM 1/C (holding his dog Snatch), Lt Vernon L. Tebo, Warren H. Lloyd ARM 1/C. Courtesy of Robert Capella and Michael Nearing. "Robert Tuggle, Jr.," accessed December 16, 2020, http://www.shipleybay.com/tuggle.htm.

reportedly even clapped their hands in excitement. Everyone started to talk about this being a good way to vent hostile feelings and a way to improve morale among the Japanese soldiers as several had died earlier that day during the air raid.[21]

Japanese Naval officers ordered men to dig a pit, measuring roughly two meters long and one meter deep, at the chosen execution site. When the Japanese soldiers were informed of the execution and invited to attend, several were reportedly so excited that they asked for permission to take part in the execution. At around 11:00 p.m. Tebo, Tuggle, and Lloyd were placed in a truck and taken to the execution site. All along the way, guards severely beat them. Once they arrived at the site, guards removed Tebo and Tuggle from the truck and made them kneel next to the pit. Surely frightened and aware of what was about to happen, they were beaten by the guards, who then beheaded them one at a time and callously kicked their bodies into the pit.

Next, guards brought Lloyd from the truck and tied him to a pole in front of the pit. Despite the aid of the bright full moon, several guards shined flashlights on Lloyd and the area surrounding the pit. He was then brutally beaten by at least fourteen men, who had eagerly volunteered. Still conscious and very much alive, Lloyd continued to suffer the brunt of the viciousness as forty men took turns using his body for bayonet practice. A Japanese doctor who was present at the execution reported that Tebo and Tuggle died immediately but Lloyd struggled in agony for nearly ten minutes before he died from his wounds. Afterward, guards threw his lifeless body in the pit and filled it in with dirt. In the immediate days after the war, orders were given to disinter the remains of the three flyers, cremate them, and dispose of their ashes in the sea so that no traces of an execution would be left behind when the occupation forces landed on the island.[22]

At the postwar tribunal forty-five perpetrators stood trial for their role in these cruel crimes. Trial evidence indicates that Japanese officers chose Lloyd to be bayonetted because their soldiers lacked experience and this would help prepare them for battle. This treatment was surely a form of revenge as well, as the men involved in Lloyd's interrogation allegedly felt that he acted arrogant when he answered their questions. After the incident, participants gathered in the officers' quarters and congratulated each other, in particular the men who wielded the swords, on their skill and spirit. While the perpetrators denied that they killed the flyers out of revenge for the deaths of two Japanese officers who died during the air raid, the emotions and reactions following the aerial attack surely influenced the perpetrators' attitude when they confronted Tebo, Tuggle, and Lloyd, whom they could hold responsible.[23]

The tribunal sentenced forty-one of the tried perpetrators to death. The vast majority of these individuals received reduced sentences, ranging from two years to life imprisonment, due largely to their relatively young ages. Following appeals, six men were acquitted of any wrongdoing. After the war, memorials were constructed in both Japan and in the United States to honor the ultimate sacrifice Tebo, Tuggle, and Lloyd made during the war, to memorialize the atrocities committed against them, and to remember the Allied flyers who were victims of Axis atrocities during World War II (figure 2.9).[24]

Figure 2.9. Erected in 2001, the memorial on Ishigaki Island is dedicated to honor Tebo, Tuggle, and Lloyd. Courtesy of Hiroyuki Fukao.

May 25–26, 1945–Tokyo Military Prison Fire

Between January and April 1945, at least sixty-five American airmen—all B-29 crewmembers—were shot down during bombing raids over Tokyo and the surrounding area. Following their immediate capture, the flyers were sent to the local Kempeitai jail, where they were interrogated and tortured, as Japanese officials sought information relating to crewmembers, aircraft equipment, and missions and targets. For those airmen suspected of participating in indiscriminate bombings, as was the case with all of these sixty-five prisoners, they were designated as criminals (as opposed to POWs) and transferred to the Tokyo military prison. Similar to several other incidents, for example, at the Taipei Prison, the majority of the flyers sent to the military prison were gunners and radiomen—crewmembers least likely to have useful intelligence information.

Shortly around 10:30 p.m. on May 25, 1945, air raid sirens blared throughout the city of Tokyo, as an aerial armada of over four hundred B-29s thundered overhead. This was the fifth and final raid against the city of Tokyo—one of the world's most densely populated areas. Over three thousand tons of napalm-filled incendiaries were dropped on the city, killing over three thousand people, rendering over five hundred thousand people homeless, and burning sixteen square miles to the ground. While devastating, the destruction paled in comparison to the firebombing of Tokyo on March 9–10, 1945, which killed over one hundred thousand people. Known as "Operation Meetinghouse," it was the deadliest air raid in history.[25]

The following firsthand account of the Tokyo air raid on May 25–26, 1945, by Misao Kanayama, offers an insight into the terror and destruction experienced on the ground during the bombing raids. Further, it provides an attempt to comprehend the motives behind the cruelty inflicted upon downed Allied flyers. As the twenty-four-year-old railway worker recalled, he saw

> beams of light from searchlights [. . .] probing the sky for enemy planes. [. . .] [T]hey were coming in lower than ever before. I was used to seeing B-29s flying high above the clouds, but [. . . t]onight was different. [. . .] Anti-aircraft shells flashed as they exploded in the air. About ten B-29s flew over, then twenty, then another ten. There was no end to them. [. . .] Incendiary bombs started raining down. [. . .] Falling like red shooting stars, they suddenly burst into flames. Small at first, the flames expanded as they fell until they were like giant sparklers. Wherever they dropped, the ground turned bright red, and pillars of flame shot up. Although they were not yet above us, the sky

was filled with sounds of explosions, anti-aircraft fire, and the bombers' engines. [. . . I]t seemed like we were gradually being surrounded. [. . .] Apart from children and old people, both men and women were expected to stay and fight the fires. Those who ran were likely to be called traitors. [. . .]

Suddenly we heard an explosion nearby, a strange scraping sound like someone sweeping sand. I looked round and saw a huge red ball of fire falling from the sky. "Incendiary bombs! Look out!" I screamed and ducked behind a telegraph pole. As they came down, they sounded like hundreds of empty cans rolling on the ground. [. . .] The sounds of explosions, falling firebombs, and burning houses mingled with a howling wind that blew smoke in our eyes. [. . .] A torrent of incendiaries had fallen all around us. Someone was crying for help, but we couldn't even look around. [. . .] I felt dizzy and my throat was dry. Sweat was streaming down my back. About two meters away from us, globs of flame were shooting out of an incendiary stick. It was something from another world. [. . .]

Suddenly everything went quiet. We pricked up our ears. We weren't imagining it—the bombing had ended. There was no time to lose. [. . .] First, we made for the more open space of the Omotesando road leading to Meiji Shrine. Looking around as we ran, [. . .] we came across a group of men who were still madly dashing about with buckets of water. For a moment I felt ashamed that we were running away. As we turned the first corner at great speed, one of them jeered, "Escaping, are you?" and three of them started walking purposefully in our direction. [. . .] "You scum!" we heard them shouting behind us. [. . .] It was strange. A moment earlier I had felt guilty [. . . for] escaping while they risked their lives, but now those feelings had gone. [. . .]

In the howling wind, we heard the muffled sound of explosions. They had started bombing again. Looking up [. . .] we saw a whirlwind of flames [. . .] and sparks dancing in the air. [. . .] We [. . .] decided to join the flow of people making for the cemetery. [. . .] The road filled with smoke and a foul smell. [. . .] At the sound of explosions or falling incendiaries, people crouched on the ground, hugged telegraph poles, or cowered behind others. [. . .]

The smoke was so thick that we could no longer see our feet. It was getting harder to breathe and we had to stop many times to clear our throats. [. . .] People were collapsing all around me. I was no longer aware of the sound of bombing or flames from the incendiaries, only my immediate surroundings. [. . .] Tears rolled down my cheeks as I thought how my mother and father, elder brother and his wife would have no idea I was in this plight. [. . .] I thought hell must be something like this. Many people were running without noticing that their clothes were on fire. [. . .]

Dawn finally broke. [. . .] Everything was quiet now. [. . .] Beside the blackened telegraph poles and burnt debris of wooden houses, charred corpses were lying in the road. [. . .] To our horror, we found countless bodies piled up on top of each other in front of the entrance of the subway station. Resembling black logs or sticks of charcoal, most of them were no longer recognizable as human beings. To whom could we protest about this barbaric atrocity? How cruel war is![26]

Meanwhile, at the military prison, guards and several dozen Japanese prisoners organized into fire-prevention teams and frantically tried to extinguish the rapidly spreading inferno. Fanned by the strong winds and fueled by the predominately wooden structures, the firestorm quickly grew out of control. The sound of American aircraft signified the relentlessness and fortitude of the Allied war effort and offered the captured flyers an increased sense of hope that they would win the war. At the same time, however, the danger and destruction of their comrades' weapons surely caused fear and panic among the trapped and helpless airmen and whether they would escape the hellish ordeal.

Around 1:30 a.m. on May 26, the commander of the prison ordered the release of prisoners; however, only the remainder of the roughly four hundred Japanese prisoners were released. Once free from their cells, they rushed "in utter disorder towards the gate, stumbling, falling, and struggling to escape," according to the chief jailor, W/O Terazawa Fujiyoshi.[27] Prison officials later testified during the postwar trial that they were allegedly "afraid that if they [the flyers] were let out, they might be harmed by general citizens as well as Japanese prisoners who were too excited with the fierce attacks of allied planes."[28] While the Japanese government did further inflame serious resentment and ferocious hostility within the public against B-29 flyers through radio broadcasts and newspaper articles, portraying them as "ogres" and "murderers," the guards' attempt to reduce their punishment at the hands of the postwar tribunal was largely unsuccessful.[29]

As countless examples revealed during the postwar trial, prison officials ordered guards to kill any American that escaped. Japanese prisoner Abe Eihachi testified that during the air raid the Americans "had caused a commotion and a guard drew his sword and waved it to quiet them, and he kicked and stabbed those trying to break out."[30] Sometime around 2:00 a.m. the jailors fled for their lives as the flames grew out of control, leaving the helpless flyers to perish in their cells. By 6:00 a.m. the inferno had largely been suppressed, leaving behind a wasteland of rubble and ash.

After the war, between February 14 and 21, 1946, a US Graves Registration team meticulously searched for the remains of the American prisoners amidst the rubble of where the prison once stood. They discovered the bodies buried in a mass grave located at the site of the former air raid shelter (figure 2.10). It measured six feet deep, three feet across, and roughly fifty feet long. Investigators found small, charred pieces of clothing and blankets and thirty-two American identification tags as they sifted through a mixture of ash, dirt, and trash. They reported that nearly all the lower leg bones were fractured—possibly an indication of mistreatment prior to their death; however, this remained undetermined. Following the disinterment, investigators concluded that the remains totaled fifty-eight individuals; however, they admitted that "positive separation of remains was very difficult due to the advanced decomposition and the various positions of the bodies. Although the team tried their utmost to ascertain separation, it is believed if any more bodies were in the grave they were recovered as remains of other individuals."[31]

Figure 2.10. The common grave (located between the two white crosses) at the Tokyo prison, where the remains of the American flyers were disinterred after the war. Appendix to Report of Investigation Division, Legal Section by William R. Gill, February 18, 1947, US vs Toshio Tashiro et al., Yokohama, Japan, March–July 1948.

Table 2.1. List of the 65 American airmen who died in the Tokyo prison fire on May 25-26, 1945.

B-29 (42-94034)
Sgt Donald W. MacNiven
2nd Lt Clifford Manning
Sgt Donald L. Shubert

B-29 (44-69834)
Sgt Noel E. Beck
Sgt Robert K. Sedon

B-29 (44-49799)
1st Lt Alpheus G. Carle
S/Sgt Lawrence T. Duffy
2nd Lt Andew J. Litz
Pfc Edwin P. Lund
Cpl Allen L. Morsch
2nd Lt William F. Muhlenberg
Cpl Darwin J. Muller
2nd Lt John T. Price
Cpl Calvin R. Raymond
Lt Col Doyne L. Turner
T/Sgt Jim W. Verhines

B-29 (44-69871)
2nd Lt Donald L. Bartholomew
Sgt Archer S. Kronick
S/Sgt Anthony F. Scolaro
Sgt Henry L. Younge
Sgt Bertram Ware

B-29 (42-63545)
Maj Ralph H. Chapel
2nd Lt Harvey M. Glick
F/O John T. Hostey
T/Sgt Frederick E. Hulse
2nd Lt Harold J. Nelson, Jr.
2nd Lt James A. Reinhart, Jr.
Cpl Jean j. Schwartz
2nd Lt Edward Sullivan

B-29 (42-24674)
Sgt Otto J. Marek
Sgt John W. Meagher

B-29 (42-63569)
Cpl Walter C. Grubb

B-29 (42-63423)
2nd Lt Herbert Edman
Capt Elmer G. Hahn
2nd Lt Eugene J. Redinger

B-29 (42-93905)
2nd Lt Eugene A. Homyak

B-29 (44-69666)
2nd Lt David H. Gerhardt
2nd Lt Gerould L. Giddings
Sgt Harry E. McMillen
Sgt Maurice Myers
Sgt Robert H. Nead
Sgt Thaddeus J. Pasternak
2nd Lt Theordore C. Reynolds
T/Sgt Raymond C. Richmond
2nd Lt Donald J. Van Dever
Sgt Leonard J. McNeill

B-29 (42-94026)
2nd Lt Justice J. Buttala
Sgt Thomas L. Klingensmith
Sgt David H. Powell
Sgt Gilbert C. Stockinger
Sgt Douglas Bannon

B-29 (42-24644)
Sgt William W. Sutherland
Sgt John W. Welsh
S/Sgt Chester A. Johnson, Jr.
S/Sgt Irving C. Ellington

B-29 (42-93962)
2nd Lt Ray E. Harry
Sgt Reynold S. Jenkins

B-29 (42-40077)
2nd Lt John R. Jennings

B-29 (42-93893)
S/Sgt Allen K. Hill

B-29 (42-55344)
S/Sgt Alfred J. McNamara

*Italicized names indicate US Graves Registration's uncertainty regarding whether the flyer died in the Tokyo military prison during the fire.

84 | War Crimes Narratives: Pacific and Southeast Asia

The process was further complicated when Japanese officials reported that all records were destroyed in the fire; however, documents were eventually presented to the US military that indicated sixty-two American flyers had been held in the prison at the time of the fire. The Japanese attempted to argue that the additional three remains were of Japanese prisoners or guards. However, the US investigators viewed this as an attempt by the Japanese to show that they did not single out the Americans to die in the fire. Ultimately, the court determined that no Japanese died in the fire. Referencing rosters of flyers held at the local Kempeitai jail prior to the fire along with prisoner transfer lists, the investigators concluded that sixty-five American flyers perished in the Tokyo prison fire. At the postwar trial, five prison officials were tried and found guilty of malicious and deliberate mistreatment that resulted in the death of the airmen (Table 2.1). Although each perpetrator was sentenced to death, the court ultimately reduced their sentences, ranging from ten years to life imprisonment.

May 26, 1945—Choeiji Temple in Emoto, Japan

During the final raid on Tokyo on May 25–26, 1945, as described in the previous incident, 1st Lt Darwin T. Emry (bombardier) and his crew of their B-29 (44-66978) were shot down during their run on the target area. Only six of the eleven crewmembers, including Emry, survived the crash.[32] According to the radio operator, 1st Lt Harmon Reeder Jr.,

> The flak around the target area was very intense. On the bomb run we lost the No. 1 engine. We continued the bomb run and immediately after bombs away were hit by flak in No. 2 engine, bomb bays and in the radar compartment. Due to the loss of two engines on the same wing we lost altitude very rapidly from our bombing altitude of 9,300 feet to approximately 2,500 feet. The plane was full of gasoline fumes. [. . .] We were exceptionally low, my parachute opening just before I hit the ground, which probably accounts for only five of us getting out in time.[33]

Following the war, on November 23, 1945, a US Graves Registration Company was assigned to assist in recovering the remains of allied personnel believed to be buried in a Japanese cemetery near Mobara—roughly forty-five miles southwest of Tokyo. They recovered six bodies, which were eventually identified as Emry and the five missing members of his aircrew, using identification tags, laundry marks, and dental records. The body of Emry, identified in part by shorts baring his initials, was partially decomposed; however, the medical examiner, Capt Donald M. Eramwell, recognized that the "head had been all but completely severed [. . .] and in addition, ten to twelve shallow stab wounds appeared on the back of the torso." Further, both Eramwell and a member of the Graves Registration Company (S/Sgt Francis A. Tourat) testified during the postwar trial that Emry's "hands were tied behind his back [. . . and] there were strands of rope around one ankle." Due to the likelihood of a war crime, the US Judge Advocate General (JAG) opened an investigation into the death of Emry.[34]

The postwar investigation revealed that Emry and his crew stuck in their damaged B-29 crashed near Mobara during the early morning on May 26, 1945. A witness, Minoru Moriyama, revealed that Army Capt Mabuchi Masaaki, a Shinto Priest before the war, summoned him to the Choeji Temple to treat two injured American flyers. One had a severe head injury and the other a compound fracture of the bones in his thigh. Despite only being an eye doctor, Moriyama did what he could by cleansing the wounds as well as setting and splinting the fracture. He could tell that the flyers were in shock, as both had lost a large amount of blood; however, he had no morphine to ease their pain. Without further medical attention, Moriyama was certain the airmen would not survive.[35]

At around 10:00 a.m., a local farmer named Toriyama Tadashi visited the Choeiji Temple and reported seeing both airmen; however, the flyer with the head wound was dead.[36] The other airman, Emry, as it would later be determined during the postwar investigation, lay on the ground with his leg in a splint, profusely coughing up blood. Meanwhile, five unidentified US flyers had been captured and brought to the temporary collection point at Choeiji Temple. Around an hour later, Capt Uzawa Shoichi (Kempeitai) arrived and took charge of five flyers but left Emry due to the severity of his injuries. Uzawa reportedly told Mabuchi to "take care of the flyer," which he understood as "kill the suffering flyer out of mercy."[37]

Around noon, Capt Mabuchi ordered the decapitation of Emry. He argued during the postwar trial that this was necessary to end his suffering and that it was done in a proper manner, that is, in accordance with the Bushido Code. However, Emry's remains were subsequently used to practice bayoneting technique, during which a large crowd of curious villagers watched and shouted their approval. As an indication of concealing the incident, no official Japanese report of the event mentioned the decapitation or bayoneting. Mabuchi only verbally reported the beheading to his superior. When the US military discovered Emry's remains after the war, Mabuchi frantically tried to cover up the incident by writing to witnesses and suggesting what their testimony should be.[38]

86 | War Crimes Narratives: Pacific and Southeast Asia

At the postwar trial two Japanese officers were found guilty of committing inhumane atrocities and mutilating the body of Emry. Mabuchi was sentenced to death by hanging and the additional perpetrator received twenty-five years imprisonment. The tribunal concluded that

> after the execution, had it been truly a mercy-killing under the Bushido Code, steps would have been taken immediately for honorable disposal of the body. Instead [. . .] the body [. . .] was used in bayonet practice. This abuse [. . .] becomes ever more obnoxious when carried out in public view. Under these circumstances it is basically brutalizing, blood-lustful, and so shocking to the ordinary sensibilities of mankind and to common decency as to warrant execution of the death penalty upon the perpetrator. The public display with laughter, applause, and shots accompanying it indicates that this procedure was not intended as bayonet practice alone but as an act of vengeance and a further inciting of national hatred and revenge.[39]

Navigator 2nd George L. Sheridan was held at the Kempeitai headquarters in Tokyo upon capture and was transferred to a POW camp shortly before the end of the war. While Sheridan survived to be liberated, he suffered from not only the brutal interrogations but also from malaria, beri-beri, diphtheria, and malnutrition. He was evacuated to the United States aboard the *USS Benevolence*; however, after reaching the United States, he fell into a coma and died.[40]

May-June 1945—Kyushu Imperial University (Japan)

In the early evening hours on May 5, 1945, 1st Lt Marvin S. Watkins' crew aboard their B-29 (42-65305) was shot down following a bombing attack on the Tachiarai airfield near the city of Fukuoka. The bomber received major damage from fighter attacks and flak, which caused one of the four engines to burst into flames. The blaze quickly spread and grew uncontrollable, forcing the crew to bail out.

Watkins, along with four of his ten crewmembers (2nd Lt William R. Fredericks, 2nd Lt Dale E. Plambeck, S/Sgt Teddy J. Ponczka, and Cpl John C. Colehower) were captured in good condition and taken to a nearby Japanese Army camp in Fukuoka. While in custody, they were blindfolded, held in individual adjoining cells, and not allowed to speak to each other. During a postwar interview, Watkins further described how he was separated from his crewmembers and sent to Tokyo, where interrogators severely tortured him along with other B-29 airmen. Watkins described how he was forced to assume a kneeling position in front of the Japanese and during the interrogation he severely beat me about the head and hips with a short stick which was about eighteen to twenty-four inches in length and about one inch in diameter. [...] The interrogator continued to beat me until I was unable to maintain the kneeling position. [...] I was returned to my cell [...] where the blindfold, handcuffs and shoes were removed, and I was given some blankets. This was the first time the handcuffs had been removed since my capture [four days prior]. The next morning [...] I was removed from my cell and again interrogated for about two hours. [...] During this interrogation they threatened to remove my head. [...] I was interrogated about eight more times, but I did not receive any further beatings.[41]

Inquiring about the fate of his crew in 1947, Watkins wrote, "To this date I haven't heard or been able to get any information as to the whereabouts of my crew. It is my opinion that some of the men may have been taken by Jap civilians before getting into Jap military hands. It hardly seems possible that all ten would have disappeared."[42] However, as US war crimes investigators eventually discovered, Watkins was the sole survivor of his crew; even more devastating, six of his crewmembers were brutally tortured and subjected to horrific medical experiments before they were executed.

In one of the most infamous and cruelest cases of mistreatment committed against captured flyers during World War II, Japanese medical staff subjected at least eight American flyers to experiments that involved vivisection (not always with anesthetic) and dissection on four separate occasions in May and June of 1945 at the Kyushu Imperial University. The experiments included replacing the victims' blood with sea water as well as excising various organs, such as the flyers' lungs, stomach, liver, and brain. Perpetrators involved in such atrocities attempted to justify these experiments during postwar investigations by claiming that they were used as teaching tools for medical staff and to conclude ongoing experiments; however, investigators revealed that such means were also used to extract information from prisoners and to brutally eliminate enemy prisoners.

Tono Toshio, a witness to the atrocities committed against the American flyers at Kyushu Imperial University, recalled that "it's because the prisoners thought that we were doctors, since they could see the white smocks, that they didn't struggle. They never dreamed they would be dissected."[43] He continued, recalling that

88 | War Crimes Narratives: Pacific and Southeast Asia

The B-29 crews were hated in those days. [. . .] One day two blindfolded prisoners were brought to the school in a truck and taken to the pathology lab. Two soldiers stood guard outside the room. I did wonder if something unpleasant was going to happen to them, but I had no idea it was going to be that awful. [. . .] The experiments had absolutely no medical merit. They were being used to inflict as cruel a death as possible on the prisoners. I was in a state of panic, but I couldn't say anything to the other doctors. We kept being reminded of the misery US bombing raids had caused in Japan. But looking back it was a terrible thing to have happened. [. . .] The way Japan was during the war, it was impossible to refuse orders from the military. Dr. Ishiyama and the other doctors committed crimes, but in a way they were also victims of the war.[44]

Medical experiments were carried out throughout the Pacific in Japanese-occupied territory; for example, the infamous Unit 731 was involved in the research and development of biological and chemical weapons and carried out experiments, mostly in China. While the civilians and prisoners of occupied nations were largely the victims used in these experiments, Allied POWs, especially flyers, are known to have been submitted to such brutalities on two occasions—at Kyushu Imperial University and on Dublon Island (Micronesia) in July 1944. The incident on Dublon Island is particularly shocking, as one of the medical doctors (Hiroshi Iwanami) kept the skulls of four flyers as souvenirs and eventually sent them to the Naval Medical School in Japan for an anthropological study on race superiority/inferiority.[45]

A portion of the remains were cremated and ashes, along with dissected samples, were kept at the university. They were, however, eventually disposed of in an attempt to conceal the atrocities. During the night of June 19–20, 1945, an air raid inflicted serious damage on the city of Fukuoka. Seizing the opportunity to cover up their actions, the Western Army Headquarters sent a report to the War Ministry in Tokyo that indicated fifteen or sixteen enemy flyers died in the air raid. Numerous Japanese military and government officials knew the report was false; nevertheless, they signed and forwarded the report to disguise their true actions.

Following the Japanese surrender on August 15, 1945, the detention barracks in Fukuoka were torn down and burned to conceal any trace of the years of mistreatment inflicted upon POWs as well as to destroy the writings on the walls left behind by former prisoners. Perpetrators (in particular Sato, Fukushima, and Aihara) sought to further cover up the

War Crimes Narratives: Pacific and Southeast Asia | 89

experiments at Kyushu University by claiming the flyers were sent to Hiroshima and that they had died in the atomic bombing; however, while it would eventually be discovered that at least twelve American flyers did in fact die as a result of the atomic bombing of Hiroshima, enough evidence of the medical experiments at Kyushu University existed to charge and try thirty perpetrators.

Most of the individuals put on trial were medical staff (including the only known woman tried in the Pacific for committing crimes against flyers). They were charged with killing, mutilating, dissecting, and desecrating American flyers. There was even an accusation of cannibalism, following reports that the participants ate portions of an American's livers, but this charge was eventually dropped due to lack of evidence. While one perpetrator committed suicide before the trial commenced, thirty perpetrators were charged, twenty-three of whom were found guilty. The tribunal sentenced five to death, while four received life imprisonment, and the remaining fourteen received sentences ranging from three to twenty years' imprisonment. The lone woman perpetrator was convicted and sentenced to five years' imprisonment. However, with the continuation of global hostilities on the Korean peninsula in June 1950, the focus of the US government largely shifted toward suppressing the spread of communist influence during the burgeoning Cold War. As a result, any perpetrators who remained in custody were released by 1958.

The victims included 2nd Lt Fredericks, 2nd Lt Plambeck, S/Sgt Ponczka, Cpl Colehower, Cpl Robert B. Williams, and Cpl Leon E. Czarnecki. As for the circumstances surrounding the deaths of the four remaining crewmembers (2nd Lt Howard T. Shingledecker, 2nd Lt Charles M. Kearns, Cpl Robert C. Johnson, and Cpl Leo C. Oeinck), evidence indicates that they were killed either as they descended in their parachutes or immediately upon landing. Investigators determined that two additional airmen (S/Sgt Billy J. Brown and Sgt Charles E. Palmer) were also victims of Japanese experiments before they were executed (figures 2.11–2.14).

90 | War Crimes Narratives: Pacific and Southeast Asia

Figure 2.11. Back Row, Left to Right: 1st Lt Marvin S. Watkins, 2nd Lt William R. Fredericks, 2nd Lt Howard T. Shingledecker, 2nd Lt Charles M. Kearns, 2nd Lt Dale E. Plambeck. Front Row, Left to Right: Cpl Robert C. Johnson, S/Sgt Teddy J. Ponczka, Cpl Robert B. Williams, Cpl Leon E. Czarnecki, Cpl Leo C. Oeinck, Cpl John C. Colehower. Courtesy of Hiroyuki Fukao.

Figure 2.12. S/Sgt Billy J. Brown. S/Sgt Brown was a crewmember of B-29 (#42-24611) shot down on April 29, 1945. MACR 14337, accessed January 4, 2021, https:// catalog.archives.gov/id/91153218. "Billy J. Brown," accessed January 4, 2021, https://www.findagrave.com /memorial/56116417/billy-joe -brown.

Figure 2.13. Sgt Charles E. Palmer (front row, second from right). Sgt Palmer was a crewmember of B-29 (#44-69811) shot down on May 28, 1945. MACR 14522, accessed January 5, 2021, https://catalog.archives.gov/id/91155405. "Charles E. Palmer," accessed January 5, 2021, https://www.findagrave.com/memorial/56118472/charles-eugene-palmer.

Figure 2.14. Memorial to 1st Lt Marvin S. Watkins' crew (B-29 #42-65305). Courtesy of Hiroyuki Fukao.

June 19, 1945—Taipei Prison, Taiwan

Between October 1944 and February 1945, over thirty American flyers were shot down during the numerous large-scale air raids over Formosa (Taiwan) and were apprehended by the Japanese military. At least seventeen airmen, mostly senior crewmembers, were transferred to Tokyo for interrogation. Many of these flyers were sent to Okuna Naval Interrogation Center near Yokohama, where interrogators severely tortured and beat prisoners, resulting in many deaths.[46] Fourteen flyers, mostly radiomen and gunners, remained in custody in Formosa at the Taipei prison. The purpose of this was to investigate and determine whether they had indiscriminately bombed non-military targets.

Five of these American airmen (J. C. Buchanan, Delbert H. Carter, Donald K. Hathaway, John R. Parker, and Wayne W. Wilson) were members of a PB4Y-1 Navy Liberator crew, nicknamed "Queen Bee," which was shot down over the ocean south of Taiwan on January 28, 1945 (figures 2.15–2.19). After significant damage was sustained to the aircraft, pilot Lt J. G. White was forced to ditch at sea. As a result, five crew members, including White, died. The six remaining flyers were captured by Japanese forces and taken

Figure 2.15. AMM 3/C J.C. Buchanan. Courtesy of Michael Hurst. "The Taiwan POWs," accessed December 28, 2020, http://www.powtaiwan.org/The%20Men/men_list.php.

Figure 2.16. AOM3/C Delbert H. Carter. Courtesy of Michael Hurst. "The Taiwan POWs," accessed December 28, 2020, http://www.powtaiwan.org/The%20Men/men_list.php.

War Crimes Narratives: Pacific and Southeast Asia | 93

Figure 2.17. AMM 3/C Donald K. Hathaway. Courtesy of Michael Hurst. "The Taiwan POWs," accessed December 28, 2020, http://www.powtaiwan.org/The%20Men/men_list.php.

Figure 2.18. AMM 3/C John R. Parker. Courtesy of Michael Hurst. "The Taiwan POWs," accessed December 28, 2020, http://www.powtaiwan.org/The%20Men/men_list.php.

Figure 2.19. Grave of ARM 3/C Wayne W. Wilson in Ohio. Unfortunately, no photo was able to be found for Wayne W. Wilson. Courtesy of Michael Hurst. "The Taiwan POWs," accessed December 28, 2020, http://www.powtaiwan.org/The%20Men/men_list.php.

to the Taipei prison, where Army and Kempeitai officers interrogated and tortured them for months. The copilot, Ens John F. Bertrang, who injured his leg in the crash, was sent to a local hospital, where he received treatment. Apparently, the Japanese interrogators thought Bertrang could provide useful information for them, as he was subsequently transferred to a POW camp near Tokyo, where despite horrific conditions, he was the sole crewmember to survive the war. As for the remaining crew (Buchanan, Carter, Hathaway, Parker, and Wilson), the Japanese put them on trial on May 21, 1945, along with nine other American airmen who were held at the prison. In total, there were six trials with flyers grouped together by their aircraft crew. The proceedings began at 8:30 a.m. and ended around 5:30 p.m., with the longest trial lasting around two hours.[47]

Following the mock trials, during which the airmen received no defense counsel, the Americans were found guilty of indiscriminate bombing and violating the Japanese Enemy Airmen's Act. As a result, the court sentenced the flyers to death (figure 2.20). This decision, however, had largely been made already in April. Japanese Army chief of staff at Formosa, Isayama Haruki, stated in his postwar deposition that

> as many airmen as possible were captured, by request of the central government, [and] were sent to Tokyo. However, the number of prisoners steadily increased and therefore I began to realize the difficulty in the management of those in the detention houses where they were being confined. [. . . O]n April 14 a tentative decision was reached to try 14 prisoners and give them

Figure 2.20. Lt Harwood S. Sharp. Courtesy of Michael Hurst. "The Taiwan POWs," accessed December 14, 2020, http://www.powtaiwan.org/The%20 Men/men_list.php.

the severest punishment and this [decision . . .] was sent to the Minister of War [. . .] for Tokyo's instruction. [. . .] [It had to] be submitted to the central government for review. [. . .] On May 6 [. . .] the Vice-Minister of War and the Vice Chief of Staff [. . .] instructed, "[I]f anyone is recognized of perpetrating indiscriminate bombing, apply the severest punishment."[48]

With only a few months until the end of the war, the airmen were executed by firing squad at the Taipei prison on June 19, 1945, and their remains were cremated. In addition to the five men of the "Queen Bee," the other flyers executed that day included five additional US Navy flyers (figures 2.21–2.25), three crew members of a B-24 and the pilot of a P-47 Thunderbolt.

Postwar investigation revealed that many of the alleged Japanese records used at the flyers' trials were falsified. The documents were created during the immediate days following the war to cover up the war crimes.[49] Ultimately, nine perpetrators, including the judges and other high-ranking Japanese officers involved in the trials, were charged and convicted by a US postwar crimes trial for unlawfully prosecuting the American airmen under fraudulent charges and executing them. Two perpetrators received the death sentence, two were sentenced to life imprisonment, and the remaining offenders received sentences ranging from four to forty years in jail; however,

Figure 2.21. PO 1/C James R. Langiotti. Courtesy of Michael Hurst. "The Taiwan POWs," accessed December 14, 2020, http://www.powtaiwan.org/The%20Men/men_list.php.

Figure 2.22. ARM 2/C Harry H. Aldro. Courtesy of Sue Belden.

96 | War Crimes Narratives: Pacific and Southeast Asia

Figure 2.23. ARM 1/C Frederick E. McCreary. Courtesy of Michael Hurst. "The Taiwan POWs," accessed December 14, 2020, http://www.powtaiwan.org/The%20Men/men_list.php.

Figure 2.24. S/Sgt Bobby L. Lawrence. Courtesy of Michael Hurst. "The Taiwan POWs," accessed December 14, 2020, http://www.powtaiwan.org/The%20Men/men_list.php.

Figure 2.25. S/Sgt Harry J. Spivey. Courtesy of Michael Hurst. "The Taiwan POWs," accessed December 14, 2020, http://www.powtaiwan.org/The%20Men/men_list.php.

all sentences were ultimately reduced, including the death sentences, which were commuted to life imprisonment.

June 23, 1945—Terajuku, Japan

On June 23, 1945, 2nd Lt John V. Scanlan, pilot of a P-51 Mustang (44-72650), was on a mission to target Shimodate Airfield located in Ibaraki Prefecture (figure 2.26). During aerial combat near the target, however, Japanese fighters inflicted serious damage to Scanlan's aircraft that forced him to bail out. His wingman, 2nd Lt Robert S. Scamara, reported that he observed Scanlan's parachute open successfully and indicated that Scanlan landed inland near Chosi Point.[50]

Suffering from multiple bullet wounds to his chest and abdomen, Scanlon was immediately captured by Japanese forces once he reached the ground; they brought him to the 152nd division headquarters. Evidence presented at the postwar trial indicated that Scanlan's wounds were sufficient to cause death within a short period of time without proper medical attention. A large crowd of civilians gathered outside the building and allegedly demanded revenge. A short time later, guards brought Scanlan outside, where the crowd—estimated at this point to exceed two hundred people—struck and beat him to death with their fists, clubs, and various other objects at hand.

Figure 2.26. 1st Lt John V. Scanlan. "John V. Scanlan," accessed December 14, 2020, https://www.findagrave.com/memorial/79384096/john-v-scanlan.

98 | War Crimes Narratives: Pacific and Southeast Asia

At the postwar trial Col Shimoda Chiyoshi testified that he believed there were only "two or three civilians [. . . who] wished to see the prisoner" and, therefore, he permitted guards to take Scanlan outside. Shimoda admitted that he "knew it was wrong to display the prisoner to civilians" but stated that he "felt it could do no harm to permit a few civilians to gratify their curiosity."[51] The tribunal determined that Shimoda was guilty because he knew, especially as an officer,

> that it was improper, from a moral as well as military standpoint, to display a prisoner of war before a civilian crowd. [. . . T]he local populace was in an agitated state at that time, due to the air raid which had only just occurred, and to the imminent threat of invasion which had keyed the local temperament to a high degree of tension. [. . .] The issuance of the order [by Shimoda . . .] to show the prisoner to the civilian populace, under such circumstances, can only be viewed as an act of extreme barbarity and an atrocity of the most cruel and inhumane nature, calculated to further arouse the violent instincts of the people, and constituting an invitation to the crowd to commit acts of violence upon the prisoner. [. . .] It must therefore be presumed that the accused foresaw and intended the consequences of his act.[52]

Shimoda received the most severe punishment with forty years' imprisonment. Of the five additional soldiers charged, one was sentenced to three years' imprisonment while the others were acquitted of any wrongdoing. In addition, twelve civilians were charged. Five received sentences ranging from one to three years' imprisonment, and the remaining seven were acquitted due to insufficient evidence.

July 18, 1945—Kobe, Japan

During a bombing mission against the city of Kobe on March 17, 1945, a Japanese aircraft reportedly rammed the B-29 (42-24849) "Mission to Albuquerque," causing it to crash. Nine of the crewmembers died, but two flyers—2nd Lt Robert M. Nelson (navigator) and Sgt Algy S. Augunas (radio operator)—managed to survive by parachuting from the disabled aircraft (figure 2.27). Shortly after landing, Nelson and Augunas surrendered to Kobe police officers, who took them to Osaka Kempeitai headquarters. For two agonizing months, Kempeitai officials interrogated Nelson and Augunas, seeking personal information and useful intelligence about bombing raids, American aircraft, and each flyer's specific tasks aboard the B-29 (figure 2.28). Despite repeatedly arguing that they were not guilty of indiscriminate bombing, as they had no knowledge or control of where the

Figure 2.27. Photo of original crew formed in Kansas in May 1944. Front row (left to right): George Bauman, David W. Holley, Ruben A. Wray, Algy S. Augunas, John T. Barry, John L. Cutler; back row (left to right): Robert J. Fitzgerald, Robert E. Copeland, H. Conner, Robert M. Nelson, V. Caufield. George Bauman, H. Conner and V. Caufield were not part of the crew shot down on July 18, 1945. Their replacements (missing from photo) were Robert D. Cookson, Erwin A. Brousek, James C. Reed. "Crew Photo," accessed December 20, 2020, https://www.cooksontributeb29.com/z-8-mission-to-albuquerque.html.

bombs would be dropped, Kempeitai officials believed that Nelson and Augunas had participated in indiscriminate bombing and, therefore, were guilty of violating the Enemy Airman's Act. The Kempeitai reported their decision to the Japanese Army, and, following the issuance of warrants for their arrests, the flyers were transferred to Osaka Military Prison at Ishikiri.

By mid-June Army officials approved of the flyers' prosecution, and on July 18, 1945, they were put on trial, which lasted less than two hours. The death sentence had already been requested by the Army and approved by the War Ministry before the trial. Even the graves were dug before the court announced the verdict to Nelson and Augunas. When the sentence was translated, witnesses reported that Nelson vigorously protested that their actions had not violated International Law, that they were following orders, and that they were not responsible for the bombing policy of the United States.⁵³ However, his final plea fell on deaf ears.

Later that afternoon, guards escorted the prisoners to a secluded spot at the Yokoyama gun range. The guards were ordered to decapitate Nelson and Augunas; however, they were unable to complete the task despite several attempts. As a result, the guards shot each flyer in the head. Their lifeless bodies were then buried in an unmarked grave at the Sanadayama military cemetery, and all witnesses were instructed to maintain absolute secrecy about the incident. In an attempt to conceal the crimes, the perpetrators disinterred the remains on August 23, 1945, cremated them and then reburied the ashes in wooden boxes in the same grave—just one week before the war ended.⁵⁴

After the war, the perpetrators took further steps to conceal their actions by reporting that the flyers had died in a bombing raid. Acting on orders of the War Ministry, all records pertaining to the trial were destroyed after the war. However, the Japanese Demobilization Ministry apparently knew of the incident and instructed the individuals involved to tell the truth to US officials. As a result, eight high-ranking Japanese Army officers were tried for failing to afford Nelson and Augunas a fair and impartial trial, and unlawfully killing the flyers. One perpetrator was sentenced to death, but this was later reduced to life imprisonment. Seven others received sentences that ranged from three to thirty years' imprisonment.⁵⁵

Figure 2.28. "Mission to Albuquerque." "Mission to Albuquerque," accessed December 14, 2020, https://www.cooksontributeb29.com /z-8-mission-to-albuquerque.html.

July–August 1945—Osaka Kempeitai Headquarters (Japan)

Between May and July 1945, dozens of American airmen were shot down during missions over Kobe and Osaka and held at the Osaka Kempeitai headquarters (table 2.2).[56] While POWs were under the jurisdiction of the Japanese Army and typically held at Army guardhouses before they could be sent to POW camps, the role of the Kempeitai increased in the final year of the war as the Army requested assistance in the interrogation process, during which beatings and torture became common practice.

By June 1945, the Army generally refused to take accountability for the increased number of downed airmen due to a shortage of detention cells. As a result, increased responsibility was placed on the Kempeitai, which ultimately caused friction with the Army, as the Kempeitai was not equipped to handle large numbers of prisoners. Its facilities, food, and medical supplies were far too limited. Because of this, severe measures became a preferred means to deal with captured airmen. The destruction of shrines, the damage

Table 2.2. Names of the known American flyers executed in July/ August 1945.

B-29 (42-65336) "Assid Test II"	B-29 (42-24809) "Indian Maid"
Cpl Clarence E. Scritchfield	Sgt James M. Fitzgerald
Capt William A. McCarty	Sgt Harvey B.Kennedy, Jr.
S/Sgt Dillard R. Jackson	
F/O Robert F.T. Barrett	**B-29 (44-69655)**
T/Sgt Clifford A. Welter	1st Lt Louis W. Lehnen
Cpl Norman C. Anderson	1st Lt Harold T. Cobb
B-29 (42-65348)	**B-29 (44-46389)**
Sgt Lawrence W. Beecroft	Capt Jack K. Ort
1st Lt Harrison K. Wittee	
S/Sgt Russell W. Strong	**B-29 (44-70132)**
T/Sgt Alvin R. Hart	2nd Lt James R. Price
B-29 (44-69899)	**P-51 (44-63409)**
S/Sgt Erle P. Flanagan	2nd Lt Harry W. Norton, Jr.
S/Sgt Logan M. Sparks	
2nd Lt Joe S. McSpadden	**B-29 (42-63600)**
2nd Lt Harry J. Foley	Capt Richard H. Hamilton
B-29 (44-69766) "City of Burbank"	**B-29 (44-70008)**
1st Lt Donald J. Schiltz	S/Sgt John R. Vincent
S/Sgt George C. Reed	
	TBM-Avenger (VT-6, USS Hancock)
	Ens Norman B. Bitzegaio

102 | War Crimes Narratives: Pacific and Southeast Asia

to the Imperial Palace, and the suffering of the Japanese population at large further amplified the widespread desire to mistreat downed airmen. By July 1945, the commander of the Central District Kempeitai (Maj Gen Tsugio Nagatomo) received a top-secret letter from the Army chief of staff with the instruction to "solemnly dispose [*shobun*] as you see fit of the B-29 airmen on the spot. [. . .] It is requested that you maintain absolute secrecy and reveal it to no one." Interpreting "solemnly dispose" to mean "execute," Nagatomo transmitted the orders to his subordinates.[57]

Around July 4, 1945, Kempeitai officials executed a group of five American airmen at the Shinodayama military training grounds. Then around July 20, 1945, between fourteen and seventeen flyers (the exact number remains unknown) were executed by a firing squad at the military training grounds and Jonan gun range.[58] An additional mass shooting occurred on August 3, 1945, at the Jonan gun range and resulted in the execution of fifteen American airmen.[59] These flyers were executed without being tried by a military tribunal. Depicted as punishment for the flyers' alleged role in indiscriminate bombing, this was a sinister means to alleviate their problems of taking care of the prisoners and seek revenge in the final days of the war.

Despite hearing the emperor's radio broadcast of Japan's surrender on August 15, 1945, Nagatomo ordered a third execution later that afternoon.[60] Guards loaded the five remaining prisoners in a truck and drove them to the Sanadayama Military Cemetery in Osaka. During the postwar trials, W/O Hamamoto Jiro, a member of the execution squad, recalled that

> everyone at that time was in an excited mood and was anxious to finish the executions as quickly as possible. There were many persons at the executions who asked to be allowed to kill an airman. I was one of them. These requests were not due to curiosity about killing but arose from the feeling of spiritual confusion resulting from the realization that we had been defeated.[61]

The guards argued whether the emperor's radio broadcast was authentic or American propaganda; however, as Hamada Tomekichi described, they ultimately agreed that if they spared any prisoners, the previous incidents would be exposed.[62] Therefore, the guards carried out the executions as ordered. Hamada testified after the war that first two airmen were blindfolded and made to kneel along the edge of the oblong pit that had been dug at the cemetery. As Hamada described, "I struck with the sword with all my mind and spirit so that there would be no mistake. It was splendid work. Everyone admired me, saying that the sword was good, but it was carried out with extraordinary skill. I felt slightly dizzy after executing two persons by myself, so I sat down. [Then . . .] four or five men with pistols lined up behind the remaining flyers and simultaneously shot them."[63]

After the war, a US Graves Registration team discovered two common graves at the Shinodayama training grounds. Fifteen bodies were disinterred from the first grave, and another five bodies were found in the second grave. While thirty flyers are known to have been identified, the trial determined that there were ultimately fifty-seven American victims. In total, twenty-eight men were prosecuted for their roles in willfully and unlawfully killing the American POWs. Five Army officers were sentenced to life imprisonment, ten perpetrators received sentences ranging from one to forty years' imprisonment, and twelve were acquitted. However, this was not the only instance of flyers being executed after Japan's surrender. At least seventeen other American airmen were executed on August 15, 1945, at Aburayama Military Cemetery.[64]

3 War Crimes Narratives: Europe

The following eleven narratives are examples of instances involving the mistreatment committed against downed American flyers in Europe. Their comparison with the incidents in the Pacific underscores the similarity in the forms of violence as well as the comparable justifications and motivations behind the perpetrators' actions. Despite factors unique to each Axis nation, along with each individual perpetrator, the mistreatment committed against downed airmen was generally a retaliation for the devastation and destruction inflicted by the Allied air war. Further, the abuse was the result of the Axis nations' inability to deter or effectively defend against the Allies' attacks. While the role of Axis soldiers in mistreating POWs is rather well-established, the increased participation of civilians' involvement in carrying out acts of terror on behalf of the Axis regime is becoming clearer.[1]

April 26, 1943—Grosseto, Italy

On April 26, 1943, Easter Monday, the citizens of Grosseto, Italy (located halfway between Rome and Florence, near the Tyrrhenian Sea), enjoyed a break from the chaos of war by celebrating the holiday. Although the city had been left relatively unscathed from the destruction of war, the situation quickly turned dire in the afternoon as American bombers attacked the nearby airport, located along the western edge of the city. Taken by surprise, due to the lack of an air raid warning system, the frightened and panicked civilians attempted to flee to the fields surrounding the city or seek refuge in cellars and air raid shelters; however, the attack inflicted many civilian casualties, including dozens of children at a nearby amusement park, due to the proximity of the target to the city and the often inaccuracy of the attacks. The loss of life, along with the fact that the attack occurred on a holy day, enraged the civilians.

During this air raid, German flak shot down at least one B-17, the crew of "Axis Axes" (42-5377). Six of the ten crewmembers were killed during the attack, but four (1st Lt Richard B. Charlton, 2nd Lt Richard Buskin, 2nd Lt Sumner Locke, and 2nd Lt Robert H. Calkins) safely parachuted to the ground. The copilot, Calkins, landed in a field near the airport where a large group of civilians had taken refuge. Enraged by the bombing raid, the civilians attacked Calkins, kicking and beating him with their fists and whatever objects they had available. A short time later, the local fire brigade arrived to take custody of the airman. Seeing the mob beating the flyer, a member of the fire guard, Guiseppe Toncelli, rushed to rescue him. As Toncelli was leading Calkins away from the mob toward a nearby road, another member of the fire guard, Ido Turchi, rushed toward them and struck Calkins in the head and torso with the butt of his rifle, knocking him to the ground.[2]

Toncelli helped Calkins to his feet as Turchi turned to leave; however, after just a few steps, Turchi turned and stabbed Calkins in the chest with a bayonet. In severe agony, Calkins managed to only walk around twenty steps with the assistance of Toncelli before he collapsed. Thinking that the flyer was dead, Toncelli then folded Calkins's arms across his body and left him under guard; however, it was later realized that Calkins was still alive, and guards took him to a nearby hospital in Grosseto. After two days in the hospital, Italian authorities transferred Calkins to a hospital in Lucca, where he was reunited with the three surviving members of his crew. While in the hospital, the flyers discussed their experiences at the hands of civilian mobs. They all had been severely beaten. The bombardier, Locke, had been beaten unconscious upon capture and was carried through Grosseto on a truck, being held up and shown to the civilians like some sort of war trophy. Calkins's condition worsened following an operation, and he eventually succumbed to his injuries on May 24, 1943. His remains were buried in Lucca until they were discovered by US forces after the war.

The attack on Grosseto filled the front page of newspapers throughout the world. Quoting an article by fascist journalist Virginio Gayda, the *London Evening Post* reported that Mussolini was

> calling for reprisals against captured Allied airmen and threatening Americans with bombing. [. . .] Foreign airmen who bailed out have admitted carrying out orders to make a low-level attack on civilians. These barbaric violations of civilized laws must be blamed on the airmen as well as their chiefs. The peoples of the Tripartite Powers must reply with the same implacability. The Americans think they are immune because the ocean separates them from Europe, but their turn will come. [Further,] Gayda alleged that the American airmen [. . .] hit a maternity home and a Red Cross hospital and machine-gunned a group of children on a roundabout and killed some of these little innocents on their wooden horses.[3]

106 | War Crimes Narratives: Europe

Nazi Germany and Japan issued similar demands to their citizens to act against downed Allied airmen in an attempt to suppress the overwhelming destruction inflicted by the aerial attacks in the burgeoning war.

After the war, US officials investigated the incident and apprehended Turchi. Members of the fire brigade and hospital staff testified about the incident and the extent of Calkins's injuries. Charlton supported these witness testimonies, confirming that Calkins's death was caused by the beating he received at the hands of the mob and because of the inadequate medical attention he received.[4] A US war crimes tribunal convicted Turchi for mistreating Calkins and sentenced him to death. Upon review of the sentence, however, the presiding judge, Lt Gen John C. H. Lee, reduced the sentence to life imprisonment. Lee determined that,

> because of the casualties and destruction, the population of the area, including the accused, seeing for the first time the horrible results of the war, were in a highly excited and emotional state of mind. While the emotional disturbance was not of such a nature as to constitute a legal ground for reducing the sentence nor condone the dastardly offense committed, I am of the opinion [. . .] that the circumstances should be considered in mitigation and extenuation.[5]

April 22, 1944–Chimay, Belgium

Following a morning attack on Halberstadt, Germany, on January 11, 1944, German fighters shot down the B-17 (42-30782) "Rationed Passion" near Rijssen in the Netherlands. As the navigator, 1st Lt Ivan E. Glaze, recalled in a postwar report,

> After a running fight [. . .] we were shot down by five FW 190's. The pilot pulled the plane out of a spin and gave the order to bail out. I was thrown out of the bomb bay at about 18,000 feet. I opened by parachute at about 8,000 feet and landed in a tree. I was slow in getting out of the harness and almost before I could do anything a Dutch farmer was there to help me. Two Dutchmen took me to a farm, fed me, and gave me civilian clothes. A man came, looked at my dog tags, and asked me a lot of questions. When these people were satisfied that I was an American I was taken to a place from which my journey was arranged. I later met Sgt [Warren W.] Cole and we traveled together.
>
> After many weeks, when we got down to the French-Belgian border, our helpers could take us no further, and we were left on our own. We went to a farmhouse, explained who we were, and asked for help. The farmer at first was most distrustful since we were in civilian clothes, and he feared that we

were a Gestapo "plant." But we managed to convince him that we were all right and he took us to another farmer. From there our journey was once again arranged.

We were moved to a number of places. We were with a very active resistance group and when things became hot for them a large group of us [flyers] were assembled in a very crowded shelter in the woods. Some weeks later we started to build a larger house in another woods to shelter us more comfortably until we could be evacuated. We could see that there was little chance of going for some time, so we decided to set out on our own, as we had long been wanting to do.[6]

This group of flyers consisted of three additional B-17 crews—2nd Lt Robert J. Benninger, 2nd Lt George W. Eike, Sgt John Pindroch, 2nd Lt Billy H. Huish, Sgt Vincent J. Reese, S/Sgt John J. Gemborski, T/Sgt Orian G. Owens, T/Sgt Charles A. Nichols—who hid in the woods near Chimay (figures 3.1–3.5).[7] As Glaze reported, by the beginning of April, he and Cole decided they would take the risk and head south to Paris in hopes of eventually reaching Spain. They were ultimately successful, reaching Gibraltar

Figure 3.1. Original crew of the "Rationed Passion" (42-30782). Back row (left to right): S/Sgt Joseph G. O'Connell (POW), *S/Sgt John J. Gemborski* (POW/KIA), S/Sgt Albert C. Schaeffler (KIA), S/Sgt Warren W. Cole (Evd), Sidney Gormez, T/Sgt Orian G. Owens (Evd); front row (left to right): 1st Lt Ivan E. Glaze (Evd), 2nd Lt Norman J. Sansom, Bruce J. McMahon, 1st Lt Willard D. Reed (POW). For this fateful mission, Reed replaced McMahon as pilot; 1st Lt Myron J. Dmochowski (POW) replaced Norman as bombardier; T/Sgt Charles A. Nichols (Evd) replaced Gomez as radio operator; MACR 1931, accessed June 8, 2021, https://catalog.archives.gov/id/90913698. See also, accessed June 8, 2021, https://www.aircrewremembered.com.

Figure 3.2. Crew of the "Susan Ruth" (42-31499). Back row (left to right): S/Sgt Roy K. Holbert (POW), Sgt Louis L. Colwart, Jr. (KIA), T/Sgt Ross L. Kahler (KIA), *Sgt John Pindroch* (POW/KIA), S/Sgt Joseph J. Musial (POW), S/Sgt William D. Slenker (Evd); front row (left to right): 1st Lt Howard J. Snyder (Evd), 2nd *Lt George W. Eike* (POW/KIA), 2nd *Lt Robert J. Benninger* (POW/KIA), 2nd Lt Richard L. Daniels (POW). "Robert J. Benninger," accessed June 8, 2021, http://www.americanair museum.com/person/191318. MACR 2493, accessed June 8, 2021, https://catalog.archives.gov/id/90922998.

on June 26, 1944; however, they were the only airmen from this group of ten to survive the war.[8]

A few weeks after Glaze and Cole departed for Gibraltar, Gestapo officials, tipped off by an informant, searched a wooded area near Chimay on the morning of April 22. Along with the airmen, roughly thirty Belgian citizens, who had provided the Americans and the resistance fighters with food, first aid, and other assistance, were arrested and interrogated. The Belgians were imprisoned and eventually sent to concentration camps in Germany, where many died. The eight flyers, all of whom were still wearing their identification tags, were separated from the resistance fighters and interrogated at a local school. Later that afternoon, Gestapo officials loaded the men into a truck and transported them back to the woods where they had been captured. Two guards accompanied each flyer, the flyers' hands tied behind their backs, and escorted them into the woods. Following the signal by the officer in

Figure 3.3. Crew of "Women's Home Companion" (42-39795). Back row (left to right): 1st Lt William C. Osborn (POW), 2nd Lt Nelson Campbell (Evd), 2nd Lt Lawrence D. Ross, 2nd Lt Jack Jernigan, Jr.(POW); front row (left to right): S/Sgt George L. Daniel (POW), Sgt William E. Wolff (Evd), Sgt Lyle W. Fitzgerald (KIA), Sgt Vincent J. Reese (KIA), Sgt Earl D. Wolfe (POW), Sgt Lawrence B. Evans (KIA). For this fateful mission, 1st Lt Edward L. Cobb (POW) replaced Ross as navigator. "Mission No. 93," accessed June 8, 2021, http://www.303rdbg.com/missionreports/093.pdf. MACR 1931, accessed June 8, 2021, https://catalog.archives.gov/id/90913698.

charge, the guards opened fire, killing the flyers. Their remains were retrieved later that day and transported to the Luftwaffe airfield in Gosselies and buried in a mass grave.

After the war, US war crime investigators were unable to identify the perpetrators who executed these eight American flyers; however, a Belgian military tribunal did prosecute five Belgian police and military officers for their role in the slayings. While four perpetrators received the death penalty and the fifth was sentenced to ten years' imprisonment, it remains unknown whether these sentences were carried out or if they were commuted.[9]

Figure 3.4. 2nd Lt Billy H. Huish (POW/KIA), navigator aboard "Skunkface" (42-29656). "Billy Hugo Huish," accessed June 8, 2021, https://www.findagrave.com/memorial/56299997/billy-hugo-huish/photo.

Figure 3.5. Wreckage of "Skunkface" (42-29656) near Lens, Belgium. MACR 5628, accessed June 8, 2021, https://catalog.archives.gov/id/90986730, NND735001.

May/June 1944—Marquise, France

One of the most shocking cases uncovered in Europe, thus far, involved a Luftwaffe doctor, Max Schmid, who killed and mutilated the body of a downed American flyer in Marquise, France, during the summer of 1944. The injured airman, who had a fractured back, was brought into the shower room of the dispensary at Marquise. There were no visible wounds reported by the medical staff; however, instead of attempting to treat the flyer, Schmid gave him three injections of an unknown substance. As a result, the flyer died, reportedly from bleeding of the lungs, within minutes. The following morning, a witness reported that Schmid told him, "From now on, all Allied airmen will have the same fate."[10]

However, this was only the beginning of Schmid's ghastly mistreatment of the flyer. As Schmid described during his postwar testimony, following the flyer's death, he cut off the head and prepared the skull by boiling, skinning, and finally soaking it in hydrogen peroxide. He alleged that he needed it for instructional purposes during June and July 1944. He claimed that this act was "for scientific reasons and not as an expression of hatred for Americans." However, he eventually sent the flyer's skull home to his wife in Germany as a "souvenir." This was not the only instance of such a ghastly act, as an article in *Life Magazine* from May 1944 reported that a US Naval officer sent his girlfriend in Arizona the skull of a Japanese soldier from New Guinea.[11] In return for Schmid's confession to mutilating the flyer's remains, the court dropped the charges of murder and convicted him of maltreating a dead body. He received ten years' imprisonment for his actions.[12]

June 10, 1944—St. Sulpice Sur Risle, France

Four days after the D-Day invasion in Normandy, a P-47—most likely flown by 2nd Lt Daniel T. Loyd (42-25981)—was struck by flak during a strafing mission over France at around 8:30 a.m.[13] Unable to extinguish the engine fire that resulted from being hit by flak, the pilot made a forced landing near Bois-Arnault (roughly a mile from Rugles), located west of Paris. A French farmer, Armand Cote, witnessed the flyer's forced landing near his house and recounted that he had suffered a head wound. He reported that a short time later German soldiers arrived at the aircraft wreckage and escorted the flyer away.[14]

Postwar investigators maintained that the German soldiers (who included Sgt Hugo Wolf) escorted the airman to an orphanage in Rugles where SS troops were stationed; from there, they took him to the command post.

112 | War Crimes Narratives: Europe

SS officers allegedly interrogated the pilot, most likely for information regarding his previous and latest missions as well as any knowledge of the ongoing Allied invasion of Europe. Cecile Marie Gruart, a young girl who lived with her family across from the SS command post, testified after the war that Wolf came to her house and discussed the incident with her father. She told investigators how Wolf had said, "There's one more [flyer] who will not go back to America. [. . . They] do not take any SS prisoners; therefore, the SS will not take any prisoners."[15]

Locals reported that, prior to being shot down, American fighters had been strafing vehicles in the area and, in addition to destroying an ambulance, had killed two German officers. Because of this, SS officials took the flyer to the castle in St. Sulpice, where the Twelfth SS Panzer Division (Hitler Youth Division) was stationed. An alleged summary court, consisting of Lt Hildebrand, Sgt Kohlmeir, and Lt Karl Kirchner, was hastily convened and tried him for indiscriminately attacking a nonmilitary target. Following this mock trial, during which no witnesses were called to confirm the allegations and no translation or defense counsel were provided, he was found guilty and sentenced to death by shooting.[16]

Following the execution, SS guards stripped the body of all means of identification, including uniform and personal items. After the war, a French civilian, Marthe Franchini, testified that Kirchner was billeted at her home at the time of the incident and, following the execution of the flyer, Kirchner left the flyer's uniform, which was marked with the name *D. T. Loyd*, in her home and bragged about killing him.[17]

US investigators determined that no ambulance or vehicles with Red Cross markings had been attacked during the strafing, after Kirchner eventually confessed that no ambulance was attacked, but that two SS officers were killed when their command car was strafed. He and his fellow comrades sought revenge by executing the captured American flyer. Further, a former judge advocate in the Germany army, Dr. Max Buerger, testified at the postwar US trial as to the nature of such summary hearings in the Germany army. He explained the numerous illegalities of the proceedings (even according to German military standards), for example, "one who appointed such a court could not also sit as a member [as Kirchner had done]; that an interpreter would be necessary [. . .]; and that [. . .] while such a court could in emergency cases order its own sentence executed, this applied only to German soldiers." Ultimately, the postwar US tribunal found both Karl Kirchner and Hugo Wolf guilty and sentenced them to death by hanging.[18]

June 18, 1944—Mittenwald, Germany

In the afternoon of June 18, 1944, a four-engine American bomber—most likely a B-24 (41-28782)—crash landed roughly one and a half miles from the Bavarian town of Mittenwald, located along the alpine border north of Innsbruck, Austria.[19] Members of the German Army reportedly captured nine crewmembers; however, a large crowd of curious civilians gathered as word spread quickly throughout the rural area.

Falling into the hands of the German military surely offered a sense of relief for the flyers, as rumors circulated among Allied airmen about numerous incidents in which SS, Gestapo, Nazi officials, and in particular civilians (especially women) brutally beat and killed captured airmen.[20] However, it did not take long for the crowd to become hostile and unleash vengeful attacks against the air crew. Their relief of surviving being shot down now turned to fear of their fate at the hands of the mob that, in the meantime, had reportedly grown to upwards of one thousand people, at least 80 percent of whom were women.[21]

It only took one individual to lash out at the flyers for the entire mob to roar into a frenzy. Drastically outnumbered, the German soldiers had little chance at defending the airmen even if they wanted to. Members of the crowd punched and kicked the airmen and used various objects and tools to beat the men; some were even knocked unconscious. Witnesses recounted how several women in the crowd screamed hysterically and shouted their hatred for the enemy airmen, as they scratched, punched, and spit in the flyers' faces. Despite the confusion and turmoil, the incensed crowd had a lone objective, namely, to seek revenge for their personal and material losses suffered during the war, largely as a result from the aerial bombardments. For the civilians, the encounter with enemy flyers provided an occasional, and much desired, opportunity at releasing their pent-up frustration and soothe their anguish.

A member of the crowd, Charlotte V. Battalo, admitted after the war that "she was in a great wrath when she saw the unharmed pilots come along chewing gum." Such a simple act—even a smirk—was excuse enough for individuals to release their repressed rage. Battalo further acknowledged that she used profane language and physically assaulted the airmen. As far as she knew, she "was the first who physically mistreated the flyers."[22] Despite cuts, bruises, and concussions, the air crew survived this ordeal. A postwar tribunal prosecuted six members of the mob (including Battalo and one other woman). The court sentenced them all to between one and two years' imprisonment.[23]

August 15, 1944—Wolfisheim, France

During a bombing raid on industrial targets in Ludwigshafen and Mannheim on August 14, 1944, a bomber—most likely a B-17 (42-97852)—was hit by flak, which caused the pilot, F/O William J. Stiles, to lose reliable control of the aircraft. Nevertheless, he and his crew managed to fly the damaged aircraft nearly eighty miles south and reached Strasbourg shortly after noon. At this point, however, Stiles ordered his crew to bail out, as he feared the aircraft was becoming uncontrollable. All but three crewmembers bailed out as Stiles, along with 2nd Lt John Madeira and 2nd Lt Charles Keck Jr., flew the aircraft for another thirty minutes westward toward Paris. Apparently, Stiles managed to regain control of the war-torn bomber and continued flying until the aircraft ran out of fuel. These officers then bailed out and managed to return to Allied control.[24]

As for the flyers who bailed out over Strasbourg, Luftwaffe records indicate that four were captured. These included F/O Joseph Lojewski, S/Sgt Ralph Monteil, S/Sgt Arthur L. Varricchio, and S/Sgt Hubert P. Campney. Yet T/Sgt Thomas J. Walker was unaccounted for and remained listed as MIA.[25] After the war, US authorities investigated an incident that involved the execution of a flyer in Wolfisheim (Landkreis Strasbourg) on August 14, 1944—the exact date and location of where T/Sgt Walker went missing. While investigators were unable to positively confirm whether T/Sgt Walker was this flyer, the parallels appear to be more than coincidental.

Investigators revealed that a French family in Wolfisheim sheltered the unidentified flyer after he parachuted safely to the ground. Harboring Allied soldiers, flyers, and others on the run from Nazi officials was not without its perils. As countless memoirs have described, anyone caught aiding and abetting escapees and evaders faced harsh punishment that included imprisonment and even death.[26]

The parachuting of flyers and roar of aircraft flying overhead was impossible for people to miss. Similarly, the assistance of the downed airman also did not go unnoticed, and the local Kreisleiter and leader of the Gendarmerie, Karl J. Rebel, was quickly informed of the whereabouts of an enemy flyer. After conferring with the Gauleiter Otto Friedrich Isenmann, who reminded Rebel of their orders to turn captured flyers over to the Gestapo or SS for execution, both Rebel and Isenmann went to the French home and took custody of the flyer. While the circumstances that unfolded at this home remain unknown, Rebel did admit after the war that he repeatedly hit the flyer.[27]

The Gauleiter ordered both Rebel and another man to escort the flyer by car toward Wolfisheim, taking the route through the villages of Kolbsheim and Breuschwickersheim. He also informed the men that they would meet a group of men in civilian clothes from Strasbourg (either SS or Gestapo officials) and that they should give them custody of the prisoner. Yet, the guards did not meet anyone on their way to Wolfisheim and, therefore, held the flyer at the local headquarters of the gendarmerie. At around 2:00 a.m., four Gestapo/SS officials arrived from Strasbourg—located a mere three miles away—and took custody of the flyer. Later that morning, the airman's body was discovered in a wooded area roughly a mile outside of Wolfisheim.[28]

During the postwar hearing, both Gauleiter Isenmann and Kreisleiter Rebel were prosecuted and found guilty of participating in the killing of an unknown American airman. While Isenmann received life imprisonment, Rebel was sentenced to ten years' confinement; however, they were ultimately released by 1954. The triggermen were never identified.[29]

September 12, 1944—Ruppertshütten, Germany

Shortly after a bombing raid on Leipzig on September 12, 1944, the B-17 (42-31638) nicknamed "Big Gas Bird" took heavy flak damage that disabled two engines (figure 3.6). As a result, the aircraft could not keep up with the bomber formation, and the pilot, 1st Lt Ramon H. Newman, was forced to

Figure 3.6. B-17 (42-31638) "Big Gas Bird." "Hardlife Herald: Newsletter of the 358th Bombardment Group Association" 32, no. 3, September 2015, https://www.385thbga.com/wp-content/uploads/Newsletter-9-15-2.pdf.

116 | War Crimes Narratives: Europe

make an emergency landing near Ruppertshütten in the Spessart Mountains. Several crewmembers were injured, including Newman, 2nd Lt Harvey Dater, 1st Lt Edward J. Lower, and T/Sgt Robert E. Kuhn. As a group of civilians approached the wreckage, the remaining crew (S/Sgt Clifton D. Eastabrook, S/Sgt Tom H. Morrissey, S/Sgt Claude H. Lyons, Cpl John H. Fuchs, and 2nd Lt George W. Pearson) split into groups and sought shelter in the nearby forest.[30]

Meanwhile, a so-called *Jagdkommando* (search and pursuit unit) was dispatched from Würzburg, roughly thirty miles away. The unit consisted of four members from the Kripo, two from the Gestapo, four regular uniformed police officers, and a driver. By the time the unit arrived at the aircraft wreckage, a large crowd of civilians had gathered. According to witnesses, roughly eighty to one hundred people from the nearby village were present.[31]

A member of the Jagdkommando, Gottlob Hohloch, testified after the war, "We found one uninjured American soldier who showed us where in the vicinity there were two injured and one uninjured American airman." After gathering the flyers together and searching them, several members of the Jagdkommando escorted the airmen toward the woods while Hohloch and the leader of the unit, Christian Blum, remained behind to hold back the crowd. A short time later, the crowd heard the shots coming from the woods as the guards executed Newman, Dater, Lower, and Kuhn. Blum then ordered a vehicle from the village to dispose of the bodies.[32]

Hohloch later recalled, "We were told that they had been shot while attempting to escape, although the two injured ones could hardly move." Later, Blum wrote a report to his superior officer (Kriminalrat Kurt Hans) confirming this. However, Blum revealed during the postwar investigations that Hans had called a secret meeting sometime prior to this incident and informed the police officers that "no more airmen are to be taken [prisoner] but they are to be shot." Thus, the war crimes tribunal determined that the task of the Jagdkommando was to execute the flyers and that the claim that they were shot while attempting to escape was an attempt to conceal the atrocity. Further, given the airmen's injuries, it would have been impossible for them to escape.[33]

After the war, four members of the Jagdkommando were tried in August 1946 for their roles in executing the four airmen. The leader of the unit, Blum, received a mere one-year imprisonment while the remaining three Kripo officers (including Hohloch) were acquitted of any wrongdoing. The rest of the unit did not face charges as they were either dead by the time the trial commenced or could not be found.[34]

As for the remaining crewmembers who evaded capture, Luftwaffe records indicate that Eastabrook, Morrissey, and Lyons were captured on September 14 near Mömbris, located roughly twenty miles west of Frankfurt am Main. During their attempt to reach Allied lines, they managed to travel roughly fifteen miles west of their aircraft.[35] As for Fuchs and Pearson, Luftwaffe reports reveal that they managed to evade capture for nearly two weeks before they were found by German police officials near Tschirn, located roughly eighty-five miles northeast of where they landed. These five crewmembers were transferred to Dulag Luft for interrogation and managed to survive the war in POW camps.[36]

October–December 1944–Apeldoorn, the Netherlands

During a bombing mission over Berlin on the morning of April 29, 1944, 1st Lt Bill F. Moore's B-24 (42-52506) received flak damage that disabled one of the four engines.[37] Despite this, Moore and his crew managed to stay with their bomber formation and begin their return to England. Over Holland, however, Moore's aircraft lost a second engine, which made it impossible to maintain altitude and safely return to base. As a result, the crew bailed out following Moore's order to abandon ship. The flyers landed safely, scattered throughout the countryside near Apeldoorn, and most managed to evade capture after contacting the Dutch resistance. German soldiers captured one crewmember, T/Sgt Clifton L. Watts, and sent him to a Luftwaffe hospital in Amsterdam to treat his injured leg before transferring him to a POW camp in Germany. The remaining crew managed to successfully evade capture for at least several months (if not the remainder of the war) with the aid of the Dutch resistance.

On October 1, members of the SD raided the hideout where the resistance had been hiding Moore, 1st Lt John L. Low Jr. (bombardier), and several flyers from other downed aircraft. While some managed to escape, Moore and numerous resistance fighters were captured and held at the Willem III military barracks in Apeldoorn. The next day Sgt Robert W. Zercher, crewmember of the B-17 "Karen B" (42-39920), along with F/Sgt Kenneth H. C. Ingram (RAF) and eight members of the Dutch resistance, were executed by the SD at the barracks (figure 3.7).[38]

Over the following few months, the SD interrogated and tortured the airmen. A failed attempt to liberate Moore and the resistance fighters resulted in German retaliation with the execution of Moore and twelve resistance fighters on December 2, 1944 (figure 3.8). After the war, in March 1950, a Dutch war crimes trial charged a Luftwaffe officer, Oberleutnant Adolf

Figure 3.7. Sgt Robert W. Zercher (first row, second from right) with his crew. Courtesy of Brig. Gen. (ret.) RNLA Jelle Reitsma. "Robert Zercher en de bemanning van de Karen B," accessed January 29, 2021, https://www.apeldoornendeoorlog.nl/achtergronden/robert-zercher-en-de-bemanning-van-de-karen-b.

Figure 3.8. Back row (Left to Right): 1st Lt William F. Moore (POW/KIA), 2nd Lt Edgar J. Powell (POW), 1st Lt Franklin Coslett (POW), 2nd Lt Edward Verbosky (POW); front row (Left to Right): T/Sgt Clinton L. Watts (POW), Sgt James R. Anslow (Evd), S/Sgt Walter T. Kilgore (Evd), S/Sgt Henry H. Allen (POW), S/Sgt Werner G. Braun (POW), S/Sgt Robert G. Stitely (not present on final mission)—missing from picture is Command Pilot Maj Robert L. Salzarulo (POW). "William F. Moore's Crew," accessed June 5, 2021, http://www.467bg-research.com/detail.php?cCrewNumber=011-R0.

War Crimes Narratives: Europe | 119

Glück, with Moore's murder and sentenced him to three years' imprisonment; however, Glück was released and deported to Germany roughly a year later.[39]

A few weeks after Moore was captured, 1st Lt Coslett and several other downed airmen were discovered on Christmas Eve hiding in the woods near Hoenderloo. Two flyers, including Coslett, were captured and taken to the SD Headquarters in Velp, where they were interrogated. The men were put on trial for terrorism and espionage and subsequently sentenced to death. They were transferred to the De Kruisberg prison in Doetnchem until they could be executed. Despite agonizing mistreatment and horrific conditions, Coslett managed to survive and was liberated shortly before the end of the war.

December 9, 1944—Kaplice, Czech Republic

During the early afternoon of December 9, 1944, 1st Lt Woodrow Warren's B-17 (42-97739) crew was returning to their base in Amendola, Italy, following a bomb run against targets in Regensburg, Germany, and Pilsen, Czechoslovakia. Shortly after the raid, Warren radioed 1st Lt Sidney P. Upsher, pilot of another bomber in the formation, that while flying over the target area his aircraft sustained flak damage, which disabled two engines and damaged the fuel tanks. Since he was losing altitude, he was afraid that they would not make it over the Alps and informed Upsher that they would have to bail out or ditch the aircraft. Upsher wished Warren and his crew good luck shortly before he lost radio contact.[40]

Fighting to keep the aircraft in the air, Lt Warren ordered his crew to bail out. However, only five flyers managed to exit the aircraft (1st Lt Burke W. Jay, 2nd Lt William Jolly, S/Sgt Ralph E. Henry, S/Sgt Benjamin J. Sheppard, and T/Sgt Warren Anderson). The damaged bomber continued to lose altitude, and Warren had no option other than to make a forced landing. The rest of the airmen (1st Lt Donald L. Hart, T/Sgt Frank Pinto, 2nd Lt George D. Mayott, and S/Sgt Joseph A. Cox) anxiously braced themselves for the emergency landing. Warren and his copilot, Hart, successfully landed their bomber in a field near Dolní Dvořiště (also called Unterhaid in German), located a few miles south of Kaplice along the Austrian-Czechoslovakian border. The crew was safe and reportedly uninjured (figures 3.9–3.13).

Within a short period of time, numerous farmers and German soldiers, led by the Kreisleiter of Kaplice, Franz Strasser, arrived at the crash site and apprehended the five airmen. Strasser ordered guards to load the enemy airmen onto a truck allegedly to transport them to Kaplice; however, at a prearranged, secluded spot in the mountains, Strasser and his accomplices, who included Hermann Nelböck, Walter Wolf (Gestapo), Josef Pusch, Johann

Figure 3.9. 2nd Lt George D. Mayott. "Frank Pinto," *Fort Worth Star Telegram,* January 7, 1949.

Figure 3.10. T/Sgt Frank Pinto. "Frank Pinto," *Fort Worth Star Telegram,* January 7, 1949.

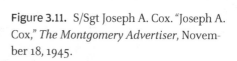

Figure 3.11. S/Sgt Joseph A. Cox. "Joseph A. Cox," *The Montgomery Advertiser,* November 18, 1945.

Figure 3.12. 1st Lt Woodrow Warren and 1st Lt Burke W. Jay. *The Evening Review*, December 19, 1945.

Figure 3.13. Lt Warren's B-17 (42-97739) after the forced landing. "Boeing B-17 42-97739," accessed January 22, 2021, http://www.leteckabadatelna.cz/havarie-a-sestrely/detail/523/.

Reichl, and Karl Lindemeyer (police officer from Kaplice), mercilessly executed the flyers.[41] Their bodies were reportedly buried in Reichenau (Rychnov nad Malši), Czechoslovakia, and in Stiegersdorf, Austria.[42]

During a postwar investigation, the accused offered conflicting statements regarding the events that unfolded that dreadful day; however, they reported that they shot the flyers after they attempted to escape. The court determined that the evidence—in particular Strasser's confession that he killed two of the flyers and the admission that Lindemeyer killed the other three men—clearly indicated that the prisoners had made no attempt to escape. Only Strasser was prosecuted for his role in the murders. Lindemeyer committed suicide after the war, shortly before Strasser's trial commenced. The court sentenced Strasser to death by hanging, and he was executed on December 10, 1945 (figure 3.14).[43]

Figure 3.14. The execution of Franz Strasser at Landsberg Prison. "He Murdered Two US Fliers," *Miami News*, January 22, 1946.

As for the fate of the five airmen who bailed out of the aircraft, 1st Lt Burke W. Jay, S/Sgt Ralph E. Henry, S/Sgt Benjamin J. Sheppard, and T/Sgt Warren Anderson were quickly captured but managed to survive the war in POW camps. However, 2nd Lt William Jolly was not as fortunate. After safely parachuting from the damaged aircraft, a crowd apprehended him and the Ortsgruppenleiter of Oppolz, Josef Wimmer, allegedly executed him. The accused was never apprehended, and Jolly's death remains unresolved.[44]

March 5, 1945—Sœr, Hungary

On March 1, 1945, 1st Lt William R. Farrington's B-24 (44-41218) crew departed Grottaglie, Italy (near Bari), for a midday bombing raid on Mossbierbaum, Austria (figure 3.15).[45] According to witnesses, Farrington and his crew had been lagging behind the formation. This was reportedly due to an inoperable engine caused by mechanical failure. Roughly seven minutes before the bomber formation reached the target, Farrington's bomber was

Figure 3.15. Back row (left to right): S/Sgt James F. Bradley, T/Sgt Donald P. Brown, S/Sgt Preston J. Hill, S/Sgt Hubert R. Burnette, S/Sgt Kenneth C. Rost, T/Sgt Felix Kozekkowski; front row (left to right): 1st Lt William Farrington, Albrecht Allen, Bob Ruff, Eugene Gosfield. 2nd Lt John P. Knox, 2nd Lt Warren F. Ames, and 1st Lt Floyd B. Bremermann replaced Albrecht Allen, Bob Ruff, and Eugene Gosfield on March 5, 1945. "Farrington Crew," accessed January 22, 2021, https://449th.com/farrington-crew/.

124 | War Crimes Narratives: Europe

last seen turning off to the right and leaving the formation. Radio logs report that north of Lake Balaton, the formation ran into heavy flak, which knocked out two of the remaining three engines on Farrington's B-24 and killed one crewmember, most likely S/Sgt Kenneth C. Rost.[46]

Roughly twenty-five miles north of Lake Balaton, Farrington ordered his crew to bail out. While at least two crewmembers were reportedly injured, they all parachuted safely to the ground and landed in the vicinity of Ácsteszér and Súr. Various groups of a voluntary Hungarian SS unit captured eight flyers and brought them to the unit headquarters in Súr.[47] Due to the conditions of the roads, the guards were unable to transport the prisoners that night to the Fourth SS Panzer Corps Headquarters in Inota, located roughly fifteen miles south. The remaining crewmember, 1st Lt Floyd B. Bremermann Jr., was captured by a different unit, became a POW, and managed to survive the war.

The following day, road conditions had improved, and SS guards (Karolyi and Schmidt) transported the three officers (1st Lt Farrington, 2nd Lt John P. Knox, and 2nd Lt Warren F. Ames) to Captain Grund in Inota. Grund inquired about the status of the remaining flyers, and he asked Karolyi why he had not brought all the flyers. Karolyi responded that they could not all fit in their vehicle. While it remains unclear what exactly was discussed between Grund and Karolyi, upon his return to Súr, Karolyi informed his superior, Major Ney, that Grund had given him the impression that the three American officers would be executed, and that the remaining five enlisted flyers (T/Sgt Donald P. Brown, T/Sgt Felix D. Kozekowski, S/Sgt James F. Bradley, S/Sgt Hubert R. Burnette, and S/Sgt Preston J. Hill) should be as well. Shortly before he left his unit in Súr for a several-day meeting, Major Ney allegedly refused to carry out these executions and ordered his subordinate (Bakos) to escort the five airmen to the Fourth Wehrmacht Calvary Brigade at Aka the next morning (March 3).[48]

Officials at the headquarters in Inota quickly received word that Ney did not plan on executing the remaining flyers. They reminded Major Ney's subordinates that they "did not consider airmen prisoners of war" and ordered the execution of the Americans. It was suggested that the easiest way to execute the airmen would be to shoot them during the night and to simulate an attempted escape. Following these orders, five guards escorted the American flyers to a nearby wooded area. The two injured crewmembers were taken by wagon while the other three walked alongside. A guard reported that one of the flyers asked what was happening, upon which he told them they were going to be executed. Allegedly, the guards gave them 15 to 20 minutes to pray before they proceeded further into the woods. Once in a secluded area, the flyers were lined up with their backs to the guards. After the executions, the guards removed the airmen's clothing, identification tags, and jewelry to hinder any future identification of the remains.[49]

In October 1945, US officials found the common grave that contained the remains of Brown, Kozekowski, Burnette, Hill, and Bradley. The circumstances surrounding the executions of the three officers remain unknown. A postwar crimes trial held at Salzburg, Austria, in the summer of 1946 tried six Hungarian SS officials involved in the killings. Despite their attempt to defend their actions based on adherence to superior orders, four were convicted and sentenced to death by hanging while two received life imprisonment.[50]

April 3, 1945—Linz, Austria

Stationed at Ramitelli Air Base in Italy, 2nd Lt Walter P. Manning was a member of the famed Tuskegee Airmen (figure 3.16). On April 1, 1945, Manning was assigned to escort bombers during a mission to attack St. Polten in Austria. Roughly eighty miles west of the target (located south of Wels), Luftwaffe fighters attacked the formation. Manning and his squadron of eight P-51 Mustangs defended the bombers and immediately engaged the enemy. As the dogfight ensued, Manning's aircraft, nicknamed "Unaka" (42-106943), was severely damaged. A witness reported seeing the fighter in a steep dive with smoke billowing from the engine and flames under the wings; it was likely an attempt to extinguish the fire.[51] Although no one observed Manning bail out, he was able to parachute from his damaged aircraft.

Figure 3.16. 2nd Lt Walter P. Manning. "Walter Peyton Manning," accessed June 6, 2021, https://www.findagrave.com/memorial/56657981/walter-peyton-manning.

He was surely filled with adrenaline but also hesitant about what awaited him once he landed, especially regarding how local Austrians would treat him as an African American.[52] Nazi propaganda not only legitimized and urged citizens to commit Lynchjustiz against downed Allied airmen but also consistently portrayed African Americans as the main representation of the Allied air war. The images and speeches presented Germans and Austrians with the history of lynching used to terrorize African Americans in the United States. Such propaganda advocated using "American justice" against Americans (figures 3.17–3.18).

After landing safely near Kematen an der Krems, Manning was quickly confronted by an enraged crowd of civilians and soldiers. Despite raising his hands to indicate that he was not a threat, members of the crowd lashed out at Manning. Before he could be seriously injured, soldiers intervened and transported him to the local Gendarmerie headquarters. According to witness reports, the local Ortsgruppenleiter, Karl Doblber, wanted to execute Manning, but soldiers prevented him from doing so. This resulted in Manning being sent to Luftwaffe officials in Hörsching, where he was detained in a cell for the next two days. Meanwhile, word quickly spread throughout the alpine region about the capture of the enemy flyer.[53]

Figure 3.17. "Negro terror flyers over the art-city of Munich—also a symbol of this war." ("Neger als Terrorflieger über der Kunststadt München"), *Völkischer Beobachter* (Berlin), June 19, 1944.

How exactly the subsequent moments unfolded is not exactly known due to varying postwar testimonies; however, at some point during the early morning hours of April 4 two Wehrmacht officers, presumably under the direction of Doblber, arrived at the guardhouse and demanded the guards release the flyer into their custody. One of the guards testified during the postwar criminal investigation that the officers presented him with written orders that "a certain negro prisoner of war was to be released and transported to Munich." Without hesitation, the guards released Manning, and, once outside, the two Wehrmacht officers mercilessly beat him. They then tied his hands behind his back and hanged him from a nearby telegraph pole. A few hours later his body was discovered, with a sign around his neck that read "We help ourselves!"[54] The Luftwaffe commander of the air base allegedly attempted to investigate the incident; however, Gestapo and Nazi party officials prevented any further inquiries in an attempt to cover it up. Thereafter, when discussing the incident, locals referred to Manning as the "straw doll" or "negro doll" hanging from the lamppost. Manning's body was buried on the grounds of the base and subsequently discovered by US officials after the war.[55]

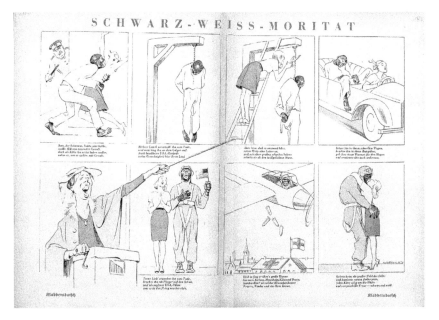

Figure 3.18. Eleanor Roosevelt presenting this "Black-White *Moritat*," *Kladderadatsch*, April 16, 1944, page 5-6, accessed June 6, 2021, http://digi.ub.uni-heidelberg.de/diglit/kla1944/0186.

128 | War Crimes Narratives: Europe

Unlike most of the known cases involving the mistreatment of airmen, the incident involving Manning is unique, as he was the only known African American flyer to be hanged. Despite a brief investigation by US authorities after they recovered his remains and acknowledging that Manning was murdered, none of the perpetrators were found or brought to justice. In 2018, thanks to the research conducted by Hoffmann, a memorial plaque that commemorates Manning was placed at the site of his execution. It is one of few memorials that acknowledges the extensive Axis violence unleashed against downed Allied airmen.

4 US Postwar Flyer Trials

For the perpetrators of this macabre and ghoulish blood orgy to escape proper
and just punishment would shock people of good conscience and good will
everywhere. [. . .] Stern justice must be meted out [. . .] for the terrible atrocity
that occurred, but it will be the type of justice that is tempered with mercy
and grounded in the interest of humanity and the common good.

—Lt Col Allan R. Browne,
Review of the Staff Judge Advocate, January 13, 1949

Throughout the four years after World War II, the postwar trials conducted
by the Allied nations offered an opportunity, albeit brief, for the world to
examine and comprehend the horrors and atrocities committed during the
conflict. The most well-known postwar hearings were the Tokyo and Nuremberg trials. The International Military Tribunal (held at Nuremberg)
tried twenty-four high-ranking German officials for conspiracy to wage war,
war crimes, and crimes against humanity and lasted from November 20,
1945, to October 1, 1946. In the Pacific, the International Military Tribunal
for the Far East (IMTFE) charged twenty-eight high-ranking Japanese military and government officials with conspiracy to wage war (Class A crimes)
and lasted two and a half years, beginning in May 1946.[1]

Each Allied nation also tried thousands of perpetrators throughout Europe and the Pacific after the well-known Nuremberg and Tokyo trials. Most
of the US trials in the Pacific were carried out in Yokohama, Japan; however,
for logistical reasons, the United States also held trials closer to the locations
where crimes were committed, for example, in Shanghai, Guam, Manila,
Singapore, Rangoon, Rabaul, the Marshall Islands, and Morotai Island in
Indonesia. These hearings focused primarily on war crimes (Class B) and
crimes against humanity (Class C). The victims largely included civilians of
occupied nations and POWs. Similarly, in Europe the United States conducted twelve subsequent trials in Nuremberg (December 9, 1946–April 13,

130 | US Postwar Flyer Trials

1949) that prosecuted German industrialists and military officers primarily for use of slave labor, plundering occupied nations, human experimentation, and mass murder. In addition, the United States carried out the so-called Dachau trials, which took place at the former Dachau concentration camp (among other locations in the US-occupied zone) and focused mainly on crimes committed against American citizens and POWs. Most of these proceedings focused on the so-called *Lynchjustiz* (lynch justice) committed against hundreds of captured American airmen.[2]

The court records of lower-level perpetrators are valuable sources as they assist in understanding the extent of violence committed against captured American airmen, for example; who mistreated the flyers (their ages, educational background, and careers prior to the outbreak of war); along with how the atrocities were committed and the number of downed airmen involved. Moreover, these trials permit a closer examination of "ordinary" citizens' willing involvement in crimes and provide an opportunity to not only understand how prevalent and similar mistreatment of downed airmen was throughout the war, but they also provide an attempt to comprehend perpetrators' motives. While the trials analyzed in this study surely do not describe every instance relating to the mistreatment of downed airmen, they provide a key opportunity to advance the discourse on the mistreatment committed against downed airmen in World War II. Further, the comparison of the US flyer trials in Germany and Japan offers an opportunity to fill the gaps related to this topic due to the scarcity of remaining documents and has the potential to assist in resolving unanswered questions regarding the circumstances surrounding the death of missing US servicemen.

The Flyer Trials

The flyer trials in the Pacific and in Europe were quite elaborate. In the Pacific, the trials lasted on average just over one month. In comparison, the proceedings in Germany averaged less than one week. While investigations in both theaters were plagued by the difficulty in apprehending accused perpetrators and collecting evidence (especially finding witnesses), the remoteness of crime scene locations that spanned much of the Pacific theater often caused delays in proceedings. Nevertheless, the trials in the Pacific benefited from the precedents set at the Nuremberg and Dachau trials, which had the advantage of commencing investigations and hearings much sooner, as the war concluded more than three months earlier in Europe.

Hearings in both theaters similarly included extensive judicial sources, for example, investigative files, transcripts of court proceedings, detailed depositions (and translations thereof), appeals for clemency, occasionally autopsy reports when the victims' bodies were recovered, and justifications for verdicts. However, following the trials, the inability to identify numerous flyers lingered due to either the lack of remains or the poor condition thereof. While this issue did occur in Europe, it was particularly problematic in the Pacific, as Japanese officials often ordered the cremation of flyer's remains after their execution, many of which were then dispersed at sea, or officials ordered the disposal of the airmen's bodies in an attempt to conceal the crimes.[3] As a result, the standard evidence for conviction at hearings in both Europe and the Pacific often relied, out of necessity, on witness testimonies, which largely included hearsay. Thus, the critical analysis of the trial documents is imperative to reliably determine how and why the violence committed against flyers unfolded.

An examination of seventy flyer trials held in the Pacific between 1945 and 1949 revealed that 394 perpetrators were charged with, for example, unlawful torture and execution of flyers; the desecration, mutilation, and dissection of their bodies; as well as prosecuting captured airmen for indiscriminate bombing. The victims included over four hundred American airmen, nearly all of whom were killed. This number is increased by several hundred when taking into consideration the flyers who survived their mistreatment. While numerous flyers remained unknown by the end of the trials, most victims have since been identified, though the extent to which perpetrators sought to conceal their actions significantly hindered the identification process and surely hindered uncovering additional cases. This was similar to the incidents that occurred in Nazi Germany. Compared to analysis of 179 flyer trials held in Germany between 1945 and 1948, where 490 perpetrators were charged with committing assaults and killing downed American airmen, the victims included a comparable number of flyers, 310, over 70 percent of whom were killed.[4]

At the time of the trials in the Pacific, the average age of perpetrators was thirty-seven years old, with an age range between nineteen and sixty-five years. They were far younger than the accused perpetrators in Germany, whose average age was forty-five years old, though, the age range was comparable at nineteen to seventy-two years (table 4.1). However, two gleaming differences between the perpetrators in the Pacific and in Europe are apparent. The first is the large representation of civilians implicated in Germany. While surely an underestimate of the actual number of civilians who took part in the mob violence, they represented 39 percent of all perpetrators tried and nearly 70 percent of offenders involved in committing assaults on flyers. In the Pacific, however, less than 8 percent of individuals prosecuted were civilians, nearly half of whom were medical personnel

Table 4.1. Comparison between Age of Perpetrators Tried in Japan and Nazi Germany

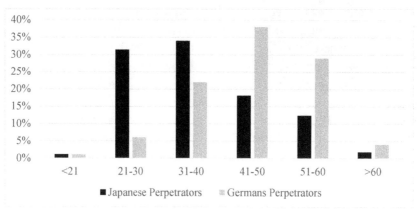

implicated in conducting medical experiments on airmen. The second noticeable difference is the influence of the Nazi Party and rhetoric. Roughly 50 percent of the perpetrators were known NSDAP members and one third were considered *Alte Kämpfer*—members who joined the Nazi Party before 1933. This relatively high percentage indicates not only that the war crime trials pursued party members but also that the party members were influential in the violence.[5]

In my analysis of the German flyer trials, I categorized the perpetrators into six main groups—civilians, police, security forces, party officials, military personnel, and government officials— to best represent the broader German society (table 4.2). Based on the perpetrators' testimonies, each of these groups had distinct motives that influenced their actions. For example, civilians acted primarily out of rage and distress. Their actions were a direct response to their experiences with the aerial bombing raids and strafing attacks. Party officials used the tense emotional situation to further incite the broader public to seek revenge against captured enemy flyers. The second-largest group tried was the German police, who included, for example, criminal police, order police, and Gendarmerie, along with rural and auxiliary police forces. These individuals acted largely in adherence to orders from party officials and security force members. The latter group consisted of SS, SD, and Gestapo and was the most likely to be involved in killing captured airmen. Party officials and security force members were prosecuted mainly for passing on orders to mistreat and kill captured flyers; however, their

Table 4.2. Percentage of German Perpetrators (by group) Tried for Mistreating Captured Airmen*

*Figure 4.7, Hall, *Terror Flyers*, 139.

personal participation in violence was not uncommon. As for the military personnel and government officials, they represented the groups least likely to mistreat airmen. Military personnel, especially members of the Luftwaffe, generally felt a sense of camaraderie with US airmen; when soldiers were involved in mistreating flyers, it was often out of revenge for lost family members or for fear of retaliation for disobeying orders. Government officials rarely had contact with enemy aviators.[6]

The overwhelming majority (roughly 89 percent) of perpetrators tried in the Pacific trials were either members of the Army, Navy, or Kempeitai (military police). The majority (70 percent) of these military personnel were officers, whose ranks ranged from Lieutenant to Vice Admiral (table 4.3). While the number of civilians tried for mistreating airmen is relatively minimal with less than 8 percent, of whom the majority were medical physicians working with the Japanese Army, there were far more civilians involved in mistreating downed airmen than indicated by the trials.[7]

While the mistreatment of downed airmen was most prevalent in the main territory of Imperial Japan and Nazi Germany, where the bombing raids were most prevalent, violence occurred wherever flyers were shot down and in nearly every country involved in the war (figures 4.1–4.2).[8] Given the increased number of bomber crewmembers compared to fighter pilots

Table 4.3. Percentage of Japanese Perpetrators (by group) Tried for Mistreating Captured Airmen

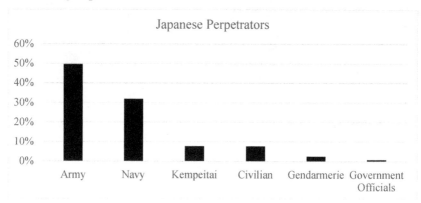

in general, which resulted in an augmented number of bomber crew being captured, roughly 90 percent of victims (in both theaters of operation) were bomber crewmembers. Their association with, and participation in, aerial bombing raids gravely influenced their mistreatment at the hands of Axis citizens and during their imprisonment.

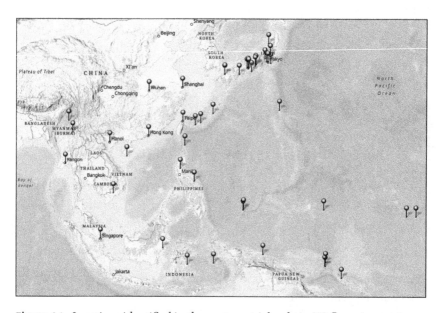

Figure 4.1. Locations identified in the postwar trials where US flyers were mistreated throughout the Pacific. Created by author. See Kevin T Hall, "Downed American Flyers: Forgotten Casualties of Axis Atrocities in World War II," *Journal of Perpetrator Justice* 4, no. 1 (2021): 208.

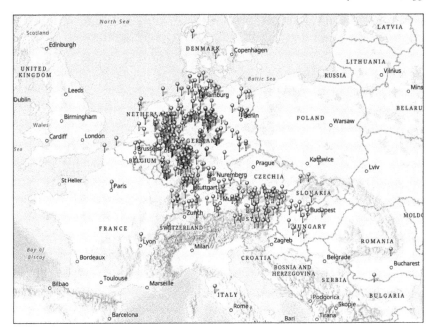

Figure 4.2. Locations identified in the postwar trials where US flyers were mistreated throughout Europe. Created by author. See Kevin T Hall, "Downed American Flyers: Forgotten Casualties of Axis Atrocities in World War II," *Journal of Perpetrator Justice* 4, no. 1 (2021): 208.

In the Pacific, the mistreatment of flyers began much sooner and lasted far longer (table 4.4). This was due, in part, to the Doolittle Raid on April 18, 1942. As a result of the raid, the Japanese enacted the "Enemy Airmen's Act" (an ex post facto law) on August 13, 1942, which declared the death penalty for any Allied flyer who participated in indiscriminate bombing or targeted nonmilitary targets. The peak of violence committed against American airmen occurred in the final months of the war, especially after May 1945 as Japanese military and government officials ordered the disposal of enemy flyers who lacked any valuable intelligence information. The execution of the three Doolittle raiders was, and remains, the most well-known incident in the Pacific that involved reprisal killings of downed airmen.

In Europe, however, the violence committed against airmen largely began at the end of 1943/beginning of 1944 and climaxed between July and August 1944. This was a result of not only the increased Allied bombing raids but also a response to Nazi propaganda minister Joseph Goebbel's newspaper article in May 1944 in which he publicly validated violence (*Lynchjustiz*) to be committed against captured airmen.[9] A final surge in violence occurred

Table 4.4. Timeline of American Airmen Mistreated by Theater of Operation*

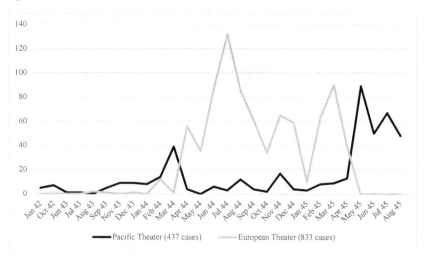

*Figure 4.7, Hall, *Terror Flyers*, 139.

in the final months of the war, largely by civilians and security forces who heeded the Nazi regime's call for a final stand to defend the Reich. While there was not an official law in Germany equivalent to Japan's "Enemy Airmen's Act," the Nazi regime did determine by May 1944 that any enemy flyer suspected of indiscriminate bombing would not be considered as a POW but rather as a criminal, to circumvent proper treatment provided by international law. No trials are known to have occurred in Germany as they did in Japan; however, the possibility was discussed among high-ranking Nazi officials.[10] Nevertheless, Nazi officials permitted and encouraged civilians to vent their anger and frustration by seeking revenge against captured flyers (table 4.5). The most widely known incident that involved reprisal killings of downed flyers during World War II was the Rüsselsheim massacre, which occurred on August 26, 1944. Following the most devastating air raid on the city of Rüsselsheim, German soldiers marched eight American airmen through the town on their way to Dulag Luft for interrogation. With the citizens still in an excited condition following the destructive bombing raid, a crowd quickly gathered around the airmen. The mob viciously beat the airmen with fists and blunt objects. Six flyers died but two managed to escape and survived the war.[11]

Despite women's involvement in beating captured flyers, only one woman is known to have been tried for participating in the mistreatment

Table 4.5. Number of Known US Flyers Mistreated in Japan and Nazi Germany (excluding occupied territories)*

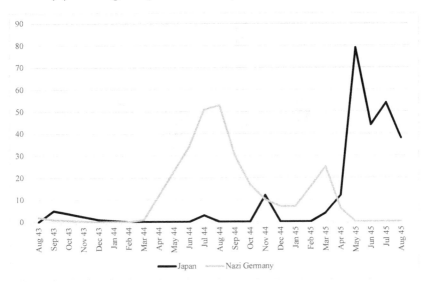

*Data is based on my analysis of US postwar crimes trials held at Yokohama and in Germany.

of Allied airmen. As a medical staff member involved in the vivisection experiments on American airmen at Kyushu Medical University in May/June 1945, the nurse received five years' imprisonment. In Germany, however, eight women were tried and sentenced for their roles in the mob violence; however, this is a serious underestimate, as the number of undocumented women (and men) involved was undoubtedly higher. Most trials in Germany, and countless personal accounts from aviators, depicted the brutality suffered at the hands of large civilian mobs and suggest that the dark figure is certainly high. Witnesses reported that these crowds could reach several hundred participants, of which women represented a significant portion.

Trial Sentencing

In both Japan and Germany, the largest percentage of sentences resulted in death; however, US military review boards reduced a significant number of sentences following appeals for clemency (tables 4.6–4.7). Some convictions were even overturned due to insufficient evidence. Once the Federal Republic of Germany was established in 1949, many more convicted perpetrators were pardoned or received additionally reduced sentences. By 1955, the West

Table 4.6. Distribution of Sentences (by percent)

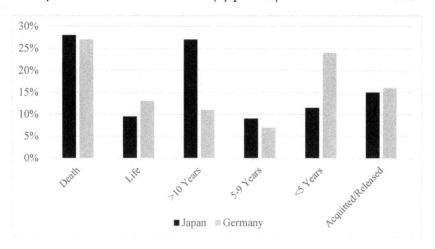

Table 4.7. Death Sentences Administered each Year

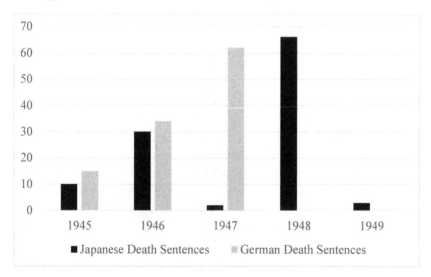

German government paroled most perpetrators, in part due to various pressure groups through the United States and Germany. Similarly, in 1958 the Japanese government released the remaining convicted war criminals.

With most perpetrators in the Pacific belonging to the military, their typical defense was based on superior orders and, had they not obeyed such orders, that they themselves would have faced imprisonment or even death. Similar defenses were put forth by German soldiers, security forces, and Nazi officials. However, the judges refused to accept such arguments, as most of these perpetrators were officers and as such knew—or at least should have known—the illegality of their actions. US prosecutors (at least in Germany) pointed out that even Goebbels acknowledged this in his May 1944 article, in which he condemned the Allied air raids and encouraged citizens to seek revenge against downed flyers. Ironically, he argued that "it is not provided in any military law that a soldier in the case of a despicable crime is exempt from punishment because he blames his superior, especially if the orders of the latter are in evident contradiction to all human morality and every international usage of warfare."[12] As for the civilians who took part in the mob violence, they argued that the trauma inflicted by the war, especially the air raids, induced their vicious and cruel actions in hopes of seeking revenge for their losses. Particularly in Germany, the relentless Nazi propaganda and rhetoric was influential in agitating the already anxious populace.

Prosecutors and investigators repeatedly uncovered forged documents by Japanese and German perpetrators that attempted to cover up the circumstances surrounding flyers' deaths and the extent to which mistreatment occurred. During many of the flyer trials in Germany, perpetrators reported that airmen were "shot while attempting to escape."[13] While countless downed airmen did indeed try to avoid capture, as was their duty, most of these cases revealed that flyers were shot and killed after they no longer posed a threat to their captors. In the Pacific, military officials only attempted to cover up the murders of airmen in the final days of the war and during the immediate months thereafter. Often, false trial documents, such as witness statements, and even statements allegedly made by captured flyers, were created to appear to corroborate their participation in indiscriminate bombing and therefore justify the perpetrators' actions. In addition, perpetrators actively tried to dispose of and cremate airmen's remains to conceal their actions and prevent any future consequences from the Allied occupiers.[14]

Until now, no single study has compared the mistreatment committed against downed flyers. Combining the few studies that have dealt with this topic regarding Europe results in roughly one thousand identified American airmen who were mistreated (including both deaths and assaults) in Nazi Germany (including Austria) after they were shot down. Taking into consideration the flyers from the remaining Allied nations as well as the broader geographic scope of combat in Europe during World War II, a conservative estimate for the number of downed Allied flyers mistreated is around three thousand.[15]

140 | US Postwar Flyer Trials

Turning to the Pacific, while there have been numerous studies on the experiences and abuse of Allied POWs, far less analysis has been conducted on the mistreatment of downed airmen prior to being sent to a POW camp. Studies have confirmed the reduced survival rates of POWs while in custody of Japanese forces compared to German troops. The death rate of American POWs ranged from roughly one percent in Germany to over thirty percent in Japan.[16] Further, scholars have estimated that as high as several hundred Allied airmen were executed after being shot down in the Pacific, a significant number of whom were allegedly killed after summary trials and courts-martial.[17] However, analyzing seventy US postwar crimes hearings concerning the mistreatment of flyers revealed that 437 American airmen alone were executed throughout the Pacific Theater. In addition to this figure, the countless flyers whose remains were never recovered (and the circumstances surrounding their deaths have never been confirmed) need to be taken into consideration, as does the mistreatment inflicted upon flyers of the other Allied nations. Conservatively, at least one thousand Allied flyers were mistreated (both executed and assaulted) by the Japanese. Similar to the cases in Europe, the dark figure is certainly high.

Analysis of the mistreated flyers in both theaters reveals that bomber crews were most likely to experience mistreatment. This is, however, unsurprising given their increased numbers (compared to fighter pilots) and the targeted hatred of Axis civilians and soldiers toward bomber crews for their role in wreaking havoc and devastation upon the Axis home fronts (table 4.8). Interestingly, according to the postwar trial statistics, enlisted flyers were more likely to be mistreated than officers in the Pacific Theater. The opposite was confirmed in Europe (table 4.9).

This is supported by numerous statements and reports by Japanese perpetrators who ordered the transfer of flyers with useful intelligence information, which happened to include officers most often, to Tokyo for additional interrogation. Meanwhile, the remaining enlisted crewmembers were often executed to reduce the burden of taking care of them. This was especially the case as the food and supplies ran low among the Japanese soldiers. As a result, after severe torture during interrogations, many of the officers transferred to Tokyo were eventually sent to POW camps, where they fought to survive the war one day at a time. The struggle to survive in a POW camp was arduous, given the rampant abuse at the hands of the guards and being subjected to backbreaking forced labor that often resulted in death; however, the first major hurdle for downed flyers was to stay alive long enough to make it to a POW camp.

With the conclusion of World War II in 1945 and the postwar crime trials in Germany (1949) and Japan (1950), it did not take long for a new international

Table 4.8. Mistreated Flyers by Known Crew Type in Each Theater

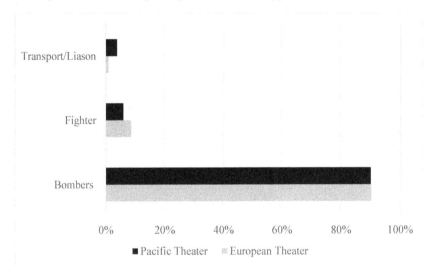

Table 4.9. Type of Mistreated Flyers by Theater

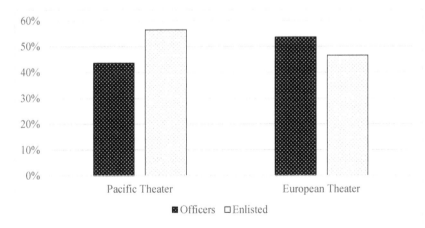

war to threaten to return the global order into chaos and unrest. The expanding threat and eventually outright combat on the Korean Peninsula quickly diverted the Allies' attention away from carrying out the punishment of war crimes. The prevention of the spread of communism and securing prodemocratic and capitalist spheres of interests took center stage. As a result, the remaining convicted perpetrators still imprisoned in West Germany were paroled by the early 1950s and by the late 1950s in Japan.

Conclusion

It is not the willingness to kill on the part of our soldiers which most concerns me. That is an inherent part of war. It is our lack of respect for even the admirable characteristics of our enemy—for courage, for suffering, for death, for his willingness to die for his beliefs, for his companies and squadrons which go forth, one after another, to annihilation against our superior training and equipment. What is courage for us is fanaticism for him. We hold his examples of atrocity screamingly to the heavens while we cover up our own and condone them as just retribution for his acts. A Japanese soldier who cuts off an American soldier's head is an Oriental barbarian, lower than a rat. An American soldier who slits a Japanese throat did it only because he knew the Japs had done it to his buddies. But, after all, we are constantly telling ourselves, and everyone else who will listen to us, that we are the upholders of all that is good and right and civilized.

—Charles A. Lindbergh, July 21, 1944

While studies have increasingly revealed the involvement—or more often indifference—of "ordinary" citizens in Axis violence, their strategic role as active participants (whether voluntarily or through coercion), for example, in mistreating downed airmen, is becoming increasingly evident.[1] For Axis citizens, downed flyers embodied the culprits of the death and destruction they experienced during the war. Incensed, vulnerable, and often encouraged to seek vengeance, some individuals who experienced the bombing and strafing raids (and even those who personally had not, but rather were influenced by propaganda and the experiences of family and friends) seized the chance for reprisal when confronted with the opportunity. The Axis regimes, especially Nazi Germany, sought to use the public's insecurity and desperation for revenge to reaffirm their loyalty to the nation and to strengthen the home front against the enemies in their midst—or at least create the guise of such a force in a failed attempt to deter future Allied aerial

144 | Conclusion

bombings. Often landing behind enemy lines in the heart of Axis territory, Allied airmen offered citizens, especially civilians, with a unique opportunity to seek, what was in their mind, justice and to contribute to the defense of the home front by making sure there would be at least one less enemy flyer who could take to the sky again; however, both Axis citizens' and flyers' fears of confronting each other, their inability to effectively communicate with one another, and the uncertainty of each other's actions further escalated an already tense situation. Often, one wrong move or expression was enough to cause the situation to go from difficult to deadly.

Considering, for example, German citizens' participation (whether through direct action or indifference of such measures) in the Nazi regime's detention, deportation, and genocide of its designated enemies, their agency in the mistreatment of thousands of captured enemy airmen expressed an added dimension in the totality of the war. Instances of mistreatment can be found throughout the timespan of the global campaigns and represent a similar approach by Nazi Germany, Imperial Japan, and Fascist Italy to counter the escalating and relentless aerial bombardments. Further, the violence reveals the willingness, and often eagerness, of "ordinary" citizens to participate (whether in an alleged defense of the nation, hometown, regime or for personal revenge) as well as the Axis regimes' growing instability and desperate reliance on civilians to carry out its desired actions.[2]

While the violence inflicted upon airmen was horrific and far more widespread than previously acknowledged, a minority of downed flyers experienced the relatively sporadic mistreatment. For flyers shot down over Japan, B-29 crewmembers were most likely to be mistreated due to their direct role in firebombing largely urban neighborhoods. Yet, in occupied territories, the combat conditions were a key influence as to whether an airman would be transferred across the vast Japanese-occupied territory to a POW camp or if the resources (e.g., food, fuel, and manpower) would be saved and the flyer executed. For most perpetrators, being held accountable for their involvement in the mistreatment committed against flyers remained an afterthought, especially since the Axis regimes did not reprimand anyone for mistreating captured Allied flyers. Only once the end of the war was definite did perpetrators begin to conceal their actions, for example, by forging or destroying documents as well as exhuming and cremating flyers' remains and disposing of their ashes at sea.

Airmen's experiences largely varied depending on when and where they were captured as well as the disposition and previous war experiences of their captors, though the influence of luck was unmistakable (figure C.1). Those detained during or immediately following an aerial attack were most

Figure C.1. 1st Lt Ernest A. Pickett, pilot of B-29 (42-6408), captured near Yawata, Japan on August 20, 1944. *Mainichi Shinbun*, August 21, 1944. K.P. Burke, Proof through the Night: A B-29 Pilot Captive in Japan, (Salem: Opal Creek Press, 2001), 93.

likely to experience mistreatment as emotions ran high. Either wild mobs of civilians formed spontaneously to seek revenge and protect their possessions, families, and communities or Axis soldiers and government officials organized such responses based on superior orders to defend against aerial attacks.[3] Ultimately, as Barak Kushner confirmed, the "domestic support of the war effort required the battlefront to be linked to the home front." While the aerial attacks on urban and industrial neighborhoods and Axis propaganda bridged these fronts and instilled hatred for Allied flyers, the personal contact between downed airmen and Axis citizens often provided the pivotal spark for violence.[4]

The Axis powers constructed similar xenophobic and strict militaristic societies in which each nation's military and government comparably sought to circumvent international law to combat the unrelenting (though controversial) aerial attacks. On one hand, the Axis regimes portrayed their citizens as victims of the escalating Allied air war to garner domestic support of combating captured flyers. On the other hand, they attempted to appeal to both global and domestic audiences by portraying the violence committed

146 | Conclusion

against Allied airmen as morally justified. Examination of propaganda and government documents reveal that German civilians were far more conditioned and encouraged to aggressively seek revenge against captured enemy flyers. This is not to say that Japanese (or other Axis) civilians did not abuse, and even murder, downed airmen, as numerous cases exist; however, the number of Japanese civilians who participated in the execution of Allied aviators appears to have been far less than Axis civilians in Europe—at least according to the postwar trials. While these trials do not include every instance of violence inflicted upon downed flyers, they do offer the best collection of available documents. Generally, the Japanese government and military sought to conceal the widespread atrocities (for example, the mutilation and torture of POWs and civilians) to try and preserve the honor of both the perpetrators and the nation—often contorting such claims as inflated Allied propaganda or, as a last resort, justifying the actions taken against Allied aviators as reasonable justice for their attacks on civilians and nonmilitary targets.[5]

Although it often remains difficult to uncover the details of the personal confrontations between flyers and Axis citizens, the previous chapters have documented examples that involve both Axis and Allied flyers. As postwar trials reveal, security forces (e.g., SS, Gestapo, and Kempeitai) represented a significant driving force in the mistreatment inflicted on captured airmen. For soldiers, in addition to following orders, a further motive to mistreat flyers was to impress their comrades and superiors. While many perpetrators revealed during postwar interrogations that military superiors often asked for volunteers to participate in the executions, few refused.[6] As for civilians, their involvement often helped distinguish themselves in the eyes of not only local military and government officials but also even among their neighbors, friends, and family. Overall, the violence directed at downed flyers was stimulated by multiple factors that involved, for example, deep-seated pressures of group cohesion, conformity, situational circumstances, but ultimately personal choice.

Two main factors resulted in a disproportionate number of victims among Allied flyers. First, the main locations of combat were in Axis territory and, therefore, an increased number of Allied airmen were shot down in enemy territory, thereby increasing the chances for contact between Axis citizens and downed Allied airmen. While more prominent in Nazi Europe, the second stimulus involved the Axis propaganda campaign that explicitly condoned and urged citizens to commit violence against captured enemy airmen. Additional factors such as the location and phase of the war as well as the diverse war experiences of the perpetrators also contributed to the motivation of citizens to participate in violence. Similar to what social psychologist James Waller outlined in his investigation of how and why "ordinary" people became willing participants of Nazi terror, "the cultural construction of worldview, the psychological construction of the 'other,' and the social construction of cruelty [. . .] converge[d] interactively to impact individual behavior in situations of collective violence."[7]

When analyzing the mistreatment of downed airmen during World War II, the following inevitable question arises: how accurate were the Axis claims that captured airmen targeted nonmilitary targets and civilians? The issue of whether some of the Doolittle Raiders had attacked civilians has remained rather taboo, as has investigating the general methods implemented in the Allied air war (e.g., bombing and strafing civilians and urban neighborhoods), as the flyers have come to represent courageous national heroes who avenged the attack on Pearl Harbor and ultimately helped stem the tide of Axis atrocities. Nevertheless, Michel Paradis's sound study on the complex aftermath of the Doolittle Raid reveals that, like in any war, transgressions are often committed in the heat of battle, and the Allies were no exception. Confronted with the complex choice of risking their safe return to base or ending up in the hands of the enemy, many flyers—often scared and impressionable young men—chose to drop their bombs on targets of opportunity, as they were often suggested to do. Further, aviators were often hindered by the weather and the technological capabilities of the time. While downed flyers were mistreated prior to the US entrance into World War II, for example, the relatively minor abuse of a few Luftwaffe flyers in England during the Blitz, the Doolittle Raid prompted the most well-known case of mistreatment committed against captured airmen during the war and greatly influenced the treatment of downed flyers throughout the remaining conflict.[8]

Daniel Hedinger has revealed the transnational influence of National Socialist ideology (and fascism in general) on Japan and Italy, especially during the 1930s and 1940s, as well as how Nazi Germany's Blitzkrieg victories in the spring of 1940 further radicalized Japanese elites and helped pave the way to attack Pearl Harbor.[9] However, this influence flowed in both directions, as both Berlin (Goebbels) and Rome (Mussolini) looked (to a degree) to Tokyo as an imperial model for Europe. For example, Japan's response to the aerial attack set a dangerous precedent in motion for the rest of the war and directly influenced Nazi Germany's (and Fascist Italy's) procedures for dealing with captured Allied airmen in Europe. As the war dragged on, the visceral hatred for the enemy (experienced by combatants and often by noncombatants) intensified; it reflected the desire for retribution, further

148 | Conclusion

amplified the brutality in combat, and relaxed the constraints of moral tolerance.[10] As Margaret MacMillan explained, "civilians often hate the enemy more than those doing the fighting."[11]

The boundaries of warfare became distorted as Axis regimes increasingly suffered setbacks and defeats, and in response the violence inflicted upon noncombatants, downed flyers, and other POWs escalated. Further, civilians became more involved (whether as bystanders or participants) in the mobilization of society. Drawing on lessons from the past, previous war experiences influenced individuals' boundaries of moral acceptability along with their physical and psychological limits.[12] In Nazi-occupied Europe, for example, the average age cohort of convicted perpetrators (forty-five years old) supports the findings of numerous studies regarding the impact of experiencing World War I as adolescents. As Isabel V. Hull confirmed, "The Great War was disfigured by wave after wave of violent reprisals exercised with lethal stubbornness, particularly against prisoners of war."[13] Despite its relatively limited use, aerial attacks (largely against military objectives located in cities) became an increasingly acceptable means for reprisal against German raids on London and Paris, as well as the treatment of POWs and civilians. Further, Hull revealed that German military and government officials assumed that "reprisals were the only effective way to affect their enemy's (putative) behavior; effectiveness was the only criterion; therefore, disproportion was acceptable or even sometimes required."[14] As a result, the possibility of civilian deaths caused by aerial bombardments became increasingly tolerable by Allied military and government officials.

With the signing of the Treaty of Versailles on June 28, 1919, Germany's humiliating defeat, individuals' tragic war experiences, the economic and social struggles that followed, and especially the rise of ethnic nationalism in the 1930s conditioned individuals' propensities of accepting, and at times demanding, reprisals against the new enemies in their midst. Further, as Hedinger described, during the 1930s, Nazi Germany, Imperial Japan, and Fascist Italy exhibited "reciprocal and cumulative radicalization."[15] Especially throughout the escalating wars in Spain and China, the fascist character of the three regimes intensified. Both Guernica and Nanking became symbols of the increasing brutality that would be generally accepted, and often encouraged, by the Axis regimes during World War II. Further, the early foundations of the doctrine of strategic bombing set in World War I were advanced during the interwar years and grew to include civilian morale as a tolerable objective of aerial warfare. "Bombing from the sky," according to MacMillan, was believed by many to be "a cheap and easy way to bring recalcitrant civilians under control, especially if they were regarded [. . .] as less-civilized peoples." With the increased use of aerial attacks to defend world order from Axis terror in World War II, the death and destruction enflamed latent sentiments (particularly among civilians, but also within the military) concerning the Allies' (largely reprisal) bombing of cities in World War I. Ultimately, the Axis regimes' widespread acceptance, and even encouragement, of reprisals against downed Allied airmen were triggered by their desperation and insecurity caused by the Allied air war as well as their inability to effectively provide a means of defense against such attacks.[16]

Similar stimuli influenced perpetrators in Japan. Although the average age of convicted perpetrators was nearly a decade younger (thirty-seven years old) than the German perpetrators, these individuals similarly grew up during an influential era of violent conflicts (e.g., the Siberian Intervention, Invasion of Manchuria, and eventually the Second Sino-Japanese War), economic downturn, as well as the rise of nationalism, militarism, expansionism, and totalitarianism.[17] Further, Japan incorporated aerial attacks during most of these conflicts, especially against cities and civilian morale. As Karl Hack and Kevin Blackburn revealed, Japanese soldiers were taught during the Russo-Japanese War to regard surrender as dishonorable. They explained that "this ethos increased with the rise of the militarists in the 1920s and 1930s [. . .] and reinforced the Japanese troops' contempt for POWs and accelerated the acceptance of the militarists' culture of violent discipline." Further, Hack and Blackburn confirm that "as early as 1932 Japanese military and police [in China . . .] were authorized to use *genju-shobun* (severe punishment) or *genchi-shobun* (on the spot punishment), leading to massacres. [. . .] By 1941 the Japanese military were schooled in these more ad hoc and sometimes brutal practices."[18] And captured prisoners, especially flyers, became a prime target.

Beginning in 1942 the radicalization of combat escalated to new levels: Germany's Blitz against Great Britain failed to extinguish their willingness to fight, and its advance on the Eastern Front was stagnated by harsh weather, the vastness of the front, and the might of the resilient Soviet forces; Italy failed to secure North Africa and eventually capitulated in 1943; and Japan gradually lost ground throughout the Pacific and Southeast Asia. Yet, despite controlling roughly one-third of the world population, the Axis regimes did not have an answer as to how they could best defeat the Allies.[19] As a result, the Axis powers further escalated the violence against their enemies, in particular downed airmen, whose ambiguous status and role in attacking the home front elicited an often-violent response. Japan became an "Über-Blitzkrieger," according to Hedinger, following the heavy defeats and setbacks.[20] The mistreatment of captured flyers and other POWs often became

150 | Conclusion

an outlet to channel the anger and insecurity caused by the bombing war and the ultimate collapse of the Axis powers away from the regimes.[21]

With the end of the war in Europe, the US government sent Charles A. Lindbergh from the Pacific to Germany in May 1945 to assess German aircraft technology. This was of great importance, as both the United States and Soviet Union vied for collecting Nazi intelligence, technology, and individuals with key skills and know-how. As Lindbergh flew over Mannheim—a rather large city with a population of roughly 280,000 in 1939 that sank to around 105,000 by 1945—he was taken aback by the devastation.[22] Echoing the radicalization of aerial warfare since World War I, he recorded in his journal, "It reminded me of a Dali painting, which in its feel of hellish death so typifies the excessive abnormality of our age—death without dignity, creation without God."[23]

The violent mistreatment inflicted upon downed flyers represented a complex combination of both calculated and spontaneous responses to the intense and devastating Allied aerial attacks that razed cities and killed hundreds of thousands of civilians. The Allies accepted civilian deaths as a tolerable consequence to defeating the Axis nations' attack on world safety; however, unlike Axis violence, the Allied nations did not pursue the explicit extermination of civilians during the war. As a result, the Axis home front no longer afforded civilians safety from the effects of war. Despite increased technological advancements and the growing reliance on aircraft to support combat operations, aerial attacks were often far from precise, and strategic bombing sought to attack centers of industry and cities to hinder future military production and cripple the enemy's will to fight. The air war brought death to the doorsteps of Axis citizens, as industrial targets were often located near urban centers. This was further augmented with the firebombing of Japanese residential and commercial neighborhoods. Nevertheless, as Hedinger confirmed, "More than 80 percent of those killed [during the war] were from the Allied countries. [. . . Whereas] the majority [. . .] (two-thirds or three-quarters) of those killed by the Allies were members of the Axis military. Even the Allied bombing campaign, which is inextricably linked to the destruction of cities [and consequently civilian deaths, . . .] does not change these relations."[24] Ultimately, however, the conflict deteriorated at times into an all-out, retaliatory melee and resulted in reoccurring intrusions on the boundaries of moral acceptability (by both combatants and noncombatants) during the fog of total war.[25]

Appendix

Index of Analyzed US Flyer Trials Held
in the Pacific and Southeast Asia

Trial Number/Location/Date	Airmen	Aircraft/Unit	Date Shot Down	Date of Incident (*Death)	Location	Japanese Trial	Accused	Offender's Status	Age	Profession	Sentencing	Outcome
No. 25 Yokohama April 5–20, 1946	2nd Lt Darwin T. Emry	504th B.G. 313th B.W. B-29 (44-69978) MACR 14503	May 25, 1945	May 26, 1945*	Choeiji Temple (Emoto, Hiyosh-mura)	No	Mabuchi Masaki	Army Capt	33	Shinto Priest	Death	
							Kikuchi Jutaro	Army 2nd Lt	24	Student	25 Years	
No. 32 Shanghai July 1–25, 1946	S/Sgt Bobbie L. Lawrence	90th B.G. 319th B.S. B-24 (44-49432) MACR14438	February 18, 1945	June 19, 1945*	Taihoku, Taiwan		Isayama Harukei	Army Lt. Gen.			Life	
	S/Sgt Harry J. Spivey	90th B.G. 319th B.S. B-24 (44-49432) MACR14438	February 18, 1945	June 19, 1945*			Furukawa Seiichi	Army Col			Death	Reduced to Life
	S/Sgt Merlin W. Riggs	90th B.G. 319th B.S. B-24 (44-49432) MACR14438	February 18, 1945	June 19, 1945*			Sugiura Naritaka	Army Lt Col			Death	Reduced to Life

Trial Number/ Location/ Date	Airmen	Aircraft/Unit	Date Shot Down	Date of Incident (*Death)	Location	Japanese Trial	Accused	Offender's Status	Age	Profession	Sentencing	Outcome
	ARM 1/c Frederick E. McCreary	SB2C Helldiver (*USS Intrepid*)	October 12, 1944	June 19, 1945*			Nakano Yoshio	Army Capt			Life	
	ARM/2c Harry H. Aldro	TBF Avenger (*USS Enterprise*)	January 5, 1944	June 19, 1945*			Ito Tadao	Army Capt			20 Years	
	AOM/2c Charles E. McVay	TBF Avenger (*USS Enterprise*)	January 5, 1944	June 19, 1945*			Matsui Masaharu	Army Capt			40 Years	
	Lt Harwood S. Sharp	SB2C Helldiver (*USS Bunker Hill*)	October 25, 1944	June 19, 1945*			Date Jitsuo	Army 1st Lt			30 Years	
	PO/1c James R. Langiotti	SB2C Helldiver (*USS Bunker Hill*)	October 25, 1944	June 19, 1945*			Fujikawa Ken	Army 1st Lt			30 Years	
	AMM/3c J. C. Buchanan	PB4Y (VPB-117) "Queen Bee"	January 28, 1945	June 19, 1945*								
	AOM/3c Delbert H. Carter	PB4Y (VPB-117) "Queen Bee"	January 28, 1945	June 19, 1945*								
	AMM/3c Donald K. Hathaway	PB4Y (VPB-117) "Queen Bee"	January 28, 1945	June 19, 1945*								
	AMM/3c John R. Parker	PB4Y (VPB-117) "Queen Bee"	January 28, 1945	June 19, 1945*								

Trial Number/ Location/ Date	Airmen	Aircraft/Unit	Date Shot Down	Date of Incident (*Death)	Location	Japanese Trial	Accused	Offender's Status	Age	Profession	Sentencing	Outcome
No. 66 Yokohama June 9–24, 1947	S/Sgt Serafino Morone	29th B.G. 314th B.W. B-29 (44-87664) "Thunderbird" MACR 14820	August 8, 1945	August 8, 1945*	Nishiki Primary School (Tachikawa)	No	Yajima Shichisaburo	Kempetai Maj			Life	
No. 78 Yokohama March 24– July 8, 1948	Sgt Leonard J. McNeill	500th B.G. 881st B.S. B-29 (44-69666) MACR14230	April 1, 1945	May 26, 1945*	Tokyo Military Prison (Shibuya)	No	Tashiro Toshio	Prison Warden	60	Soldier	Death	Reduced to 60 Years
	2nd Lt Clifford Manning	29th B.G. 6th B.S. B-29 (42-94034) MACR14271	April 16, 1945	May 26, 1945*			Kambe Hatsuaki	Prison Guard	30	Truck Driver	Death	Reduced to Life
	Sgt John W. Welsh	499th B.G. 878th B.S. B-29 (42-24644) MACR14237	April 14, 1945	May 26, 1945*			Okubo Mataishi	Prison Guard	33	Office Clerk	Death	Reduced to Life

Appendix | 155

Trial Number/Location/Date	Airmen	Aircraft/Unit	Date Shot Down	Date of Incident (*Death)	Location	Japanese Trial	Accused	Offender's Status	Age	Profession	Sentencing	Outcome
	Sgt Robert K. Sedon	9th B.G. 5th B.S. B-29 (44-69834) MACR 14474	April 15, 1945	May 26, 1945*			Kamimoto Keiji	Prison Guard	30	Mining Company Clerk	Death	Reduced to Life
	Pfc Edwin P. Lund	330th B.G. 458th B.S. B-29 (44-69799) MACR14240	April 13, 1945	May 26, 1945*			Koshikawa Masao	Prison Guard	53	Soldier	Death	Reduced 10 Years
	Sgt Archer S. Kronick	19th B.G. 30th B.S. B-29 (44-69871) MACR 14269	April 16, 1945	April 19, 1945*?								
	2nd Lt Justice J. Buttala	19th B.G. 28th B.S. B-29 (42-94026) MACR14312	April 24, 1945	May 26, 1945*								
	S/Sgt Anthony F. Scolaro	19th B.G. 30th B.S. B-29 (44-69871) MACR14269)	April 16, 1945	May 26, 1945*								

Trial Number/ Location/ Date	Airmen	Aircraft/Unit	Date Shot Down	Date of Incident (*Death)	Location	Japanese Trial	Accused	Offender's Status	Age	Profession	Sentencing	Outcome
	Sgt William W. Sutherland Jr.	499th B.G. 878th B.S. B-29 (42-24644) MACR14237	April 14, 1945	May 26, 1945*								
	Maj Ralph H. Chapel	9th B.G. 5th B.S. B-29 (42-63545) MACR14250	April 15, 1945	May 26, 1945*								
	2nd Lt Harvey M. Glick	9th B.G. 5th B.S. B-29 (42-63545) MACR14250	April 15, 1945	May 26, 1945*								
	2nd Lt Harold J. Nelson Jr.	9th B.G. 5th B.S. B-29 (42-63545) MACR14250	April 15, 1945	May 26, 1945*								
	2nd Lt James A. Reinhart Jr.	9th B.G. 5th B.S. B-29 (42-63545) MACR14250	April 15, 1945	May 26, 1945*								

Trial Number/ Location/ Date	Airmen	Aircraft/Unit	Date Shot Down	Date of Incident (*Death)	Location	Japanese Trial	Accused	Offender's Status	Age	Profession	Sentencing	Outcome
	2nd Lt Edward S. Sullivan	9th B.G. 5th B.S. B-29 (42-63545) MACR14250	April 15, 1945	May 26, 1945*								
	F/O John T. Hostey	9th B.G. 5th B.S. B-29 (42-63545) MACR14250	April 15, 1945	May 26, 1945*								
	T/Sgt Frederick E. Hulse	9th B.G. 5th B.S. B-29 (42-63545) MACR14250	April 15, 1945	May 26, 1945*								
	Sgt John W. Meagher	29th B.G. 6th B.S. B-29 (42-24674) MACR 13625	April 7, 1945	May 26, 1945*								
	Lt Col Doyne L. Turner	330th B.G. 458th B.S. B-29 (44-69799) MACR 14240	April 13, 1945	May 26, 1945*								

158 | Appendix

Trial Number/Location/Date	Airmen	Aircraft/Unit	Date Shot Down	Date of Incident (*Death)	Location	Japanese Trial	Accused	Offender's Status	Age	Profession	Sentencing	Outcome
	Capt Elmer G. Hahn	497th B.G. 870th B.S. B-29 (42-63423) MACR 11620	January 27, 1945	May 26, 1945*								
	1st Lt Eugene J. Redinger	497th B.G. 870th B.S. B-29 (42-63423) MACR 11620	January 27, 1945	May 26, 1945*								
	2nd Lt John T. Price	330th B.G. 458th B.S. B-29 (44-69799) MACR 14240	April 13, 1945	May 26, 1945*								
	2nd Lt David R. Gerhardt	500th B.G. 881st B.S. B-29 (44-69666) MACR14230	April 1, 1945	May 26, 1945*								
	Sgt Donald W. MacNiven	29th B.G. 6th B.S. B-29 (42-94034) MACR 14271	April 16, 1945	May 26, 1945*								

Trial Number/ Location/ Date	Airmen	Aircraft/Unit	Date Shot Down	Date of Incident (*Death)	Location	Japanese Trial	Accused	Offender's Status	Age	Profession	Sentencing	Outcome
	2nd Lt Andew J. Litz	330th B.G. 458th B.S. B-29 (44-69799) MACR 14240	April 13, 1945	May 26, 1945*								
	Cpl Walter C. Grubb	19th B.G. 28th B.S. B-29 (42-63569) MACR 13822	March 10, 1945	May 26, 1945*								
	2nd Lt Eugene A. Homyak	29th B.G. 43rd B.S. B-29 (42-93905) MACR12972	March 10, 1945	May 26, 1945*								
	2nd Lt John R. Jennings	90th B.G. 319th B.S. B-29 (42-40077) MACR 4926)	April 12, 1945	May 26, 1945*								
	S/Sgt Allan K. Hill	9th B.G. 1st B.S. B-29 (42-93893) MACR 14278	April 15, 1945	May 26, 1945*								

Trial Number/ Location/ Date	Airmen	Aircraft/Unit	Date Shot Down	Date of Incident (*Death)	Location	Japanese Trial	Accused	Offender's Status	Age	Profession	Sentencing	Outcome
	Sgt Otto J. Marek	29th B.G. 6th B.S. B-29 (42-24674) MACR 13625	April 7, 1945	May 26, 1945*								
	S/Sgt Alfred J. McNamara	499th B.G. 879th B.S. B-29 (42-55344) MACR 11598	April 15, 1945	May 26, 1945*								
	Cpl Darwin J. Muller	330th B.G. 458th B.S. B-29 (44-69799) MACR 14240	April 13, 1945	May 26, 1945*								
	2nd Lt William F. Muhlenberg	330th B.G. 458th B.S. B-29 (44-69799) MACR 14240	April 13, 1945	May 26, 1945*								
	2nd Lt Theodore C. Reynolds	462nd B.G. 881st B.S. B-29 (44-69966) MACR 14230	April 1, 1945	May 26, 1945*								

Trial Number/ Location/ Date	Airmen	Aircraft/Unit	Date Shot Down	Date of Incident (*Death)	Location	Japanese Trial	Accused	Offender's Status	Age	Profession	Sentencing	Outcome
	Sgt Donald L. Schubert	29th B.G. 6th B.S. B-29 (42-94034) MACR14271	April 16, 1945	May 26, 1945*								
	T/Sgt James W. Verhines	330th B.G. 458th B.S. B-29 (44-69799) MACR 14240	April 13, 1945	May 26, 1945*								
	Sgt Thomas L. Klingensmith	19th B.G. 28th B.S. B-29 (42-94026) MACR14312	April 24, 1945	May 26, 1945*								
	Sgt Gilbert C. Stockinger	19th B.G. 28th B.S. B-29 (42-94026) MACR14312	April 24, 1945	May 26, 1945*								
	S/Sgt Chester A. Johnson Jr.	499th B.G. 878th B.S. B-29 (42-24644) MACR14237	April 14, 1945	May 26, 1945*								

162 | Appendix

Trial Number/ Location/ Date	Airmen	Aircraft/Unit	Date Shot Down	Date of Incident (*Death)	Location	Japanese Trial	Accused	Offender's Status	Age	Profession	Sentencing	Outcome
	Cpl Allen L. Morsch	330th B.G. 458th B.S. B-29 (44-69799) MACR14240	April 13, 1945	May 26, 1945*								
	2nd Lt Donald L. Bartholomew	19th B.G. 30th B.S. B-29 (44-69871) MACR14269	April 16, 1945	May 26, 1945*								
	1st Lt Alpheus G. Carle	330th B.G. 458th B.S. B-29 (44-69799) MACR14240	April 13, 1945	May 26, 1945*								
	S/Sgt Lawrence T. Duffy	330th B.G. 458th B.S. B-29 (44-69799) MACR14240	April 13, 1945	May 26, 1945*								
	2nd Lt Ray E. Harry	9th B.G. 99th B.S. B-29 (42-93962) MACR 14276	April 16, 1945	May 26, 1945*								

Appendix | 163

Trial Number/ Location/ Date	Airmen	Aircraft/Unit	Date Shot Down	Date of Incident (*Death)	Location	Japanese Trial	Accused	Offender's Status	Age	Profession	Sentencing	Outcome
	Sgt Henry L. Younge	19th B.G. 30th B.S. B-29 (44-69871) MACR14269)	April 16, 1945	May 26, 1945*								
	Sgt Douglas Bannon	19th B.G. 28th B.S. B-29 (42-94026) MACR14312	April 24, 1945	May 26, 1945*								
	Cpl Calvin R. Raymond	330th B.G. 458th B.S. B-29 (44-69799) MACR14240	April 13, 1945	May 26, 1945*								
	1st Lt Herbert Edman	497th B.G. 870th B.S. B-29 (42-63423) MACR 11620	January 27, 1945	May 26, 1945*								
	Sgt Noel E. Beck	9th B.G. 5th B.S. B-29 (44-69834) MACR 14474	April 15, 1945	May 26, 1945*								

Trial Number/ Location/ Date	Airmen	Aircraft/Unit	Date Shot Down	Date of Incident (*Death)	Location	Japanese Trial	Accused	Offender's Status	Age	Profession	Sentencing	Outcome
	2nd Lt Gerould L. Giddings	500th B.G. 881st B.S. B-29 (44-69666) MACR14230	April 1, 1945	May 26, 1945*								
	Cpl Glenn H. Hodak	19th B.G. 93rd B.S. B-29 (44-69686) MACR 13857	March 10, 1945	May 26, 1945*								
	Sgt Harry E. McMillen	500th B.G. 881st B.S. B-29 (44-69666) MACR14230	April 1, 1945	May 26, 1945*								
	Sgt Maurice Myers	500th B.G. 881st B.S. B-29 (44-69666) MACR14230	April 1, 1945	May 26, 1945*								
	Sgt Robert H. Nead	500th B.G. 881st B.S. B-29 (44-69666) MACR14230	April 1, 1945	May 26, 1945*								

Trial Number/ Location/ Date	Airmen	Aircraft/Unit	Date Shot Down	Date of Incident (*Death)	Location	Japanese Trial	Accused	Offender's Status	Age	Profession	Sentencing	Outcome
	Sgt Thaddeus J. Pasternak	500th B.G. 881st B.S. B-29 (44-69666) MACR14230	April 1, 1945	May 26, 1945*								
	Sgt Kenneth A. Pettersen	498th B.G. 874th B.S. B-29 (42-93999) MACR 13762	April 2, 1945	May 26, 1945*								
	Cpl James M. Pettit	29th B.G. 52nd B.S. B-29 (42-65301) MACR 12975	March 10, 1945	May 26, 1945*								
	Sgt David H. Powell	19th B.G. 28th B.S. B-29 (42-94026) MACR14312	April 24, 1945	May 26, 1945*								
	T/Sgt Raymond C. Richmond	500th B.G. 881st B.S. B-29 (44-69666) MACR14230	April 1, 1945	May 26, 1945*								

166 | Appendix

Trial Number/ Location/ Date	Airmen	Aircraft/Unit	Date Shot Down	Date of Incident (*Death)	Location	Japanese Trial	Accused	Offender's Status	Age	Profession	Sentencing	Outcome
	Cpl Jean J. Schwarz	9th B.G. 5th B.S. B-29 (42-63545) MACR14250	April 15, 1945	May 26, 1945*								
	2nd Lt Donald J. Van Dever	500th B.G. 881st B.S. B-29 (44-69666) MACR14230	April 1, 1945	May 26, 1945*								
	Sgt Bertram L. Ware	19th B.G. 30th B.S. B-29 (44-69871) MACR 14269	April 16, 1945	May 26, 1945*								
	2nd Lt James O. Warren Jr.	39th B.G. 52nd B.S. B-29 (44-69882) MACR 14270	April 16, 1945	May 26, 1945*								
	Cpl Laverne J. Zehler	19th B.G. 93rd B.S. B-29 (44-69686) MACR 13857	March 10, 1945	May 26, 1945*								

Trial Number/ Location/ Date	Airmen	Aircraft/Unit	Date Shot Down	Date of Incident (*Death)	Location	Japanese Trial	Accused	Offender's Status	Age	Profession	Sentencing	Outcome
	S/Sgt Irvin C. Ellingson	499th B.G. 878th B.S. B-29 (42-24644) MACR14237	April 14, 1945	May 26, 1945*								
	Sgt Reynold E. Jenkins	9th B.G. 99th B.S. B-29 (42-93962) MACR 14276	April 16, 1945	May 26, 1945*								
No. 123 Yokohama July 18– August 28, 1947	2nd Lt Robert W. Nelson	500th B.G. 881st B.S. B-29 (42-24849) MACR 13079	March 17, 1945	July 18, 1945*	Kobe	Yes	Uchiyama Eitaro	Army Lt. Gen.	59	Soldier	30 Years	
	Sgt Algy S. Augunas	500th B.G. 881st B.S. B-29 (42-24849) MACR 13079	March 17, 1945	July 18, 1945*			Otahara Kiyotomi	Army Maj. Gen., Judicial Dept.	65	Lawyer	Death	Reduced to Life
							Yamanaka Norio	Army Intel. Maj.	33	Soldier	25 Years	

Trial Number/ Location/ Date	Airmen	Aircraft/Unit	Date Shot Down	Date of Incident (*Death)	Location	Japanese Trial	Accused	Offender's Status	Age	Profession	Sentencing	Outcome
							Ono Buichi	Army	42	Post Office Official	30 Years	
							Matsumori Hideo	Army 1st Lt	40	Economist	10 Years	Suspended Sentence
							Ogiya Yorio	Army Capt	27	Lawyer	3 Years	
							Nakamichi Kanji	Army Capt	51	Prison Warden	3 Years	
							Kunitake Michio	Army Lt. Gen.	54	Soldier	3 Years	
No. 152 Yokohama February 25– March 15, 1948	Sgt Theodore W. Prince	468th B.G. 793rd B.S. B-29 (44-70084) MACR 14672	June 22, 1945	July 24, 1945*	Kochi Army Hospital	No	Yamamoto Takeo	Kempetei Capt	32	Farmer	Life	Reduced to 10 Years
							Tamura Hajime	Army Capt	33	Medical Doctor	25 Years	Reduced to 5 Years
							Takami Shuniciro	Army 2nd Lt	36	Medical Doctor	20 Years	Suspended Sentence
							Tsutsui Hajime	Army Capt	44	Medical Doctor	5 Years	Suspended Sentence

Trial Number/ Location/ Date	Airmen	Aircraft/Unit	Date Shot Down	Date of Incident (*Death)	Location	Japanese Trial	Accused	Offender's Status	Age	Profession	Sentencing	Outcome
No. 208 Yokohama September 12, 1947 (See no. 32)	1st Lt Ralph R. Hartley	140th F.S. P-47 (42-29068) MACR13608	February 27, 1945	June 19, 1945*	Taipei Military Prison	Yes	Koike Kaneichi	Army Capt	38	Lawyer	4 Years	Reduced to 3 Years
No. 217 Yokohama April 29, 1947 (See no. 66)							Seki Noboru	Kempetai W/O	34	Soldier	20 Years	
No. 251 Yokohama January 22– March 4, 1948 (See no. 289)							Ito Nobuo	Army Maj	39	Lawyer	Death	Reduced to Life
							Matsuo Kaiji	Army Maj	44	Farmer	20 Years	
							Kataura Toshiatsu	Army Lt	27	Lumbermill Owner	15 Years	

Trial Number/ Location/ Date	Airmen	Aircraft/Unit	Date Shot Down	Date of Incident (*Death)	Location	Japanese Trial	Accused	Offender's Status	Age	Profession	Sentencing	Outcome
							Santo Hirokichi	Army Lt	46	Judge	20 Years	
No. 258 Yokohama November 26, 1947–March 16, 1948	Lt Vernon L. Tebo	Squadron VC-97 TBM Avenger (68767) (USS Makassar Strait)	April 15, 1945	April 15, 1945*	Ishigaki Island	No	Akatsuka Hanji	Navy	39	Plasterer	Death	Reduced to 5 Years
	Amm/1c Warren H. Lloyd	Squadron VC-97 TBM Avenger (68767) (USS Makassar Strait)	April 15, 1945	April 15, 1945*			Enomoto Muneo	Navy 1st Lt	43	Farmer	Death	
	AOM/1c Robert Tuggle Jr.	Squadron VC-97 TBM Avenger (68767) (USS Makassar Strait)	April 15, 1945	April 15, 1945*			Fujinaka Matsuo	Navy Petty Officer	36	Farmer/ Miner	Death	
							Fukumoto Norio	Navy	41	Farmer	5 Years	Reduced to 2 Years
							Furuno Masaji	Navy	35	Miner	Death	Reduced to 22 Years

Trial Number/ Location/ Date	Airmen	Aircraft/Unit	Date Shot Down	Date of Incident (*Death)	Location	Japanese Trial	Accused	Offender's Status	Age	Profession	Sentencing	Outcome
							Goto Toshio	Navy	41	Restaurant Owner	Death	Reduced to Life
							Hagido Morimitsu (Seiko)	Navy	40	Barber	Death	Reduced to 5 Years
							Ikehara Shigeichi	Navy	32	Farmer	Death	Reduced to 5 Years
							Ikemiyagi Morikaji (Seiki)	Navy	32	Farmer	Acquitted	
							Inami Yoshiaki	Navy	29	Farmer	Death	Reduced to 20 Years
							Inoue Katsutaro	Navy Lt	25	University Student	Death	
							Inoue Otohiko	Navy	50	Contractor	Death	
							Kamishin-bara Taneyoshi	Navy	22	Farmer	Death	Reduced to Life
							Kawahira Kenji	Navy	30	Farmer	Acquitted	
							Kimoto Kazuo	Navy	32	Contractor	Death	Reduced to 5 Years
							Kitada Mitsuno	Navy	32	Laborer	Death	Reduced to 25 Years
							Kohama Seisho	Navy	19	Farmer	Death	Reduced to 5 Years

Trial Number/ Location/ Date	Airmen	Aircraft/Unit	Date Shot Down	Date of Incident (*Death)	Location	Japanese Trial	Accused	Offender's Status	Age	Profession	Sentencing	Outcome
							Kubo Hisayoshi	Navy	24	Farmer	Death	Reduced to 10 Years
							Kuwae Ryoyu	Navy	33	Farmer	Death	
							Kuwano Sahachi	Navy	45	Factory Worker	Death	Reduced to 25 Years
							Maejima Yuichi	Navy Lt	49	Banker	Death	Reduced to 25 Years
							Maeuchihara Takeshi	Navy	22	Farmer	Death	Reduced to 5 Years
							Makuda Minoru	Navy Lt	29	Office Worker	Death	
							Matake Kakutaro	Navy	37	Factory Worker	Death	Reduced to 5 Years
							Miyahara Fusao	Navy	39	Factory Worker	Death	Acquitted
							Morooka Yoshiyuki	Navy Lt	26	Book Publisher	Death	Acquitted
							Mukumoto Shimpei	Navy	26	Government Worker	Death	Reduced to 5 Years
							Nadahara Iwayoshi	Navy	25	Office Worker	Death	Reduced to Life
							Nakazono Hirotoshi	Navy	36	Carpenter	Death	Reduced to 5 Years
							Narisako Tadakuni	Navy	25	Farmer	Death	

Trial Number/ Location/ Date	Airmen	Aircraft/Unit	Date Shot Down	Date of Incident (*Death)	Location	Japanese Trial	Accused	Offender's Status	Age	Profession	Sentencing	Outcome
							Oshiro Eikichi	Navy	20	Farmer/ Fisherman	Death	Reduced to 5 Years
							Seyama Tadayuki	Navy	39	Carpenter	Death	
							Shirakata Yoshio	Navy	23	Farmer	Death	Reduced to Life
							Somoya Masonori	Navy	34	Farmer	Death	Reduced to 5 Years
							Sumitoko Shizuo	Navy	32	Farmer	Death	
							Taguchi Yasumasa	Navy	26	Government Worker	Death	
							Taike Nobuyuki	Navy	24	Railway Worker	Death	Acquitted
							Takamura Naoichi	Navy	40	Farmer	Death	Acquitted
							Tauchi Yoshio	Navy	40	Farmer	Death	Reduced to 5 Years
							Terashima Seichi	Navy	43	Farmer	Death	Reduced to 5 Years
							Tezuka Takashi	Navy	20	Fisherman	Death	Reduced to 10 Years
							Uchikura Masonori	Navy	29	Farmer	Death	Reduced to Life
							Urayama Tameichi	Navy	37	Farmer	Death	Reduced to 5 Years

Trial Number/ Location/ Date	Airmen	Aircraft/Unit	Date Shot Down	Date of Incident (*Death)	Location	Japanese Trial	Accused	Offender's Status	Age	Profession	Sentencing	Outcome
							Yamakawa Yoji	Navy	31	Clerk	Death	Reduced to 5 Years
							Yoshihara Tsuyoshi	Navy	25	Farmer	Death	Reduced to 2 Years
No. 265 Yokohama December 23, 1947–January 16, 1948	2nd Lt Leland P. Fishback	19th B.G. 314th B.S. B-29 (44-69686) MACR 13857	March 10, 1945	March 10, 1945*	Tokyo	No	Ichinoe Kimiya	Army Lt Col	47	Soldier	Death	
							Kuwabara Masao	Kempeitai	31	Farmer	Life	
							Matsumoto Shoichiro				Acquitted	
							Motokawa Sadamu	Kempeitai 2nd Lt	42	Soldier	Death	
							Sonobe Rokuro	Army 1st Lt	40	Medical Doctor	2 Years	
							Yamanaka Goro				Acquitted	
							Yanagizawa Kenichi				Acquitted	

Appendix | 175

Trial Number/ Location/ Date	Airmen	Aircraft/Unit	Date Shot Down	Date of Incident (*Death)	Location	Japanese Trial	Accused	Offender's Status	Age	Profession	Sentencing	Outcome
No. 270 Yokohama January 7–21, 1948 (See no. 25)							Sakaino Takayoshi	Army Sgt Maj	35	Farmer	Life	
No. 276 Yokohama April 12–May 13, 1948	1st Lt John V. Scanlan Jr.	15th F.G. 47th F.S. P-51 (44-72650) MACR 14983	June 23, 1945	June 23, 1945*	Sahara-Cho Primary School (Terajuku)	No	Nozaki Seiji	Army Lt Gen	59	Soldier	Acquitted	
							Shimoda Chiyoshi	Army Col	47	Farmer	40 Years	Reduced to 12 months
							Shingo Yoshio	Army Maj	39	Farmer	5 Years	Reduced to 3 Years
							Kasai Hyoma	Army Maj	52		Acquitted	
							Taka Toichi	Army 1st Lt	31	Logger	5 Years	Acquitted
							Sakai Yoso	Army 1st Lt	36	Farmer	Acquitted	
							Motomiya Unosuke	Civilian	46	Logger	5 Years	Reduced to 3 Years
							Yanagizawa Tojiro	Civilian	62	Laborer	1 Year	
							Ishii Isaburo	Civilian	57	Dyer	1 Year	

Trial Number/ Location/ Date	Airmen	Aircraft/Unit	Date Shot Down	Date of Incident (*Death)	Location	Japanese Trial	Accused	Offender's Status	Age	Profession	Sentencing	Outcome
							Ishihara Tazuko	Civilian	30		Acquitted	
							Hagihara Wakako	Civilian	23		Acquitted	
							Fujisaki Seitaro	Civilian			Acquitted	
							Ishida Naozo	Civilian			Acquitted	
							Sakakibara Kazuya	Civilian	63	Factory Worker	1 Year	
							Nemoto Kanji	Civilian	45	Government Worker	Acquitted	
							Aoyagi Jimbei	Civilian	56	Plasterer	Acquitted	
							Sugo Shotaro	Civilian	44	Laborer	Acquitted	
							Suzuki Tomoichi	Civilian	46	Store Owner	1 Year	
No. 288 Yokohama October 11– December 29, 1948	M/Sgt Robert J. Aspinall	505th B.G. 484th B.S. B-29 (44-69887) MACR 14400	May 7, 1945	June 20, 1945*	Fukuoka Girls High School	No	Aihara Kajuro	Army Capt	51	Officer Worker	5 Years	Acquitted

Appendix | 177

Trial Number/Location/Date	Airmen	Aircraft/Unit	Date Shot Down	Date of Incident (*Death)	Location	Japanese Trial	Accused	Offender's Status	Age	Profession	Sentencing	Outcome
	2nd Lt Jack M. Berry Jr.	29th B.G. 6th B.S. B-29 (42-93953) MACR 14363	May 5, 1945	June 20, 1945*			Akita Hiroshi	War College Instructor; Military Attache in Germany	46	Soldier	Acquitted	
	Pvt Merlin R. Calvin	29th B.G. 6th B.S. B-29 (42-93953) MACR 14363	May 5, 1945	June 20, 1945*			Fukushima Kyusaku	Assistant Chief of Staff, Western Army	52	Soldier	Death	Reduced to 30 Years
	Cpl Irving A. Corliss	29th B.G. 6th B.S. B-29 (42-93953) MACR 14363	May 5, 1945	June 20, 1945*			Inada Masazumi	Chief of Staff, 16th Area Army	53	Soldier	Acquitted	
	Sgt Jack V. Dengler	29th B.G. 6th B.S. B-29 (42-93953) MACR 14363	May 5, 1945	June 20, 1945*			Enatsu Tokuji	Army Officer	39		Acquitted	
	T/Sgt Edgar L. McElfresh	505th B.G. 483rd B.G. B-29 (42-63549) "Empire Express" MACR 14402	May 7, 1945	June 20, 1945*			Ito Shoshin	Army Maj Gen	55	Soldier	Death	Acquitted

Trial Number/ Location/ Date	Airmen	Aircraft/Unit	Date Shot Down	Date of Incident (*Death)	Location	Japanese Trial	Accused	Offender's Status	Age	Profession	Sentencing	Outcome
	Sgt Ralph S. Romines	505th B.G. 483rd B.G. B-29 (42-63549) "Empire Express" MACR 14402	May 7, 1945	June 20, 1945*			Jin Iichiro	Army Officer	51	Soldier	Acquitted	
	Sgt Otto W. Baumgarten	505th B.G. 483rd B.G. B-29 (42-63549) "Empire Express" MACR 14402	May 7, 1945	June 20, 1945*			Sato Yoshinao	Army Officer	49	Soldier	Death	
	F/O Charles S. Appleby	19th B.G. 28th B.S. B-29 (42-94098) MACR 14798	July 27, 1945	August 10, 1945*	Aburayama Cemetery (Fukuoka City)	No	Yakumaru Katsuya	Army Officer	43	Soldier	Life	Acquitted
	1st Lt James E. Hewitt	19th B.G. 28th B.S. B-29 (42-94098) MACR 14798	July 27, 1945	August 10, 1945*			Nakamura Minoru	Army Officer	33	Officer Worker	Acquitted	

Trial Number/ Location/ Date	Airmen	Aircraft/Unit	Date Shot Down	Date of Incident (*Death)	Location	Japanese Trial	Accused	Offender's Status	Age	Profession	Sentencing	Outcome
	Capt Louis W. Nelson	19th B.G. 28th B.S. B-29 (42-94098) MACR 14798	July 27, 1945	August 10, 1945*			Kaku Takanobu	Army Officer	25	Officer Worker	25 Years	
	Cpl Frederick A. Stearns	19th B.G. 28th B.S. B-29 (42-94098) MACR 14798	July 27, 1945	August 10, 1945*			Yokoyama Isamu	Army Officer	60	Soldier	Death	Reduced to 40 Years
	S/Sgt Ben Thornton	19th B.G. 28th B.S. B-29 (42-94098) MACR 14798	July 27, 1945	August 10, 1945*			Kuboyama Hideto	Army Officer	30	Farmer	20 Years	Reduced to 2 Years
	Sgt Jack J. Roy	6th B.G. 40th B.S. B-29 (42-93939) MACR 14750	July 10, 1945	August 10, 1945*			Inoue Mitsushige					
	1st Lt Weldon W. Dyess (Likely)	11th B.G. 98th B.S. B-29 (50958) MACR 14889	July 31, 1945	August 15, 1945*			Wako Yusei	Army Officer	40	Soldier	Death	

Trial Number/ Location/ Date	Airmen	Aircraft/Unit	Date Shot Down	Date of Incident (*Death)	Location	Japanese Trial	Accused	Offender's Status	Age	Profession	Sentencing	Outcome
	2nd Lt Robert J. Studer (Likely)	11th B.G. 98th B.S. B-29 (50958) MACR 14889	July 31, 1945	August 15, 1945*			Yukino Koshi		40	Farmer	Acquitted	
	2nd Lt Nathaniel Hoffman (Likely)	11th B.G. 98th B.S. B-29 (50958) MACR 14889	July 31, 1945	August 15, 1945*			Ikeda Kaneyoshi	Army Officer	29	Taxi Driver	20 Years	Reduced to 10 Years
	2nd Lt Serge S. Davison (Likely)	11th B.G. 98th B.S. B-29 (50958) MACR 14889	July 31, 1945	August 15, 1945*			Itezono Tatsuo	Army Officer	31	Farmer	Life	
	Sgt Aubrey B. Dixon (Likely)	11th B.G. 98th B.S. B-29 (50958) MACR 14889	July 31, 1945	August 15, 1945*			Kusumoto Tomenosuke	Army Officer	49	Business Owner	40 Years	Reduced to 10 Years
	2nd Lt Charles S. Ensey (Likely)	11th B.G. 98th B.S. B-29 (50958) MACR 14889	July 31, 1945	August 15, 1945*			Murata Sadayoshi	Army Officer	48	Lawyer	Acquitted	

Trial Number/ Location/ Date	Airmen	Aircraft/Unit	Date Shot Down	Date of Incident (*Death)	Location	Japanese Trial	Accused	Offender's Status	Age	Profession	Sentencing	Outcome
	1st Lt Robert G. Neal (Likely)	345th B.G. 498th B.S. B-25 (44-31300) MACR 14851	August 7, 1945	August 15, 1945*			Nakayama Hiroji	Army Officer	34	Construction Worker	Death	Reduced to 20 Years
	1st Lt Louis J. Winiecki Jr. (Likely)	345th B.G. 498th B.S. B-25 (44-31300) MACR 14851	August 7, 1945	August 15, 1945*			Narazaki Masahiko	Army Officer	26	University Student	Death	Reduced to 30 Years
	1st Lt Richard S. Lane (Likely)	345th B.G. 498th B.S. B-25 (44-31300) MACR 14851	August 7, 1945	August 15, 1945*			Noda Hidehiko	Army Officer	25	Medical Technician	25 Years	
	S/Sgt Robert W. Goulet (Likely)	345th B.G. 498th B.S. B-25 (44-31300) MACR 14851	August 7, 1945	August 15, 1945*			Ohno Minehiro	Army Officer	29	Lawyer	30 Years	
	S/Sgt William Cohen (Likely)	345th B.G. 498th B.S. B-25 (44-31300) MACR 14851	August 7, 1945	August 15, 1945*			Onishi Tamotsu	Army, Judicial Section	33		20 Years	Reduced to 2 Years

Trial Number/ Location/ Date	Airmen	Aircraft/Unit	Date Shot Down	Date of Incident (*Death)	Location	Japanese Trial	Accused	Offender's Status	Age	Profession	Sentencing	Outcome
	Capt Lloyd Henley Jr. (Likely)	318th F.G. 19th F.S. P-47 (44-88017) MACR 14985	August 8, 1945	August 15, 1945*			Otsuki Takahashi	Army Officer	27	Teacher	30 Years	
	2nd Lt William L. McDaniel (Likely)	507th F.G. 465th F.S. P-47 (44-88118) MACR 14871	August 14, 1945	August 15, 1945*			Toji Kentaro	Army, Air Intelligence	35	Store Owner	Death	Reduced to 40 Years
	1st Lt George A. Huck (Likely)	82nd Tac. Recon. Sqdn. P-51 (44-13138) MACR 14823	July 31, 1945	August 10 or 15, 1945*			Tomomori Kiyoharu	Army Officer	48	Officer Worker	Death	Reduced to 30 Years
	Cpl Byron H. Brewer (Likely)	504th B.G. 680th B.S. B-29 (42-94041) MACR 14797	July 27, 1945	August 10 or 15, 1945*			Yamauye Hitoshi	Army Officer	27	Farmer	25 Years	
	2nd Lt Howard T. Shingledecker (Likely)	29th B.G. 6th B.S. B-29 (42-65305) MACR 14363	May 5, 1945				Yamamoto Fukuichi	Army Officer	27	Farmer	30 Years	

Trial Number/ Location/ Date	Airmen	Aircraft/Unit	Date Shot Down	Date of Incident (*Death)	Location	Japanese Trial	Accused	Offender's Status	Age	Profession	Sentencing	Outcome
	2nd Lt Charles M. Kearns (Likely)	29th B.G. 6th B.S. B-29 (42-65305) MACR 14363	May 5, 1945				Yoshida Kanji	Army Officer	39	Lawyer	30 Years	
	Cpl Robert C. Johnson (Likely)	29th B.G. 6th B.S. B-29 (42-65305) MACR 14363	May 5, 1945				Tsuchiyama Tokuzo	Army Officer	30	Lawyer	20 Years	Reduced to 2 Years
	Cpl Leo C. Oeinck (Likely)	29th B.G. 6th B.S. B-29 (42-65305) MACR 14363	May 5, 1945				Maida Ichiro	Army Officer	29	Priest of Tenri Sect	Life	Reduced to 20 Years
No. 289 Yokohama March 8–May 19, 1948	S/Sgt Cleveland T. Niles Jr.	444th B.G. 678th B.S. B-29 (42-63451) "Black Jack Too" MACR 14606	June 5, 1945	June 28, 1945*	Seto	No	Okada Tasuku	Army Lt Gen	59	Soldier	Death	Reduced to Life
	S/Sgt Willard M. Chapman	444th B.G. 678th B.S. B-29 (42-63451) "Black Jack Too" MACR 14606	June 5, 1945	June 28, 1945*			Onishi Hajime	Army Col	45	Soldier	Life	Reduced to 30 Years

Trial Number/ Location/ Date	Airmen	Aircraft/Unit	Date Shot Down	Date of Incident (*Death)	Location	Japanese Trial	Accused	Offender's Status	Age	Profession	Sentencing	Outcome
	1st Lt Don A. Coulter	444th B.G. 678th B.S. B-29 (42-63451) "Black Jack Too" MACR 14606	June 5, 1945	June 28, 1945*			Yasuda Naofumi	Army Maj	31	Officer Worker	15 Years	Reduced to 10 Years
	M/Sgt Henry T. Farish Jr.	444th B.G. 678th B.S. B-29 (42-63451) "Black Jack Too" MACR 14606	June 5, 1945	June 28, 1945*			Adachi Seiichi	Army Lt Col	41	Soldier	17 Years	
	1st Lt Woodrow B. Palmer	444th B.G. 678th B.S. B-29 (42-63451) "Black Jack Too" MACR 14606	June 5, 1945	June 28, 1945*			Yonemaru Masukuma	Army Col	52	Soldier	25 Years	Reduced to 18 Years
	Sgt Eugene J. Prouty	444th B.G. 678th B.S. B-29 (42-63451) "Black Jack Too" MACR 14606	June 5, 1945	June 28, 1945*			Yamata (Yamada) Rikio	Army Capt	32	Agriculture Association Employee	20 Years	Reduced to 10 Years

Trial Number/ Location/ Date	Airmen	Aircraft/Unit	Date Shot Down	Date of Incident (*Death)	Location	Japanese Trial	Accused	Offender's Status	Age	Profession	Sentencing	Outcome
	T/Sgt Elgie L. Robertson	40th B.G. 44th B.S. B-29 (42-24894) MACR 14543	May 29, 1945	June 28, 1945*			Fujita Takayas	Army Sgt	33	Executive, Haruta Compaty	10 Years	Suspended Sentence
	Sgt Peter Sabo	444th B.G. 678th B.S. B-29 (42-63451) "Black Jack Too" MACR 14606	June 5, 1945	June 28, 1945*			Furuyama Mataichi	Army Cpl	35	Officer Worker	10 Years	Suspended Sentence
	1st Lt Owen P. Walls	444th B.G. 678th B.S. B-29 (42-63451) "Black Jack Too" MACR 14606	June 5, 1945	June 28, 1945*			Hayashi Shigeaki	Army Pfc	28	Police	10 Years	Suspended Sentence
	1st Lt Robert F. Dailey	444th B.G. 678th B.S. B-29 (42-63451) "Black Jack Too" MACR 14606	June 5, 1945	June 28, 1945*			Tsuchiyama Keishi	Army Cpl	33	Buddhist Priest	10 Years	Suspended Sentence

Trial Number/ Location/ Date	Airmen	Aircraft/Unit	Date Shot Down	Date of Incident (*Death)	Location	Japanese Trial	Accused	Offender's Status	Age	Profession	Sentencing	Outcome
	S/Sgt Joseph W. Romanelli	444th B.G. 678th B.S. B-29 (42-63451) "Black Jack Too" MACR 14606	June 5, 1945	June 28, 1945*			Yamamoto Eijiro	Army Sgt	27	Office Worker	10 Years	Suspended Sentence
	Sgt John H. Cox	504th B.G. B-29 (42-24882) "Pappys Pullman" MACR 14907	June 22, 1945	July 15, 1945*	Tokai	·	Kondo Kiyoshi	Army Sgt	27	Clerk	10 Years	Suspended Sentence
	M/Sgt George N. Davis	504th B.G. B-29 (42-24882) "Pappys Pullman" MACR 14907	June 22, 1945	July 15, 1945*			Kawakami Suetaka	Army Sgt	44	Farmer	10 Years	Suspended Sentence
	S/Sgt Maurice W. DuBois Jr.	504th B.G. B-29 (42-24882) "Pappys Pullman" MACR 14907	June 22, 1945	July 14, 1945*			Kuwada Haruo	Army Sgt Maj	31	Farmer	10 Years	Suspended Sentence

Trial Number/ Location/ Date	Airmen	Aircraft/Unit	Date Shot Down	Date of Incident (*Death)	Location	Japanese Trial	Accused	Offender's Status	Age	Profession	Sentencing	Outcome
	1st Lt Harry P. Polgar	468th B.G. 793rd B.S. B-29 (44-69665) MACR 14390	June 5, 1945	June 28, 1945*			Tsudruda Yoshitaka	Army Sgt Maj	25	Cosmetic Retail Store Worker	10 Years	Suspended Sentence
	1st Lt Vincent L. Garman	468th B.G. 793rd B.S. B-29 (44-69665) MACR 14390	June 5, 1945	June 28, 1945*			Nobuta Hideshi	Army Sgt	29	Teacher	10 Years	Suspended Sentence
	2nd Lt Richard M. Hurley	40th B.G. 44th B.S. B-29 (42-24894) MACR14543	May 29, 1945	June 28, 1945*			Sugai Yasui	Army 2nd Lt	40	Glass Worker	10 Years	Suspended Sentence
	Cpl. Theodore J. Mainiero	468th B.G. 793th B.S. B-29 (44-69665) MACR 14390	June 5, 1945	June 28, 1945*			Tanabe Mitsuo	Army Probationary Officer	29	Glass Worker	10 Years	Suspended Sentence
	Sgt Joseph R. McDaniel	468th B.G. 793th B.S. B-29 (44-69665) MACR 14390	June 5, 1945	June 28, 1945*			Yatagai Kiyoshi	Army Probationary Officer	26	Banker	10 Years	Suspended Sentence

188 | Appendix

Trial Number/ Location/ Date	Airmen	Aircraft/Unit	Date Shot Down	Date of Incident (*Death)	Location	Japanese Trial	Accused	Offender's Status	Age	Profession	Sentencing	Outcome
	S/Sgt Thurman E. Newland	504th B.G. B-29 (42-24882) "Pappys Pullman" MACR 14907	June 22, 1945	July 15, 1945*			Narita Kikumoto	Army 1st Lt	30	Construction Worker	30 Years	Reduced to 20 Years
	S/Sgt Billy J. Nichols	504th B.G. B-29 (42-24882) "Pappys Pullman" MACR 14907	June 22, 1945	July 15, 1945*								
	2nd Lt John H Nuttman	504th B.G. B-29 (42-24882) "Pappys Pullman" MACR 14907	June 22, 1945	July 15, 1945*								
	1st Lt William C. Muldoon	504th B.G. B-29 (42-24882) "Pappys Pullman" MACR 14907	June 22, 1945	July 15, 1945*								

Trial Number/ Location/ Date	Airmen	Aircraft/Unit	Date Shot Down	Date of Incident (*Death)	Location	Japanese Trial	Accused	Offender's Status	Age	Profession	Sentencing	Outcome
	Sgt Jack K. Merrill	504th B.G. B-29 (42-24882) "Pappys Pullman" MACR 14907	June 22, 1945	July 12, 1945*								
	S/Sgt Lester J. Shelters	19th B.G. 28th B.S. B-29 (44-69873) MACR 14711	June 26, 1945	July 14, 1945*								
	2nd Lt Roger W. Squire	504th B.G. B-29 (42-24882) "Pappys Pullman" MACR 14907	June 22, 1945	July 15, 1945*								
	S/Sgt Charles L. Vreeland	468th B.G. 793rd B.S. B-29 (44-69873) MACR 14390	June 5, 1945	June 28, 1945*								
	2nd Lt Walter S. Roper	504th B.G. B-29 (42-24882) "Pappys Pullman" MACR 14907	June 22, 1945	July 15, 1945*								

Trial Number/ Location/ Date	Airmen	Aircraft/Unit	Date Shot Down	Date of Incident (*Death)	Location	Japanese Trial	Accused	Offender's Status	Age	Profession	Sentencing	Outcome
	F/O Melvin Wolf	468th B.G. 793rd B.S. B-29 (44-69873) MACR 14390	June 5, 1945	June 28, 1945*								
	2nd Lt Keith H. Carrier	19th B.G. 314th B.S. B-29 (44-70017) MACR 14428	May 14, 1945	July 12, 1945*								
	Cpl George R. Graziadei Jr.	19th B.G. 314th B.S. B-29 (44-70017) MACR 14428	May 14, 1945	July 12, 1945*								
	2nd Lt Elton V. Kime	19th B.G. 314th B.S. B-29 (44-70017) MACR 14428	May 14, 1945	July 12, 1945*								
	Sgt Joseph R. Shelton	19th B.G. 314th B.S. B-29 (44-70017) MACR 14428	May 14, 1945	July 12, 1945*								

Trial Number/ Location/ Date	Airmen	Aircraft/Unit	Date Shot Down	Date of Incident (*Death)	Location	Japanese Trial	Accused	Offender's Status	Age Profession	Sentencing	Outcome
	Sgt Evan L. Howell	462nd B.G. 779th B.S. B-29 (44-69966) MACR 14431	May 14, 1945	July 12, 1945*							
	Sgt Jerry W. Johnson	462nd B.G. 779th B.S. B-29 (44-69966) MACR 14431	May 14, 1945	July 12, 1945*							
	Sgt Edward R. Gentry	462nd B.G. 779th B.S. B-29 (44-69966) MACR 14431	May 14, 1945	July 12, 1945*							
	Cpl Carl H. Manson Jr.	462nd B.G. 779th B.S. B-29 (44-69966) MACR 14431	May 14, 1945	July 12, 1945*							
	Cpl Benjamin W. Prichard	462nd B.G. 779th B.S. B-29 (44-69966) MACR 14431	May 14, 1945	July 12, 1945*							

Trial Number/ Location/ Date	Airmen	Aircraft/Unit	Date Shot Down	Date of Incident (*Death)	Location	Japanese Trial	Accused	Offender's Status	Age	Profession	Sentencing	Outcome
	1st Lt Dean H. Sherman	462nd B.G. 779th B.S. B-29 (44-69966) MACR 14431	May 14, 1945	July 12, 1945*								
	2nd Lt Norman Solomon	462nd B.G. 779th B.S. B-29 (44-69966) MACR 14431	May 14, 1945	July 12, 1945*								
No. 290 Yokohama March 11–August 28, 1948	Cpl Robert B. Williams	29th B.G. 6th B.S. B-29 (42-65305) MACR 14363	May 5, 1945	May–June, 1945*	Kyushu Imperial University (Vivisection)	No	Aihara Kajuro	Army Capt	48	Electrician	20 Years	
	S/Sgt Teddy J. Ponczka	29th B.G. 6th B.S. B-29 (42-65305) MACR 14363	May 5, 1945	May–June, 1945*			Akita Hiroshi	Army Col	54	Soldier	Life	
	2nd Lt Dale E. Plambeck	29th B.G. 6th B.S. B-29 (42-65305) MACR 14363	May 5, 1945	May–June, 1945*			Fukushima Kyusaku	Army Maj Gen	49	Soldier	15 Years	

Appendix | 193

Trial Number/ Location/ Date	Airmen	Aircraft/Unit	Date Shot Down	Date of Incident (*Death)	Location	Japanese Trial	Accused	Offender's Status	Age	Profession	Sentencing	Outcome
	2nd Lt William R. Fredericks	29th B.G. 6th B.S. B-29 (42-65305) MACR 14363	May 5, 1945	May–June 1945*			Goiyama Shinju	Army Capt	43	Farmer	10 Years	
	Cpl Leon E. Czarnecki	29th B.G. 6th B.S. B-29 (42-65305) MACR 14363	May 5, 1945	May–June 1945*			Goshima Shiro	Civilian	28	University Student	6 Years	
	Cpl John C. Colehower	29th B.G. 6th B.S. B-29 (42-65305) MACR 14363	May 5, 1945	May–June 1945*			Hirako Goichi	Civilian	61	Professor of Medicine	25 Years	
	S/Sgt Billy J. Brown	498th B.G. 873rd B.S. B-29 (42-24611) MACR 14337	April 29, 1945	May–June 1945*			Hirao Kanichi	Army Probationary Officer	38	Medical Doctor	Death	
	Sgt Charles E. Palmer	9th B.G. 1st B.S. B-29 (44-69811) MACR 14522	May 28, 1945	May–June 1945*			Horiuchi Kiyoma	Army Maj Gen	60	Army Medical Officer	Acquitted	
							Inada Masazumi	Army Lt Gen	51	Soldier	7 Years	

194 | Appendix

Trial Number/ Location/ Date	Airmen	Aircraft/Unit	Date Shot Down	Date of Incident (*Death)	Location	Japanese Trial	Accused	Offender's Status	Age	Profession	Sentencing	Outcome
							Ito Akira	Civilian	43	Dentist	Acquitted	
							Ito Shoshin (Ito Akinobu)	Army Maj Gen	54	Lawyer	10 Years	
							Jin Iichiro	Army Lt Col	49	Soldier	Acquitted	
							Kishi Tatsuro	Army 2nd Lt	33	Medical Doctor	Acquitted	
							Makino Reiichiro	Civilian	32	University Student	9 Years	
							Matake Shinchiro	Army Capt	40	Medical Doctor	Acquitted	
							Mori Yoshio	Civilian	37	Medical Doctor	Death	
							Morimoto Kenji	Army 1st Lt	37	Medical Doctor	Life	
							Nogawa Nobuyoshi	Civilian	28	University Student	25 Years	
							Oda Tayuru	Civilian	39	Lab Assistant	Acquitted	
							Ryu Miki	Civilian	38	Medical Doctor	3 Years	
							Sato Yoshinao	Army Capt	40	Soldier	Death	
							Senba (Semba) Yoshitaka	Civilian	28	University Student	Life	
							Tashiro Tomoki	Civilian	29	Assistant Medical Doctor	15 Years	

Trial Number/ Location/ Date	Airmen	Aircraft/Unit	Date Shot Down	Date of Incident (*Death)	Location	Japanese Trial	Accused	Offender's Status	Age	Profession	Sentencing	Outcome
							Torisu Taro	Civilian	41	Medical Doctor	Death	
							Tsurumaru Hironaga	Army Capt	35	Medical Doctor	Acquitted	
							Tsutsui (Tsutsuo) Shizuko	Civilian	31	Nurse (Female)	5 Years	
							Yakamaru Katsuya	Army Lt Col	43	Soldier	Life	
							Yokoyama Isamu	Army Lt Gen	57	Soldier	Death	
							Kubo Toshiyuki	Civilian	27	Medical Doctor	15 Years	
							Tashiro Jiro	Army 1st Lt	32	Medical Doctor	15 Years	
No. 294 Yokohama March 1–2, 1948	2nd Lt Andrew J. Litz (See no. 78)	330th B.G. 458 th B.S. B-29 (44-69799) MACR 14240	April 14, 1945	May 26, 1945*	Kempeitai HQ (Tokyo)	No	Hikita Toyokzu	Army	26	Radio Operatr	4 Years	
	S/Sgt Walter W. Dickerson	6th B.G. 24th B.S. B-29 (44-70116) MACR 14786	July 20, 1945	July 28, 1945			Tanabe Kiyoshi	Army	31	Clerk	2 Years	

Trial Number/ Location/ Date	Airmen	Aircraft/Unit	Date Shot Down	Date of Incident (*Death)	Location	Japanese Trial	Accused	Offender's Status	Age	Profession	Sentencing	Outcome
	S/Sgt Thomas W. Peel	27th BG		May 26, 1945*								
	Capt Gordon P. Jordan	6th B.G. 24th B.S. B-29 (44-70116) MACR 14786	July 20, 1945	July 28, 1945								
	Sgt Lester C. Morris	29th B.G. 314th B.S. B-29 (44-87664) "Thunderbird" MACR 14820	August 8, 1945	August 8, 1945								
	Capt Vincent A. Gaudiani Jr.	21st F.G. P-51 (44-72661) "Mary One" MACR 14838	August 6, 1945	August 6, 1945								
	1st Lt Marvin S. Watkins	29th B.G. 6th B.S. B-29 (42-65305) MACR 14363	May 5, 1945	August 1945								
	James L. Green			January–August 1945								

Trial Number/ Location/ Date	Airmen	Aircraft/Unit	Date Shot Down	Date of Incident (*Death)	Location	Japanese Trial	Accused	Offender's Status	Age	Profession	Sentencing	Outcome
	F/O Mark S. Kennard	468th B.G. 792nd B.S. B-29 (42-6408) MACR 9687)	August 20, 1944	May–June 1945								
No. 295 Yokohama April 7–18, 1948 (See no. 306 and 369)							Hirano Kenji	Army 1st Lt	29	Medical Doctor	Life	
No. 296 Yokohama March 11–30, 1948	Cpl Marvin J. Greenspan	9th B.G. 313th B.S. B-29 (42-63545) MACR 14250	April 15, 1945	April 16, 1945*	Kamijiki-mura (Otaki-cho)	No	Tamura Ippei	Army 2nd Lt	27	Clerk	12 Years	
							Oku Misumasa	Army Private	35	Farmer	Acquitted	
							Minamide Tahichi	Army Private	34	Salesman	Acquitted	

Trial Number/ Location/ Date	Airmen	Aircraft/Unit	Date Shot Down	Date of Incident (*Death)	Location	Japanese Trial	Accused	Offender's Status	Age	Profession	Sentencing	Outcome
No. 306 Yokohama March 29–31, 1948 (See no. 369)							Noguchi Esuji	Kempeitai	38	Teacher	12 Years	
No. 307 Yokohama May 24–July 14, 1948	9 unidentified flyers	Navy PBY	October 1, 1944	November 24, 1944	Kendari, Indonesia	No	Furukawa Tamotsu	Navy Rear Adm	55		20 Years	
							Taniguchi Gosuke	Navy Capt	56		Acquitted	
							Sanokawa Takao (Hisao)	Navy Capt	48		Acquitted	
							Chiuma Sazae	Navy Ens	37		Not Tried	
							Moritama Yoshiyotsu	Navy Capt	54		10 Years	
							Tanabe Toshisuke	Navy Lt	28		10 Years	Reduced to 7 Years
							Nozaka Keiichi	Navy Lt	45		10 Years	Reduced to 7 Years

Trial Number/ Location/ Date	Airmen	Aircraft/Unit	Date Shot Down	Date of Incident (*Death)	Location	Japanese Trial	Accused	Offender's Status	Age	Profession	Sentencing	Outcome
							Nakata Yoshisa	Navy Ens	41		10 Years	Reduced to 7 Years
							Maeda Toshioka (Tokioka)	Navy Lt	27	Chemical Engineer	10 Years	Reduced to 7 Years
							Imai Katsuto (Katsushito)	Navy Ens	34		Acquitted	
No. 310 Yokohama May 24– October 13, 1948	2nd Lt John S. Houghton	498th B.G. 874th B.S. B-29 (42-93999) "Filthy Fay II" MACR 13762	April 2, 1945	April 11, 1945*	Kempeitai HQ (Tokyo)	No	Kono Shoji	Chief of Eastern Army Medical Department	58	Medical Doctor	Acquitted	
	Sgt Seth Rigby	29th B.G. 6th B.S. B-29 (42-94034) MACR 14271	April 16, 1945	April 16, 1945*			Toyama Toshio	Army Capt	40	Lawyer	Life	
	2nd Lt Roland F. Nelson	9th B.G. 5th B.S. B-29 (44-69834) MACR 14474	April 15, 1945	April 18, 1945*			Wachi Nobushige	Kempeitai 2nd Lt	36	Soldier	8 Years	Redcued to 5 Years

Trial Number/ Location/ Date	Airmen	Aircraft/Unit	Date Shot Down	Date of Incident (*Death)	Location	Japanese Trial	Accused	Offender's Status	Age	Profession	Sentencing	Outcome
	Sgt William H. Osborn	499th B.G. 877th B.S. B-29 (42-24650) "Jug Haid II" MACR 13763	April 2, 1945	April 18, 1945*			Fujino Ranjo	Kempeitai Lt Col	46	Soldier	5 Years	
	Sgt Walter E. Walk	499th B.G. 878th B.S. B-29 (42-24644) MACR 14237	April 14, 1945	May 1, 1945*			Nemoto Tsune	Kempeitai 1st Lt	46	Officer Worker	3 ½ Years	
	M/Sgt Erwin R. Griffin	9th B.G. 5th B.S. B-29 (44-69834) MACR 14474	April 15, 1945	April 24, 1945*								
	Cpl Stanley Forystek	499th B.G. 877th B.S. B-29 (42-63513) "Ramp Queen" MACR 14512	May 26, 1945	May 27, 1945*								

Trial Number/ Location/ Date	Airmen	Aircraft/Unit	Date Shot Down	Date of Incident (*Death)	Location	Japanese Trial	Accused	Offender's Status	Age	Profession	Sentencing	Outcome
	Cpl Elmer H. Bertsch Jr.	40th B.G. 44th B.S. B-29 (42-62538) "Winged Victory the 2nd" MACR14507	May 25, 1945	May 26, 1945*								
	1st Lt Robert L. Williams	15th F.G. 78th F.S. P-51	June 8, 1945	June 26, 1945*								
	Sgt Warren L. Olson	499th B.G. 877th B.S. B-29 (42-63513) "Ramp Queen" MACR 14512	May 26, 1945	June 5, 1945*								
	T/Sgt Harold E. Halldorson	444th B.G. 777th B.S. B-29 (42-24724) "Her Majestry" MACR 14494	May 25, 1945	June 5, 1945*								
	Sgt Charles W. Snell	6th B.G. 39th B.S. B-29 (42-63558) "Tokyo Trolley" MACR 14505	May 25, 1945	June 4, 1945*								

202 | Appendix

Trial Number/ Location/ Date	Airmen	Aircraft/Unit	Date Shot Down	Date of Incident (*Death)	Location	Japanese Trial	Accused	Offender's Status	Age	Profession	Sentencing	Outcome
	1st Lt Francis F. Jensen Jr.	505th BG B-29		June 8, 1945*								
	1st Lt Theodore H. Fox	21st F.G. 531st F.S. P-51 (44-63911) "Ted's Little Helper" MACR 14801	July 28, 1945	August 8, 1945*								
	2nd Lt George L. Sheridan	504th B.G. 398th B.S. B-29 (44-69978) MACR 14503	May 25, 1945	October 29, 1945*								
	Sgt Kenneth A. Pettersen	498th B.G. 874th B.S. B-29 (42-93999) "Filthy Fay II" MACR 13762	April 2, 1945	May 26, 1945*								
No. 317 Yokohama August 5–13, 1948 (See no. 318)	Lt David C. Kincannon	Shangri-La CV-38 FG1D Corsair (67876)		May 1, 1945*	Kikai Island (Ryukyus)		Oshima Munehiko	Navy Lt	27	Electrician	7 Years	

Trial Number/ Location/ Date	Airmen	Aircraft/Unit	Date Shot Down	Date of Incident (*Death)	Location	Japanese Trial	Accused	Offender's Status	Age	Profession	Sentencing	Outcome
							Sato Isamu	Navy Cmdr	39	Factory Manager	20 Years	
No. 318 Yokohama July 19–26, 1948	Ens Arthur L. Thomas	Essex CV-9 SB2C Helldiver (20732)		April 1, 1945*	Kikai Island (Ryukyus)	No	Taniguchi Tetsuo	Navy Ens	36	Farmer	Death	
							Sato Isamu	Navy Cmdr	39	Factoy Manager	Death	
							Kida Satohiko	Navy Capt	48	Soldier	40 Years	
							Yoshida Masayoshi	Navy Lt	37	Farmer	40 Years	
No. 328 Yokohama August 2, 1948–January 3, 1949 (See no. 364)	Sgt Lawrence W. Beecroft	497th B.G. 869th B.S. B-29 (42-65348) MACR 14593	June 1, 1945	July 20, 1945*	Shinodayama Military Cemetery (Osaka)	No	Anjo Hiroshi	Kempeitai Lt Col	45	Soldier	4 Years	Reduced to 2 ½ Years

Trial Number/ Location/ Date	Airmen	Aircraft/Unit	Date Shot Down	Date of Incident (*Death)	Location	Japanese Trial	Accused	Offender's Status	Age	Profession	Sentencing	Outcome
	Sgt James M. Fitzgerald	505th B.G. 482nd B.S. B-29 (42-24809) "Indian Maid" MACR 14603	June 5, 1945	July 20, 1945*			Fujioka Hideo	Kempeitai Lt Col	44	Soldier	Life	
	S/Sgt Erle P. Flanagan	497th B.G. 871st B.S. B-29 (44-69899) MACR 14365	May 5, 1945	July 20, 1945*			Hamada Tomekichi	Army	31	Clerk	2 Years	Reduced to 1 Year
	Capt Richard H. Hamilton	501st B.G 21st B.S. B-29 (42-63600) MACR 14395	May 8, 1945	July 20, 1945*			Ishida Otogoro	Kempeitai Lt Gen	56	Soldier	1 Year	
	Sgt Harvey B. Kennedy Jr.	505th B.G. 482nd B.S. B-29 (42-24809) "Indian Maid" MACR 14603	June 5, 1945	July 20, 1945*			Kobayashi Hideichi	Kempeitai W/O	37	Farmer	Acquitted	

Appendix | 205

Trial Number/ Location/ Date	Airmen	Aircraft/Unit	Date Shot Down	Date of Incident (*Death)	Location	Japanese Trial	Accused	Offender's Status	Age	Profession	Sentencing	Outcome
	S/Sgt George C. Reed	330th B.G. 459th B.S. B-29 (44-69766) "City of Burbank–Old Soldiers' Home" MACR 14602	June 5, 1945	July 20, 1945*			Konishi Shinpachi	Army Cpl	27		Acquitted	
	Cpl Clarence E. Scritchfield	462nd B.G. 770th B.S. B-29 (42-65336) "Assid Test II" MACR 14394	June 5, 1945	July 20, 1945*			Kunitake Michio	Army Lt Gen	55	Soldier	Life	
	S/Sgt Logan M. Sparks	497th B.G. 871st B.S. B-29 (44-69899) MACR 14365	May 5, 1945	July 20, 1945*			Matsuda Sadaya	Army	30	Seaman	Acquitted	
	S/Sgt John R. Vincent	29th B.G. 52nd B.S. B-29 (44-70008) MACR 14604	June 5, 1945	July 20, 1945*			Mori Takao	Kempeitai	34	Clerk	2 Years	Released after trial for time served

Trial Number/ Location/ Date	Airmen	Aircraft/Unit	Date Shot Down	Date of Incident (*Death)	Location	Japanese Trial	Accused	Offender's Status	Age	Profession	Sentencing	Outcome
	1st Lt Harrison K. Wittee	497th B.G. 869th B.S. B-29 (42-65348) MACR 14593	June 1, 1945	July 20, 1945*			Morimoto Shigemi	Kempeitai	32	Clerk	Acquitted	
	Capt William A. McCarty	462nd B.G. 770th B.S. B-29 (42-65336) "Assid Test II" MACR 14394	June 5, 1945	July 20, 1945*			Nagatomo Tsugio	Army Maj Gen	55	Soldier	Life	
	S/Sgt Dillard R. Jackson	462nd B.G. 770th B.S. B-29 (42-65336) "Assid Test II" MACR 14394	June 5, 1945	July 20, 1945*			Nakano Masamoto	Civilian Interpretor for Army	31	Shop Manager	2 Years	Released after trial for time served
	F/O Robert F.T. Barrett	462nd B.G. 770th B.S. B-29 (42-65336) "Assid Test II" MACR 14394	June 5, 1945	July 20, 1945*			Oba Kojiro	Army Col	46	Soldier	10 Years	Reduced to 8 ½ Years

Trial Number/ Location/ Date	Airmen	Aircraft/Unit	Date Shot Down	Date of Incident (*Death)	Location	Japanese Trial	Accused	Offender's Status	Age	Profession	Sentencing	Outcome
	T/Sgt Clifford A. Welter	462nd B.G. 770th B.S. B-29 (42-65336) "Assid Test II" MACR 14394	June 5, 1945	July 20, 1945*			Oikada Takekazu	Army	29		Acquitted	
	Cpl Norman C. Anderson	462nd B.G. 770th B.S. B-29 (42-65336) "Assid Test II" MACR 14394	June 5, 1945	July 20, 1945*			Okido Sanji	Kempeitai Lt Gen	58	Soldier	Life	
	2nd Lt James R. Price	444th B.G. 677th B.S. B-29 (44-70132) MACR 14792	July 24, 1945	July 13, 1945*	Central District Military Police Headquarters, Osaka		Ono Buichi	Army Capt	43	Lawyer	Acquitted	
	S/Sgt Russell W. Strong	497th B.S. 869th B.S. B-29 (42-65348) MACR 14593	June 1, 1945	July 13, 1945*			Shiuchi Ikoma	Army 2nd Lt	43	Miner	Life	
	3 unidentified flyers			August 3, 1945*			Sugiura Ryuzaburo	Kempeitai W/O	32	Farmer	Acquitted	

Trial Number/ Location/ Date	Airmen	Aircraft/Unit	Date Shot Down	Date of Incident (*Death)	Location	Japanese Trial	Accused	Offender's Status	Age	Profession	Sentencing	Outcome
	1st Lt Louis W. Lehnen	499th B.G. 877th B.S. B-29 (44-69655) MACR 14911	June 26, 1945	August 5, 1945*	Jonan Rifle Range, Osaka		Takahashi Izou	Army	30	Railway Worker	Acquitted	
	1st Lt Harold T. Cobb	499th B.G. 877th B.S. B-29 (44-69655) MACR 14911	June 26, 1945	August 15, 1945*	Shinodayama Military Cemetery (Osaka)		Takayama Hiroaki	Army	38		Acquitted	
	1st Lt Joe S. McSpadden	497th B.G. 871st B.S. B-29 (44-69899) MACR 14365	May 5, 1945	August 15, 1945*			Takeda Chikara	Army Sgt Maj	32	Farmer	Acquitted	
	Capt Jack K. Ort	21st F.G. 46th F.S. P-51 (44-46389)		August 15, 1945*			Tateno Ryoichi	Army	32	Government Worker	Acquitted	
	1st Lt Donald J. Schiltz	330th B.G. 459th B.S. B-29 (44-69766) "City of Burbank—Old Soldiers' Home" MACR 14602	June 5, 1945	August 15, 1945*			Tsuno Kazuyoshi	Army	30	Farmer	Acquitted	

Appendix | 209

Trial Number/ Location/ Date	Airmen	Aircraft/Unit	Date Shot Down	Date of Incident (*Death)	Location	Japanese Trial	Accused	Offender's Status	Age	Profession	Sentencing	Outcome
	2nd Lt Harry J. Foley	497th B.G. 871st B.S. B-29 (44-69899) MACR 14365	May 5, 1945	August 15, 1945*			Uchiyama Eitaro	Army Lt Gen	61	Soldier	40 Years	Reduced to 37 Years
	1st Lt Harry W. Norton Jr.	21st F.G. 72nd F.S. P-51 (44-63409) MACR 14813	July 30, 1945	July 30, 1945*	Fujioka		Wada Yasuo	Army W/O	34		5 Years	Reduced to 2 ½ Years
	Ens Norman B. Bitzegaio	VT-6 TBM Avenger (USS Hancock)	July 30, 1945	July 30, 1945*			Yamamura Yoshio	Kempeitai Lt Col	52	Soldier	1 Year	
							Yamanaka Norio	Army Maj	35	Soldier	8 Years	Reduced to 5 ½ Years
No. 335 Yokohama July 6–26, 1948	Ens Joseph F. Florence III	Santee CVE-29 TBM Avenger (68688)	April 1945	July 11, 1945*	Miyako Jima Island	No	Tonomura Okuji	Army 1st Lt	26	Radio Station Employee	9 Years	
							Hatano Kozo	Army Cpl	30		3 Years	
							Mutsuro Fujio	Army Lt Col	44		35 Years	
							Takeuchi Jiro	Army Sgt Maj	29		3 Years	

Trial Number/ Location/ Date	Airmen	Aircraft/Unit	Date Shot Down	Date of Incident (*Death)	Location	Japanese Trial	Accused	Offender's Status	Age	Profession	Sentencing	Outcome
No. 340 Yokohama September 13–19, 1948	Capt William L. Uhler (possibly)	38th B.G. 71st B.S. B-25 (41-30221) MACR 4698	August 2, 1943	September 1, 1943*	Kairiru Island, New Guinea	No	Haraguchi Kaname	Navy Lt	28	Teacher	8 Years	
	2nd Lt Owen H. Salvage (possibly)	38th B.G. 71st B.S. B-25 (41-30221) MACR 4698	August 2, 1943	September 1, 1943*			Mura (Munehei Takeyoshi) Sohei	Navy Lt	29	Teacher	8 Years	
	1st Lt Donnelly R. McMillan (possibly)	38th B.G. 71st B.S. B-25 (41-30221) MACR 4698	August 2, 1943	September 1, 1943*			Murase Tenjiro	Navy Petty Officer	33	Boiler Repairman	5 Years	
	S/Sgt Joseph H. McDonough (possibly)	38th B.G. 71st B.S. B-25 (41-30221) MACR 4698	August 2, 1943	September 1, 1943*			Yamakawa Kuramatsu	Navy Ens	38	Navy	15 Years	
	S/Sgt Gerard H. Fortier (possibly)	38th B.G. 71st B.S. B-25 (41-30221) MACR 4698	August 2, 1943	September 1, 1943*			Akiba Genzo	Navy	28	Farmer	Acquitted	
							Akita Teruo	Navy Petty Officer	26	Vegetable Salesman	3 Years	

Trial Number/ Location/ Date	Airmen	Aircraft/Unit	Date Shot Down	Date of Incident (*Death)	Location	Japanese Trial	Accused	Offender's Status	Age	Profession	Sentencing	Outcome
							Takano Shusaku	Navy Petty Officer	24		5 Years	
							Kasatani (Kasaya)Eiichi	Navy Petty Officer	24	Farmer	5 Years	
							Katayama Daisaku	Navy Petty Officer	26	Farmer	5 Years	
							Hasegaw (Nishino) Jiro	Navy Petty Officer	27	Farmer	3 Years	
							Okura Sakae	Navy	23	Farmer	5 Years	
							Shiro Toshio	Navy Seaman	23	Electrician	3 Years	
							Shiroshita Takeji	Navy Seaman	24	Farmer	Acquitted	
							Tajima Isaburo	Navy Petty Officer	43		4 Years	
							Yasukawa Shinryu	Navy Petty Officer	27	Priest	Acquitted	
							Yamanaka Koichiro	Navy Petty Officer	34	Farmer	4 Years	
No. 342 Yokohama August 23– September 9, 1948	S/Sgt Charles L. Suey	345th B.G. 500th B.S. B-25 (43-27888) MACR 14225	April 9, 1945	May 13, 1945*	Sanya	No	Yoshida Kiichi	Navy Capt.	56	Soldier	6 Years	

Trial Number/ Location/ Date	Airmen	Aircraft/Unit	Date Shot Down	Date of Incident (*Death)	Location	Japanese Trial	Accused	Offender's Status	Age	Profession	Sentencing	Outcome
	Capt Merritt E. Lawlis	345th B.G. 500th B.S. B-25 (43-27888) MACR 14225	April 9, 1945	May 13, 1945								
	S/Sgt Benjamin T. Muller	345th B.G. 500th B.S. B-25 (43-27888) MACR 14225	April 9, 1945	May 13, 1945								
No. 344 Yokohama September 27–October 8, 1948	Maj Sidney F. Wharton Jr.			December 1943	Maika Bougainville Island	No	Ito Taichi	Kempeitai Maj	49		1 Year	
No. 348 Yokohama October 6–18, 1948	1st Lt Robert F. Burgie	71st R.G. 17th R.S. B-25 (44-29271) MACR 12932	March 6, 1945	March–May 1945*	Kodokan (Hainan Island)	No	Nomi Minoru	Navy Capt	56	Soldier	Life	

Appendix | 213

Trial Number/ Location/ Date	Airmen	Aircraft/Unit	Date Shot Down	Date of Incident (*Death)	Location	Japanese Trial	Accused	Offender's Status	Age	Profession	Sentencing	Outcome
	1st Lt John D. Holbrook	71st R.G. 17th R.S. B-25 (44-29271) MACR 12932	March 6, 1945	March–May 1945*			Yokoyama Yutaka	Navy Lt	27	Soldier	8 Years	
	S/Sgt David R. Morgan	71st R.G. 17th R.S. B-25 (44-29271) MACR 12932	March 6, 1945	March–May 1945*			Suzuki Akira	Navy Lt	28		8 Years	
	4 unidentified flyers			March–May 1945*			Shiinoki Hisayoshi	Navy	33	Textile Designer	8 Years	
No. 357 Yokohama October 11–15, 1948	3 unidentified flyers		October 1944	November 20, 1944*	Batan Island, Philippines	No	Taira Seizo	Army 2nd Lt	28		1 Year	
No. 358 Yokohama October 15, 1948 (See no. 265)				March 10, 1945			Sugihara Eiichi	Kempeitai Lt Col	42	Soldier	5 Years	

Trial Number/ Location/ Date	Airmen	Aircraft/Unit	Date Shot Down	Date of Incident (*Death)	Location	Japanese Trial	Accused	Offender's Status	Age	Profession	Sentencing	Outcome
No. 362 Yokohama December 15–29, 1948 (See no. 288)							Akamine Teruo	Army 1st Lt	32		Life	Reduced to 20 Years
							Inoue Mitsushige	Army Sgt Maj	27	Store Owner	10 Years	Reduced to 2 Years
No. 363 Yokohama December 20–22, 1948	1 unidentified flyer			March 1945*	Hainan Island	No	Umino Hajime	Navy Lt	25	Clerk	7 Years	
No. 364 Yokohama December 27, 1948–January 3, 1949 (See no. 123 & No. 328)							Hamamoto Jiro	Kempei Tai W/O	34	Truck Driver	15 Years	

Trial Number/ Location/ Date	Airmen	Aircraft/Unit	Date Shot Down	Date of Incident (*Death)	Location	Japanese Trial	Accused	Offender's Status	Age	Profession	Sentencing	Outcome
No. 365 Yokohama December 22–29, 1948 (See no. 288)							Hashiyama Noboru	Army	29	Clerk	Life	Reduced to 20 Years
No. 366 Yokohama January 26– February 1, 1949 (See No. 288)							Matsuki Suekatsu	Army Sgt Maj	29	Clerk	20 Years	Reduced to 2 Years
No. 368 Yokohama March 21–25, 1949 (See no. 288)							Nagaoka Masaji	Army Cpl	27		10 Years	Reduced to 2 Years

Trial Number/ Location/ Date	Airmen	Aircraft/Unit	Date Shot Down	Date of Incident (*Death)	Location	Japanese Trial	Accused	Offender's Status	Age	Profession	Sentencing	Outcome
No. 369 Yokohama April 25–September 13, 1949 (See no. 306 & No. 295)	2nd Lt Dwight Knapp	29th B.G. 314th B.W. B-29 (44-69728) MACR 14510	May 26, 1945	May 28, 1945*	New Senju Bridge (South River Bank)	No	Otani Keijiro	Kempeitai Cmdr	51	Soldier	10 Years	
	Cpl Jack D. Krone	29th B.G. 14th B.S. B-29 (42-93905) MACR 12972	March 10, 1945	March 20, 1945*								
No. 370 Yokohama April 11–13, 1949 (See no. 288)				August 10, 1945*	Aburayama Cemetery (Fukuoka City, Kyushu)		Otosu Norifumi	Army 1st Lt	27	Store Owner	30 Years	

Appendix | 217

Trial Number/ Location/ Date	Airmen	Aircraft/Unit	Date Shot Down	Date of Incident (*Death)	Location	Japanese Trial	Accused	Offender's Status	Age	Profession	Sentencing	Outcome
No. 371 Yokohama September 22–October 3, 1949 (See no. 348)							Yussa Tarao	Navy Lt	30		8 Years	
Army Pacific Case No. 48-371 Guam November 1947	2nd Lt Wallace F. Kaufman	494th B.G. 867th B.S. B-24 (44-42058) "Brief" MACR 14351	May 4, 1945	May 24, 1945*	Koror Island, Palau	No	Koichi Hiroe				25 Years	
							Katsuyama Totsuji				25 Years	
							Onose Ichiro				25 Years	
							Tsuchiya Naohiko				Acquitted	

Trial Number/ Location/ Date	Airmen	Aircraft/Unit	Date Shot Down	Date of Incident (*Death)	Location	Japanese Trial	Accused	Offender's Status	Age	Profession	Sentencing	Outcome
Navy Case Guam November– December 1945	F/O John A. Johnston	41st B.G. 867th B.S. B-25 (41-30613) MACR 1900	January 19, 1944	February 2, 1944*	Mille Atoll, Marshall Islands	No	Abe Masanaki	Navy Capt			Life	
	1st Lt Peter Duval	41st B.G. 867th B.S. B-25 (41-30613) MACR 1900	January 19, 1944	February 2, 1944*			Kadota Yasuyoshi	Navy 1st Lt			20 Years	
	2nd Lt David W. Kimmey	41st B.G. 867th B.S. B-25 (41-30613) MACR 1900	January 19, 1944	February 2, 1944*			Motomura Harushi	Navy Ens			20 Years	
	S/Sgt James L. Quinn	41st B.G. 867th B.S. B-25 (41-30613) MACR 1900	January 19, 1944	February 2, 1944*			Tanaka Yutaka	Navy Ens			Life	
	S/Sgt James A. Wages Jr.	41st B.G. 867th B.S. B-25 (41-30613) MACR 1900	January 19, 1944	February 2, 1944*			Oishi Chisato	Navy Col			Death	

Trial Number/ Location/ Date	Airmen	Aircraft/Unit	Date Shot Down	Date of Incident (*Death)	Location	Japanese Trial	Accused	Offender's Status	Age	Profession	Sentencing	Outcome
	S/Sgt James G. Walker Jr.	41st B.G. 867th B.S. B-25 (41-30613) MACR 1900	January 19, 1944	February 2, 1944*			Nakao Otokiti	Navy Maj			Death	
							Takarada Chojiro	Navy Maj			Death	
							Moori Yashuo	Navy 1st Lt			Death	
							Manako Tasuichi	Navy W/O			Death	
Navy Case Guam October 27, 1948	2 unidentified flyers			20. Jun 44*	Dublon Island, Micronesia	No	Hara Chuichi	Navy Vice Admiral			6 Years	Reduced to 3.5 Years
	3 unidentified flyers			10. Mar 44*	Marshall Islands							
Navy Case Guam March 28– April 28, 1949	3 unidentified flyers	B-24		September 4, 1944*	Babelthuap Island, Palau	No	Inoue Sadae				Death	
							Tada Tokuchi				4 Years	

Trial Number/ Location/ Date	Airmen	Aircraft/Unit	Date Shot Down	Date of Incident (*Death)	Location	Japanese Trial	Accused	Offender's Status	Age	Profession	Sentencing	Outcome
							Nakamura Kazue				Death	
							Kokubo Chihiro				Death	
							Nagatome Yoshimori				Acquitted	
Navy Case Guam April 1946	Petty Officer 2nd Lloyd R Woellhof	SB2C Helldiver (USS Yorktown)	July 4, 1944	August 6, 1944*	Chichi-Jima	No	Yoshio Tachinbana				Death	
	SMN/3c Grady A. York Jr.	TBF Avenger (USS Bennington)	February 18, 1945	February 26, 1945*			Yoshihisa Ito				Death	
	AOM/2c Glenn C. Frazier Jr.	SB2C Helldiver	February 18, 1945	February 24, 1945*			Matsuyu Matoba				Death	
	ARM/3c Marvelle W. Mershon	SB2C Helldiver	February 18, 1945	February 24, 1945*			Noboru Nakajima				Death	
	SMN James W. Dye Jr	TBF Avenger (USS Bennington)	February 18, 1945	February 25, 1945*			Sizuo Yoshii				Death	
	2nd Lt. Warren E. Vaughn	F4U Corsair (USS Bennington)	February 23, 1945	March 15, 1945*			Ito Kukuji				Death	

Trial Number/ Location/ Date	Airmen	Aircraft/Unit	Date Shot Down	Date of Incident (*Death)	Location	Japanese Trial	Accused	Offender's Status	Age	Profession	Sentencing	Outcome
	Ens Floyd E. Hall	SB2C Helldiver	February 18, 1945	March 25, 1945*			Higashigi Seiji				Life	
No. 83-J Singapore March 28–April 3, 1946	T/Sgt Allen W. Nicks	380th B.G. 529th B.S. B-24 (44-42329) MACR 14622	June 12, 1945	July 5, 1945*	Long Thanh Airfield, Saigon, Vietnam	No	Shundo Tomono	Army W/O			Death	
	T/Sgt Joseph A. De Maria	380th B.G. 529th B.S. B-24 (44-42329) MACR 14622	June 12, 1945	July 5, 1945*								
No. 110-J Singapore December 17–29, 1947	8 unidentified flyers	PB4Y	July–August 1945	July–August 1945*	Nee Soon Rifle Range, Singapore	No	Okamoto Toshio	Navy Lt Cmdr			Death	Reduced to 20 Years
	Unidentified flyers	B-29	April–May 1945	April–August 1945*			Kobayashi Kelichiro	Navy Lt			20 Years	
							Too Shizuo (Noboruo Shizuo)	Navy P.O.			7 Years	

Trial Number/ Location/ Date	Airmen	Aircraft/Unit	Date Shot Down	Date of Incident (*Death)	Location	Japanese Trial	Accused	Offender's Status	Age	Profession	Sentencing	Outcome
Singapore February 9–27, 1948							Shigeru Fukudome	Navy Vice Admiral			3 Years	
							Bunji Asakura	Navy Rear Admiral			2 Years	
							Ino Eiichi	Navy Cmdr			3 Years	
							Osamu Imamura	Navy Vice Admiral			8 Years	
							Gengo Matsuda	Navy Capt			2 Years	
							Yakichi Saito	Navy Capt			2 Years	
No. 111-J Singapore June 7–12, 1946	1 unidentified flyer		May 1945	June 1945*	Saigon, Vietnam	No	Setsuo Mabuchi	Army Maj, Medical Corps			Death	Reduced to Life
							Kinji Nakamura	Army Maj, Medical Corps			Death	
							Hitoshi Wakamatsu	Army Capt, Medical Corps			Death	Reduced to Life

Appendix | 223

Trial Number/ Location/ Date	Airmen	Aircraft/Unit	Date Shot Down	Date of Incident (*Death)	Location	Japanese Trial	Accused	Offender's Status	Age	Profession	Sentencing	Outcome
							Shigehiro Hisakawa	Kempeitai Capt			Death	
No. 112-J\n\nSingapore\n\nMay 30–June 5, 1946	Capt Claude H. Lamar	345th B.G. 501st B.S. B-25 (44-29580) MACR 13500	March 21, 1945	April 1945*	Saigon, Vietnam	No	Tsugio Kuwahata	Kempeitai 2nd Lt			1 Year	
	S/Sgt Harold M. Balonier	345th B.G. 501st B.S. B-25 (44-29580) MACR 13500	March 21, 1945	April 1945*			Isao Murakami	Kempeitai Sgt Maj			1 Year	
No. 116-J\n\nRangoon\n\nJune 6–19, 1946	Sgt Norman E. Albinson	308th B.G. 374th B.S. B-24 (42-73312) MACR 1205	November 17, 1943	August 18, 1944*	Rangoon Central Jail, Myanmar	No	Motozo Tazumi	Army Capt			7 years	
	Sgt John E. Leisure Jr.	341st B.G. 22nd B.S. B-25 (42-53417) MACR 241	August 3, 1943	August 18, 1944*			Akio Onishi	Army Lt			Death	Reduced to Life

Trial Number/ Location/ Date	Airmen	Aircraft/Unit	Date Shot Down	Date of Incident (*Death)	Location	Japanese Trial	Accused	Offender's Status	Age	Profession	Sentencing	Outcome
	T/Sgt John W. Boyd	341st B.G. 22nd B.S. B-25 (42-53417) MACR 241	August 3, 1943				Kiyoshi Ueno	Army Sgt Maj			3 Years	
	T/Sgt Charles A. Pittard	7th B.G. 8th B.S. B-24 (41-24126) MACR 936	October 18, 1943	June 8, 1944*			Koigetsu Uneo	Army Pvt			15 Years	
	Corp Julius F. Yackie	1st Air Commando Gp Glider MACR 332	March 6, 1944	August 18, 1944*								
	1st Lt Robert D. Drummey	341st B.G. 490th B.S. B-25 (43-4905) MACR 11697	October 17, 1944	January 11, 1945*								
	S/Sgt Jack R. Sheets	1st L.G. 71st L.S. L-5 (42-98863) MACR 9614	October 25, 1944	November 19, 1944*								

Trial Number/ Location/ Date	Airmen	Aircraft/Unit	Date Shot Down	Date of Incident (*Death)	Location	Japanese Trial	Accused	Offender's Status	Age	Profession	Sentencing	Outcome
	1st Lt Burdett C. Goodrich	80th F.G. 459th F.S. P-38 (42-67001) MACR 5378	June 6, 1944	February 27, 1945*								
	Capt Armin J. Ortmeyer Jr.	80th F.G. 459th F.S. P-38 (42-6990) MACR 1204	November 28, 1943	January 14, 1945*								
	2nd Lt Joseph C. Rich	308th B.G. 373rd B.S. B-24 (43-73245) "Maxwell House II" MACR 15125	November 27, 1943	September 13, 1944*								
	2nd Lt Burdette H. Baker	341st B.G. 491st B.S. B-25 (41-30367) MACR 1492	December 30, 1943	November 19, 1944*								
	1st Lt James M. Grey	311th F.G. 530th F.S. P-51 (43-6296) MACR 1212	November 27, 1943	August 12, 1944*								

Trial Number/ Location/ Date	Airmen	Aircraft/Unit	Date Shot Down	Date of Incident (*Death)	Location	Japanese Trial	Accused	Offender's Status	Age	Profession	Sentencing	Outcome
	S/Sgt Frank Rodriquez	8th B.G. 9th B.S. B-24 (42-73055) MACR 1277	December 1, 1943	August 27, 1944*								
	Capt Wayne R. Westberg	12th B.G. 434th B.S. B-26 (43-3896) MACR 11383	May 20, 1944	August 22, 1944*								
	2nd Lt Everitt E. Briggs Jr.	311th F.G. 503rd F.S. P-51		December 28, 1944*								
	1st Lt Paul E. Almand	29th T.G. 99th T.S. C-46 (41-5171) MACR 1234	November 7, 1943	March 27, 1945*								
	2nd Lt Gene Gambale	7th BG. 9th B.S. B-24 (42-73435) MACR 3999	April 5, 1944	August 10, 1944*								
	Sgt J. Brown											

Trial Number/ Location/ Date	Airmen	Aircraft/Unit	Date Shot Down	Date of Incident (*Death)	Location	Japanese Trial	Accused	Offender's Status	Age	Profession	Sentencing	Outcome
No. 117-J Rangoon June 21–25, 1946	1st Lt John C. Kelley	7th B.G. 493rd B.S. B-24 (42-73059) MACR 1108	November 14, 1943	December 17, 1943*	Rangoon Central Jail, Myanmar	No	Kumejiro Ikeda	Army Sgt Maj			Acquitted	
	T/Sgt Thomas P. Hopes	7th B.G. 493rd B.S. B-24 (42-73059) MACR 1108	November 14, 1943	November 22, 1943*								
	S/Sgt Francis E. Jordan	7th B.G. 493rd B.S. B-24 (42-73059) MACR 1108	November 14, 1943	November 27, 1943*								
	2nd Lt Thomas P. Hogan Jr.	7th B.G. 493rd B.S. B-24 (42-73059) MACR 1108	November 14, 1943	November 20, 1943*								
	T/Sgt Urvan A. Aubuchon	7th B.G. 493rd B.S. B-24 (42-73059) MACR 1108	November 14, 1943	November 26, 1943*								

Trial Number/ Location/ Date	Airmen	Aircraft/Unit	Date Shot Down	Date of Incident (*Death)	Location	Japanese Trial	Accused	Offender's Status	Age	Profession	Sentencing	Outcome
Rangoon May 3–21, 1946	1st Lt Robert F. Angell	311th F.G. 530th F.S. P-51 (43-6040) MACR 1211	November 28, 1943	February 15, 1944*			Nagahara Kenzo	Kempeitai Capt			4 Years	
	2nd Lt Royal D. Butterfield	308th B.G. 373rd B.S. B-24 (43-73345) "Maxwell House II" MACR 15125	November 27, 1943	June 24, 1944*			Yamazaki Kaname	Kempeitai Capt			Acquitted	
	1st Lt Joseph F. Zizlavsky	341st B.G. 491st B.S. B-25 (41-30367) MACR 1492	December 30, 1943	July 15, 1944*			Yokota Masao	Kempeitai 2nd Lt			2 Years	
	Capt Bill Wright	8th B.G. 9th B.S. B-24 (42-73055) MACR 1277	December 1, 1943	March 31, 1944*			Noda Masami	Kempeitai Cpl			Acquitted	
	1st Lt Robert L. Kavanagh	7th B.G. 492nd B.S. B-24 (41-42513) MACR 15307	May 1, 1943	June 22, 1943*			Uyeno Masakara	Kempeitai Capt			Death	Executed June 19, 1946

Trial Number/ Location/ Date	Airmen	Aircraft/Unit	Date Shot Down	Date of Incident (*Death)	Location	Japanese Trial	Accused	Offender's Status	Age	Profession	Sentencing	Outcome
	T/Sgt Edward R. Bodell	7th B.G. 492nd B.S. B-24 (41-42513) MACR 15307	May 1, 1943	July 15, 1943*								
	1st Lt Amel Boldman Jr.	80th F.G. 459th F.S. P-38 (42-66986) MACR 3998	April 5, 1944	July 11, 1944*								
	Capt William R. Gilhousen	P-51 (43-6872) MACR 5474	May 15, 1944	July 16, 1944*								
	Sgt J. H. Parker											
Manila June 1946	S/Sgt Peter P. Kosciuszek	380th B.G. 529th B.S. B-24 (42-40351) "Big Chief Cockeye" MACR 6585	July 5, 1944	August 29, 1944*	Ambon, Indonesia (Ceram Island)	No	Nogi Harumichi	Navy Lt			30 Years	

Trial Number/ Location/ Date	Airmen	Aircraft/Unit	Date Shot Down	Date of Incident (*Death)	Location	Japanese Trial	Accused	Offender's Status	Age	Profession	Sentencing	Outcome
	S/Sgt J. D. F. Hawthorne	380th B.G. 529th B.S. B-24 (42-40351) "Big Chief Cockeye" MACR 6585	July 5, 1944	August 29, 1944*			Yoshizaki Kiyosato	Navy W/O			25 Years	Reduced to 12 Years
	S/Sgt Kenneth H. Thoen	380th B.G. 529th B.S. B-24 (42-40351) "Big Chief Cockeye" MACR 6585	July 5, 1944	August 29, 1944*								
Manila February 12– 18, 1946	F/O James J. Lally	418th FIS P-51 (42-5592) MACR 13583	March 16, 1945	March 20, 1945*	San Jose, Philippines	No	Yoshioka Makato	Army 1st Lt			Death	Executed June 6, 1946
	Lt. Charles Del Rio	Navy		March 25 –26, 1945*			Okuda Fukumori	Army 2nd Lt			Death	Executed June 6, 1946
	1 unidentified flyer						Kai Mikio	Army 2nd Lt			40 Years	
							Wada Takeji	Army Sgt Maj			30 Years	Reduced to 10 Years

Trial Number/ Location/ Date	Airmen	Aircraft/Unit	Date Shot Down	Date of Incident (*Death)	Location	Japanese Trial	Accused	Offender's Status	Age	Profession	Sentencing	Outcome
							Inoue Shichiro	Army Sgt			30 Years	Reduced to 10 Years
							Sato Akiro	Army Pvt			30 Years	
Manila September 1946	2nd Lt Leslie W. Jacobs	358th B.S. B-24 (44-41078) MACR 12251	January 12, 1945	February 15, 1945*	Samarinda, Borneo (Indonesia)	No	Yamaguchi Sentaro	Navy Lt	39		Death	Executed April 1, 1947
	Cpl Frank J. Molinari	358th B.S. B-24 (44-41078) MACR 12251	January 12, 1945	February 13, 1945*			Tasuki Kiyoto	Navy Ens			Death	Executed April 1, 1947
	Sgt James W. Hagerty	358th B.S. B-24 (44-41078) MACR 12251	January 12, 1945	February 15, 1945*			Tsuda Koziro	Navy W/O				Not tried due to illness
							Suguwara Isaburo	Navy Petty Officer			Death	Executed April 1, 1947
Manila December 10, 1945– February 1, 1946 (See no. 357)	Capt William Burghs			November 20, 1944*	Basco, Batan Island, Philippines	No	Tajima Hikotaro	Army Lt Gen			Death	Executed April 2, 1946

Trial Number/ Location/ Date	Airmen	Aircraft/Unit	Date Shot Down	Date of Incident (*Death)	Location	Japanese Trial	Accused	Offender's Status	Age	Profession	Sentencing	Outcome
	Samuel Morris						Kamemoto Tetsu	Army Maj			25 Years	
	1 unidentified flyer						Nakashima (Nakajima) Akira	Army Maj			Life	Reduced to 25 Years
							Suzuki Masao	Army Maj			Not Tried	
							Nakabayashi Kiyonobu	Army Maj			Life	
							Sakasegawa Masumi	Army Capt			20 Years	
							Suzuki Yoshisuke	Army Capt			30 Years	
							Nishida Zenichi	Army Capt			Not Tried	
							Hirano Yoshiharu	Army Capt			10 Years	
							Hujiyama (Fukiyama) Shigekazu	Army 1st Lt			5 Years	Disapproved
							Nagata Kiyoshi	Army 1st Lt			5 Years	Disapproved
							Goto Bangaro	Army 1st Lt			Life	Reduced to
							Kawachi Masaki	Army Pvt			30 Years	Reduced to 10 Years
							Wakita Osamu	Army Pvt			10 Years	

Trial Number/ Location/ Date	Airmen	Aircraft/Unit	Date Shot Down	Date of Incident (*Death)	Location	Japanese Trial	Accused	Offender's Status	Age	Profession	Sentencing	Outcome
							Otani Fusakichi	Army Pvt			10 Years	
							Inoue Hikojiro	Army Pvt			15 Years	Reduced to 10 Years
							Hori Satoshi	Army Pvt			Not Tried	
Manila April 1946	2nd Lt Thomas Rafael	6th Photo Recon 20th Combat Mapping S. F-7B (44-40422) MACR 12423	September 30, 1944	September 30, 1944*	Sarmi, Papua, Indonesia	No	Ono Satoru	Army Capt			Death	
	Sgt Herbert G. Julian	6th Photo Recon 20th Combat Mapping S. F-7B (44-40422) MACR 12423	September 30, 1944	September 30, 1944*								
	Sgt Samuel T. Catlin	6th Photo Recon 20th Combat Mapping S. F-7B (44-40422) MACR 12423	September 30, 1944	September 30, 1944*								

234 | Appendix

Trial Number/ Location/ Date	Airmen	Aircraft/Unit	Date Shot Down	Date of Incident (*Death)	Location	Japanese Trial	Accused	Offender's Status	Age	Profession	Sentencing	Outcome
Manila February 1947 (See no. 307)				November 24, 1944	Kendari, Indonesia	No	Taniguchi Gosuke	Navy Capt			Death	Reduced to Life
							Mitani Toshio	Navy Lt			Life	
							Ogawa Yoshitake	Navy Ens			Life	
							Yamamoto Isokichi	Navy Ens			Life	
							Tanaka Tooru	Navy W/O			Life	
							Ohsugi Morikazu	Navy Vice Admiral			Life	
Shanghai February 14– 28, 1946	2nd Lt Lester R. White	462nd B.G. 770th B.S. B-29 (42-93848) MACR 9964	November 21, 1944	December 17, 1944*	Hankow (Wuhan), China	No	Kaburagi Masataka	Maj Gen, Chief of Staff, 34th Army	48		Death	Executed April 1946
	Sgt James E. Forbes Jr.	462nd B.G. 770th B.S. B-29 (42-93848) MACR 9964	November 21, 1944	December 17, 1944*			Fukumoto Kameji	Gendarmerie Col			Life	

Trial Number/ Location/ Date	Airmen	Aircraft/Unit	Date Shot Down	Date of Incident (*Death)	Location	Japanese Trial	Accused	Offender's Status	Age	Profession	Sentencing	Outcome
	Sgt Henry W. Wheaton	462nd B.G. 770th B.S. B-29 (42-93848) MACR 9964	November 21, 1944	December 17, 1944*			Sakai Sadatsuku	Gendarmerie Maj			20 Years	
							Kosaka Keisuke	Gendarmerie Capt			3 Years	
							Fujii Tsutomu	Gendarmerie W/O			Death	Executed April 1946
							Masui Shozo	Gendarmerie Sgt Maj	31		Death	Executed April 1946
							Hismatsu Minoru	Army Sgt Maj			15 Years	
							Yamaguchi Hissayoshi	Army Cpl, Propaganda			15 Years	
							Tsukada Kokichi	Gendarmerie Sgt			12 Years	
							Takeuchi Yoshiyuki	Gendarmerie Sgt			12 Years	
							Fujii Junichi	Gendarmerie Sgt			12 Years	
							Mizuta Masaru	Cpl, Propaganda, 34th Army			18 Months	
							Shirakawa Yosaburo	Gendarmerie Cpl	24		Death	Executed April 1946

Trial Number/ Location/ Date	Airmen	Aircraft/Unit	Date Shot Down	Date of Incident (*Death)	Location	Japanese Trial	Accused	Offender's Status	Age	Profession	Sentencing	Outcome
							Nishikawa Shoji	Army Pvt			15 Years	
							Masuda Koichi	Gendarmerie Sgt	23		Death	Executed April 1946
							Manabe Ryoichi	Consul, Japanese Consulate, Hankow			3 Years	
							Hamada Shohei	Consular Police			Acquitted	
							Kato Takumi	Interpreter, Liason Officer, Chinese Youth Corps	29		2 Years	
Shanghai February 27–April 15, 1946	1st Lt Dean E. Hallmark	Doolittle Raiders B-25 (40-2298) "The Green Hornet"	April 18, 1942	October 15, 1942*	Shanghai, China	Yes	Sawada Shigeru	Army Maj Gen			9 years	
	1st Lt William G. Farrow	Doolittle Raiders B-25 (40-2268) "Bat of Hell"	April 18, 1942	October 15, 1942*			Ryuhei Okada	Army 2nd Lt			5 Years	

Trial Number/ Location/ Date	Airmen	Aircraft/Unit	Date Shot Down	Date of Incident (*Death)	Location	Japanese Trial	Accused	Offender's Status	Age	Profession	Sentencing	Outcome
	Sgt Harold A. Spatz	Doolittle Raiders B-25 (40-2268) "Bat of Hell"	April 18, 1942	October 15, 1942*			Yusei Wako	Army Lt			5 Years	
							Sotojiro Tatsuta	Army Capt			5 Years	
Shanghai August 13– September 3, 1946	Maj David H. W. Houck	23rd F.G. 118th Tac. Rec. S. P-51 (44-11103)	January 15, 1945	April 6, 1945*	Hong Kong	Yes	Nishigai Kubo	Army Lt Col			Life	10 Years
							Koichi Yamaguchi	Army Capt			Life	
							Masamori Watanabe	Army Maj			50 Years	Reduced to 10 Years
							Haruo Fukuchi	Army Maj Gen			Death	Reduced to Life
							Hisakasu Tanaka	Army Gen			Death	Disapproved
							Hiroshi Asakawa	Army Capt			Acquitted	

Trial Number/ Location/ Date	Airmen	Aircraft/Unit	Date Shot Down	Date of Incident (*Death)	Location	Japanese Trial	Accused	Offender's Status	Age	Profession	Sentencing	Outcome
Shanghai June 6–9, 1946	2nd Lt Ted U. Hart	345th B.G. 501st B.S. B-25 (44-28152) "Apache Princess" MACR 14524	May 27, 1945	May 30, 1945	Taihoku, Formosa	No	Nakano Yoshio	Army Capt			Life	
							Kawai Kiyomi	Army Cpl			30 Years	
							Seki Susumu	Army Pvt			30 Years	
							Imura Hideichi	Army Cpl			25 Years	
Kwajalein Island (Marshall Islands) December 1945	3 unidentified flyers			March 10, 1944*	Aineman Island, Jaluit Atoll, Marshall Islands	No	Yoshimura Tsugio	Navy Lt			Death	
							Kawachi Mamoru	Navy Ens			Death	
							Tanaka Tadashi	Navy Ens			Death	
							Tasaki Tashimoto	Navy W/O			10 Years	

Trial Number/ Location/ Date	Airmen	Aircraft/Unit	Date Shot Down	Date of Incident (*Death)	Location	Japanese Trial	Accused	Offender's Status	Age	Profession	Sentencing	Outcome
Australian Trial Morotai Island, Indonesia December 1945	4 unidentified flyers			March 23, 1945*	Talaud Island, Indonesia	No	Yabe Tokuhiro	Army Lt			Death	
							Nomura Koichi	Army Lt			Death	
							Uchino Seizo	Army Sgt			10 Years	
Army Pacific Case 48-35-1 Guam November 1947	2 unidentified flyers			Jul 44	Dublon Island, Truk Atoll (Caroline Islands)	No	Iwanami Hiroshi	Navy Capt		Doctor		
	6 unidentified flyers			Jul 44			Okuyama Tokikazu	Navy Cmdr		Doctor		
							Nabetani Reijiro	Navy Lt		Doctor		
							Kamikawa Hidehiro	Navy Lt		Doctor		
							Oishi Totsuo	Navy Lt				

240 | Appendix

Trial Number/ Location/ Date	Airmen	Aircraft/Unit	Date Shot Down	Date of Incident (*Death)	Location	Japanese Trial	Accused	Offender's Status	Age	Profession	Sentencing	Outcome
							Asamura Shunpei	Navy Ens				
							Sakagami Shinji					
							Yoshizawa Kensaburo	Navy Corpsman Chief Petty Officer				
							Homma Hachiro	Navy Corpsman Chief Petty Officer				
							Watanabe Mitsuo	Navy Paymaster Chief Petty Officer				
							Tanabe Mamoru	Navy Corpsman Chief Petty Officer				
							Mukai Yoshihisa	Navy Corpsman Chief Petty Officer				

Trial Number/Location/Date	Airmen	Aircraft/Unit	Date Shot Down	Date of Incident (*Death)	Location	Japanese Trial	Accused	Offender's Status	Age	Profession	Sentencing	Outcome
							Kawashima Tatsusaburo	Navy Corpsman Petty Officer				
							Sawada Tsumeo	Navy Paymaster Petty Officer				
							Tanaka Tokunosuko	Navy Corpsman Petty Officer				
							Akabori Teichiro	Navy Corpsman Petty Officer				
							Kuwabara Hiroyuki	Navy Corpsman Petty Officer				
							Namatame Kazuo	Navy Corpsman Petty Officer				
							Takaishi Susumu	Navy Corpsman Petty Officer				
							Mitsuhashi Kichigero	Navy Corpsman Petty Officer				

Trial Number/ Location/ Date	Airmen	Aircraft/Unit	Date Shot Down	Date of Incident (*Death)	Location	Japanese Trial	Accused	Offender's Status	Age	Profession	Sentencing	Outcome
Army Pacific Case 48-36-1 Guam September 1947	2 unidentified flyers			June 20, 1944*	Dublon Island, Truk Atoll, Caroline Islands	No	Asano Simpei	Navy Capt				
							Ueno Chisato	Navy Lt Cmdr		Doctor		
							Nakase Shohichi	Navy Lt Cmdr				
							Eriguchi Takeshi	Navy Ens		Dentist		
							Korayashi Kazumi	Navy Corpsman W/O				

Acknowledgments

Several people offered important assistance in preparing this book. First, I would like to thank series editor G. Kurt Piehler, along with Fred Nachbaur and the editorial staff at Fordham University Press. Their support made the publication process straightforward and stress-free. Both Michael S. Bryant of Bryant University and Dan Orbach of The Hebrew University read the entire manuscript and offered helpful guidance and encouragement, for which I am thankful. I also would like to thank my recently retired advisor, Eric A. Johnson, for his committed guidance and support. As a gifted scholar, teacher, and mentor, he has had an enormous impact on my life and career. My dear friend and former colleague Sean Scally was always willing to read, discuss, and offer suggestions for the book throughout the writing process, for which I am very grateful. I would also like to thank Robert Sherwood for his archival assistance.

I am indebted to Hiroyuki Fukao for his research assistance, especially his willingness to provide photos of monuments in Japan. The inability to travel to Japan because of the global pandemic made his assistance essential. The numerous families of airmen and veterans' associations who graciously provided photos and stories also deserve a special thanks. Their support of and interest in this book not only helped further clarify the often-deadly circumstances that downed airmen faced but also assisted in preserving the memories and sacrifices of these brave young men.

Notes

Introduction

1. Letter from Morris to General Leon W. Johnson, Personnel Service Division, December 13, 1945, MACR 14820, https://catalog.archives.gov/id/91158644.

2. Review of the Staff Judge Advocate, October 8, 1948, US v. Noboru Seki, August 18–22, 1947, https://www.legal-tools.org/doc/01e350/pdf; US v. Shichisaburo Yajima, June 24, 1947, https://www.legal-tools.org/doc/obd5d8/pdf.

3. Review of the Staff Judge Advocate, October 8, 1948, US v. Noboru Seki, August 18–22, 1947.

4. "Accounts from End of WWII Reveal Divergent Fates of US B-29 Bomber Crews Crashing in Japan," accessed December 19, 2020, https://mainichi.jp/english/articles/20200819/p2a/00m/0fe/019000c; review of the Staff Judge Advocate, October 14, 1948, US v. Toyokazu Hikita et al., March 1–2, 1948, https://www.legal-tools.org/doc/f0b9e9/pdf.

5. Case No. 12-793, 12-793-1, 12-793-2, Record of US Army Europe, War Crimes Case Files (Cases Tried), 3 August 1945, 15 August 1945, 28–29 July 1947, RG549, Entry 290, Box 121, NARA. See also Hall, *Terror Flyers*, 180–87.

6. "Review and Recommendations," Case No. 12-793, 12-793-1, 12-793-2, Record of US Army Europe, War Crimes Case Files (Cases Tried), 3 August 1945, 15 August 1945, 28–29 July 1947, RG549, Entry 290, Box 121, NARA.

7. "Review and Recommendations," Case No. 12-793, 12-793-1, 12-793-2, Record of US Army Europe, War Crimes Case Files (Cases Tried), 3 August 1945, 15 August 1945, 28–29 July 1947, RG549, Entry 290, Box 121, NARA; see also, Hall, *Terror Flyers*, 180–87; Kevin T Hall, "Downed American Flyers: Forgotten Casualties of Axis Atrocities in World War II," *Journal of Perpetrator Justice*, 4.1 (2021), 192–221, here 205–8.

8. FDR's January 6, 1941, State of the Union address, known as the "Four Freedoms" speech, proposed these fundamental freedoms that people throughout the world should possess.

9. Richard Overy, *Blood and Ruins: The Great Imperial War, 1931–1945* (London: Allen Lane, 2021), 752, 790; Richard Overy, *The Bombers and the Bombed: Allied Air War over Europe, 1940–1945* (New York: Viking, 2014); Kenneth Werrell, *Blankets of Fire: US Bombers over Japan during World War II*

246 | Notes to pages 8–9

(Washington, DC: Smithsonian Books, 1996); Barrett Tillman, *Whirlwind: The Air War against Japan, 1942–1945* (New York: Simon & Schuster, 2010).

10. United States Army Air Forces (USAAF), Office of Statistical Control, Army Air Force Statistical Digest World War II, Washington, DC, 1945, 49–56; Georg Hoffmann, "'Vergeltung' im Bombenkrieg: Lynchjustiz an alliierten Flugzeugbesatzungen in Deutschland, Österreich und Ungarn, 1943–1945," in *Repressalien und Terror: "Vergeltung" im deutsch besetzten Europa 1939–1945*, ed. Oliver von Wrochem (Paderborn: Ferdinand Schöningh, 2017), 249–65, here 255; "World War II Accounting," accessed December 15, 2020, https://www.dpaa.mil /Our-Missing/World-War-II.

11. Overy, *Blood and Ruins*, 776–77; Sarah Kovner, "A War of Words: Allied Captivity and Swiss Neutrality in the Pacific, 1941–1945," *Diplomatic History* 41, no. 4 (2017): 719–46, here 719; Keith Lowe, *Savage Continent: Europe in the Aftermath of World War II* (London: Penguin, 2013); Karl Hack and Kevin Blackburn, eds., *Forgotten Captives in Japanese Occupied Asia* (New York: Routledge, 2008), 4; Brian MacArthur, *Surviving the Sword: Prisoners of the Japanese, 1942–45* (London: Abacus, 2006); Norman Davies, *Europe at War, 1939–1945: No Simple Victory* (New York: Macmillan, 2006); Flint Whitlock, *Given Up for Dead: American GIs in the Nazi Concentration Camps at Berga* (New York: Westview Press, 2005); Niall Ferguson, "Prisoner Taking and Prisoner Killing in the Age of Total War: Towards a Political Economy of Military Defeat," *War in History* 11, no. 2 (2004): 148–192; Yuki Tanaka, *Hidden Horrors: Japanese War Crimes in World War II* (Boulder: Westview Press, 1997), 2–3; Gavin Dawes, *Prisoners of the Japanese: POWs of World War II in the Pacific* (New York: William Morrow and Company, 1996); S. P. MacKenzie, "The Treatment of Prisoners of War in World War II," *Journal of Modern History* 66, no. 3 (1994): 487–520.

12. Sarah Kovner, *Prisoners of the Empire: Inside Japanese POW Camps* (Cambridge: Harvard University Press, 2020); Yuma Totani, *Justice in Asia and the Pacific Region, 1945–1952: Allied War Crimes Prosecutions* (New York: Cambridge University Press, 2015); Philip R. Piccigallo, *The Japanese on Trial: Allied War Criminals in the East, 1945–1951* (Austin: University of Texas Press, 1979).

13. Examples include Fiske Hanley III, *Accused War Criminal: An American Kempei Tai Survivor* (New York: Brown Books, 2020); Michel Paradis, *Last Mission to Tokyo: The Extraordinary Story of the Doolittle Raiders and Their Final Flight for Justice* (New York: Simon and Schuster, 2020); Sarah Kovner, *Prisoners of the Empire: Inside Japanese POW Camps* (Cambridge: Harvard University Press, 2020); Helen Fry, *MI9: A History of the Secret Service for Escape and Evasion in World War Two* (New Haven: Yale University Press, 2020); Harold H. Brown and Marsha S. Bordner, *Keep Your Airspeed Up: The Story of a Tuskegee Airman* (Tuscaloosa: University of Alabama, 2017); Will Iredale, *The Kamikaze Hunters: Fighting for the Pacific, 1945* (London: Macmillan, 2015); Donald E. Casey, *To Fight for My Country, Sir: Memoirs of a 19-Year-Old B-17 Navigator Shot Down in Nazi Germany and Imprisoned in the WWII "Great Escape" Prison Camp*

(Chicago: Sterling Cooper, 2009); Herman Bodson, *Downed Allied Airmen and Evasion of Capture: The Role of Local Resistance Networks in World War II* (London: McFarland, 2005); James Bradley, *Flyboys: A True Story of Courage* (New York: Back Bay Books, 2004); Dawn Trimble Bunyak, *The Last Mission: A World War II Prisoner in Germany* (Norman: University of Oklahoma Press, 2017); Stephan Ambrose, *The Wild Blue: The Men and Boys Who Flew the B-24s over Germany, 1944–45* (New York: Simon and Schuster, 2001); Philip D. Caine, *Aircraft Down: Evading Capture in WWII Europe* (Washington, DC: Brasseys, 1997); Philip Ardery, *Bomber Pilot: A Memoir of World War II* (Lexington: University Press of Kentucky, 1996); Mitchell G. Bard, *Forgotten Victims: The Abandonment of Americans in Hitler's Camps* (Oxford: Westview Press, 1994); Tom Bird, *American POWs in World War II: Forgotten Men Tell Their Stories* (Westport: Praeger, 1992); E. Bartlett Kerr, *Surrender and Survival: The Experience of American POWs in the Pacific, 1941–45* (New York: William Morrow, 1985); Philip R. Piccigallo, *The Japanese on Trial: Allied War Crimes Operations in the East, 1945–1951* (Austin: University of Texas Press, 1979); Levitt Clinton Beck, *Fighter Pilot* (Los Angeles: Wetzel Publishing, 1946).

14. Georg Hoffmann, *Fliegerlynchjustiz: Gewalt gegen abgeschossene alliierte Flugzeugbesatzungen, 1943–45* (Paderborn: Ferdinand Schönigh, 2015); Kevin T Hall, *Terror Flyers: The Lynching of American Airmen in Nazi Germany* (Bloomington: Indiana University Press, 2021); Toru Fukubayashi, "Allied Aircraft and Airmen Lost over the Japanese Mainland," May 20, 2007, http://www.powresearch.jp/en/archive/pilot/index.html.

15. Allan R. Millett, "Patterns of Military Innovation in the Interwar Period," 329–68, in *Military Innovation in the Interwar Period,* ed. Williamson Murray and Allan R. Millett (New York: Cambridge University Press, 2009).

16. Draft letter written by Augusto C. Sandino, October 10, 1927, in Robert Edgar Conrad, *Sandino: The Testimony of a Nicaraguan Patriot, 1921–1934* (Princeton: Princeton University Press, 1990), 114–15. See also "The Sandino Rebellion, 1927–1934: October 12, 1927, O'Shea, Engagement at Sapotillal," accessed March 17, 2021, http://www.sandinorebellion.com/pcdocs/1927/PC27 1012-OShea.html.

17. Isabel V. Hull, *A Scrap of Paper: Breaking and Making International Law during the Great War* (Ithaca: Cornell University Press, 2014), 276–90.

18. Raymond H. Fredette, *The Sky on Fire: The First Battle of Britain, 1917–1918* (Tuscaloosa: University of Alabama Press, 2007), 245; Giulio Douhet, *The Command of the Air,* trans. Dino Ferrari (Washington, DC: US Government Printing Office, 1998); William Mitchell, *Winged Defense: The Development and Possibilities of Modern Air Power—Economic and Military* (Tuscaloosa: University of Alabama Press, 2010); James S. Corum, *The Luftwaffe: Creating the Operational Air War, 1918–1940* (Lawrence: University of Kansas, 1997).

19. "Mr. Baldwin on Aerial Warfare—A Fear for the Future," *(London) Times,* November 11, 1932.

248 | Notes to pages 13–17

20. Kenneth Watkin, "Warriors without Rights? Combatants, Unprivileged Belligerents, and the Struggle Over Legitimacy," Program on Humanitarian Policy and Conflict Research, Harvard University, Winter 2005, no. 2, accessed March 22, 2022, https://reliefweb.int/sites/reliefweb.int/files/resources/52332277E2871AF7 C125704C0037CF99-hpcr-gen-09may.pdf; Heinz Marcus Hanke, "The 1923 Hague Rules of Air Warfare: A Contribution to the Development of International Law Protecting Civilians from Air Attack," *International Review of the Red Cross*, no. 292 (March 1993): 12–44, https://international-review.icrc.org/sites/default/files/ S0020860400071370a.pdf. Originally published in German, *International Review of the Red Cross*, no. 3, 139–72; Javier Guisández Gómez, *The Law of Air Warfare, International Review of the Red Cross*, No. 323, June 1998, 347–63.

21. "Convention relative to the Treatment of Prisoners of War," Geneva, July 27, 1929, https://ihl-databases.icrc.org/ihl/INTRO/305.

22. Michel Paradis, *Last Mission to Tokyo: The Extraordinary Story of the Doolittle Raiders and Their Final Fight for Justice* (New York: Simon & Schuster, 2020), 194–95.

23. Sarah Kovner, "A War of Words," 723.

24. Overy, *Blood and Ruins*, 768.

25. Jackson, *Fallen Tigers*, 34.

26. Overy, *Blood and Ruins*, 425–26, 772, 779, 788.

27. Nicholas Stargardt, *The German War: A Nation under Arms, 1939–1945* (New York: Basic Books, 2015), 8.

28. For example, see Daniel Hedinger, *Die Achse: Berlin, Rom, Tokio, 1919–1946* (Munich: C. H. Beck, 2021); Margaret MacMillan, *War: How Conduct Shaped Us* (London: Profile Books Ltd, 2021); John W. Dower, *War Without Mercy: Race and Power in the Pacific War* (New York: Pantheon, 1986).

29. Harcourt Brace Jovanovich and Charles A. Lindbergh, *The Wartime Journals of Charles Lindbergh* (New York: Harcourt Brace Jovanovich, Inc., 1970), 997–98.

30. Charles Lindbergh sought to be recommissioned in the US Army Air Corps following the attack on Pearl Harbor; however, President FDR and Secretary of War Henry L. Stimson declined his request. They questioned Lindbergh's loyalty after his involvement in the noninterventionist American First Committee in the 1930s as well as his public denunciation of the Roosevelt Administration and alleged Jewish agitators for war in Europe. Henry Ford, who similarly drew disdain for his own anti-Semitic views, hired Lindbergh to work as a technical advisor at the Willow Run plant that produced B-24 Liberator bombers. In 1943, he worked with United Aircraft as a civilian engineering consultant, and by 1944 found his way to the fighting in the Pacific, where he recommended innovative techniques to conserve fuel and improve the range of fighter escorts.

31. Jovanovich and Lindbergh, *The Wartime Journals of Charles Lindbergh*, 816–22; 834–35.

32. Jovanovich and Lindbergh, *The Wartime Journals*, 818.

33. Translated diary entry entitled "Blood Carnival" by an unknown Japanese soldier. Found in Information Bulletin No.10, "Activities of Japanese Military Personnel Contrary to the Laws of War," April 29, 1944, http://www.mansell.com /pow_resources/camplists/other/rabaul/Beheading_of_airman_1943-03-29_ATIS _2533-2534.pdf.

34. Fiske Hanley II, *Accused War Criminal: An American Kempei Tai Survivor* (New York: Brown Books, 2020), 112–22.

35. Margaret MacMillan, *War: How Conduct Shaped US* (London: Profile Books Ltd, 2021), 165.

36. Letter intercepted by US Office of Censorship, entitled "Allied flyers shot in their parachute over Denmark," October 17, 1944, Case No. 8-0, Records of the Office of the Judge Advocate General (Army), NARA RG 153, Entry 143, Box 119.

37. Jay A. Stout, *Fighter Group: The 352nd "Blue-Nosed Bastards" in World War II* (Stackpole Books, 2018); Sam Kleiner, *The Flying Tigers: The Untold Story of the American Pilots Who Waged a Secret War against Japan* (New York: Viking, 2018); William D. Pawley, *The Extraordinary Life of the Adventurer, Entrepreneur, and Diplomat Who Cofounded the Flying Tigers* (Washington, DC: Potomac Books, 2012); Patrick Bishop, *Fighter Boys: The Battle of Britain, 1940* (Penguin, 2004); Brian Cull, *Buffaloes Over Singapore: RAF, RAAF, RNZAF and Dutch Brewster Fighters in Action over Malaya and the East Indies, 1941–1942* (Haverton: Casemate, 2003).

38. S. P. MacKenzie, "The Treatment of Prisoners of War in World War II," *The Journal of Modern History* 66, no. 3, 487–520, here 493; Kenneth Watkin, "Warriors without Rights? Combatants, Unprivileged Belligerents, and the Struggle Over Legitimacy," Program on Humanitarian Policy and Conflict Research, Harvard University, Winter 2005, accessed March 22, 2022), https:// reliefweb.int/sites/reliefweb.int/files/resources/52332277E2871AF7C125704C0037 CF99-hpcr-gen-09may.pdf.

39. MacKenzie, "The Treatment of Prisoners," 519.

40. Major Laura C. Counts, "Were They Prepared? Escape and Evasion in Western Europe, 1942–1944" (thesis, Air Command and Staff College, 1986), 1; The analysis of the flyer trials in Germany is based on the research in Hall, *Terror Flyers*. The documents can be found at Deputy Theater Judge Advocate's Office, War Crimes Branch, NARA, RG 153, Entry 143, Box 155–510; The documents used in the analysis of the trials held at Yokohama and throughout the Pacific (e.g., Guam, Singapore, Rangoon, Rabaul, Manila, Shanghai, Indonesia, and Marshall Islands) can be found at Records of the Office of the Army Judge Advocate General (Army) RG 153, Entry 1021, NARA; "Yokohama—Philipps-Universität Marbug—ICWC," accessed March 12, 2021, https://www.uni-marburg.de/icwc /forschung/2weltkrieg/yokohama?order=source&order_type=asc&offset=0&count =100&name=&id_trial; "The International Military Tribunal for the Far East," https://imtfe.law.virginia.edu; "International Criminal Court Database," https:// www.legal-tools.org.

250 | Notes to pages 22–25

41. Overy, *Blood and Ruins*, 780–81.

42. Overy, *Blood and Ruins*, 816–17.

43. For example, see Herman Bodson, *Downed Allied Airmen and Evasion of Capture: The Role of Local Resistance Networks in World War II* (London: McFarland and Company, 2005); Aiden Crawley, *Escape from Germany, 1939–1945: Methods of Escape Used by RAF Airmen during World War II* (London: Stationery Office, 2001); Betty Gatewood and Jean Belkham, *Kriegie 7956: A World War II Bombardier's Pursuit of Freedom* (Shippensburg, PA: Burd Street Press, 2001); Kenneth W. Simmons, *Kriegie* (New York: Thomas Nelson and Sons, 1960); Sherri Greene Ottis, *Silent Heroes: Downed Airmen and the French Underground* (Lexington: University of Kentucky Press, 2001); Peter Eisner, *The Freedom Line* (New York: Harper Collins, 2004); Graham Pitchfork, *Shot Down and on the Run: The RCAF and Commonwealth Aircrews Who Got Home from behind Enemy Lines, 1940– 1945* (Toronto: Dundurn Group, 2003); Bruch H. Wolk, *Jewish Aviators in World War II: Personal Narratives of American Men and Women* (Jefferson, NC: McFarland, 2016); Jerome W. Sheridan, *Airmen in the Belgian Resistance: Gerald E. Sorensen and the Transatlantic Alliance* (Jefferson, NC: McFarland, 2014); McManus, *Deadly Sky*; Alexander Jefferson and Lewis H. Carlson, *Red Tail Captured, Red Tail Free: The Memoirs of a Tuskegee Airman and POW* (New York: Fordham University Press, 2005); David A. Foy, *For You the War Is Over: American Prisoners of War in Nazi Germany* (New York: Stein and Day, 1984).

44. Graham Pitchfork, *Shot Down and on the Run: The RCAF and Commonwealth Aircrews Who Got Home from behind Enemy Lines, 1940–1945* (Toronto: Dundurn Group, 2003), 55–96; Ben Macintyre, *Rogue Heroes: The History of Britain's Secret Special Forces Unit That Sabotaged the Nazis and Changed the Nature of War* (New York: Crown, 2016), 239–44; Helen Fry, *MI9: A History of the Secret Service for Escape and Evasion in World War Two* (New Haven: Yale University Press, 2020).

45. Gregory A. Freeman, *The Forgotten 500: The Untold Story of the Men Who Risked All for the Greatest Rescue Mission in World War II* (New York: NAL Caliber, 2007); Edi Šelhaus, *Evasion and Repatriation: Slovene Partisans and Rescued American Airmen in World War II* (Manhattan: Sunflower University Press, 1993); William Matthew Leary, *Fueling the Fire of Resistance: Army Air Forces Special Operations in the Balkans* (Washington, DC: US Air Force History and Museums Program, 1995).

46. Daniel Jackson, *Fallen Tigers: The Fate of America's Missing Airmen in China During World War II* (Lexington: University Press of Kentucky, 2021), xix.

47. Jackson, *Fallen Tigers*, xv–xviii, 46.

48. Photo courtesy of Richard I. Terpstra, former SACO member, during an interview with the author on February 8, 2015.

49. "Escape and Evasion in China," 7, Office of Naval Intelligence (ONI) Review, Headquarters US Naval Group China, Records of the Office of the Chief of Naval Operations, Naval Group China Papers, NARA, RG 38, Entry NHC-75, Box 37.

Notes to pages 25–33 | 251

50. "Escape and Evasion in China," 6.

51. "Escape and Evasion in China," 5; see also Jackson, *Fallen Tigers*, xv–xviii, 35; Otha Cleo Spencer, *Flying the Hump: Memories of an Air War* (College Station: Texas A&M University Press, 1992).

52. The most well-known flyer rescued during one of these missions was future US President Lt George H. W. Bush. He was shot down near Bonin Island on September 2, 1944, and picked up by the US submarine *USS Finnback*; "Escape and Evasion in China," 3–10; see also James Bradley, *Flyboys: A True Story of Courage* (New York: Back Bay Books, 2004), 79–80, 86, 105, 333–35.

1. Axis Policies to Combat Downed Enemy Flyers

1. Ronald J. Drez, *Predicting Pearl Harbor: Billy Mitchell and the Path to War* (New York: Pelican Press, 2017); James J. Cooke, *Billy Mitchell* (London: Lynne Riennner Publishing, 2002); General William Mitchell, "Report on Inspection of United States Possessions in the Pacific and Java, Singapore, India, Siam, China and Japan," October 24, 1924, William Mitchell Papers, United States Air Force Academy Archives (USAFA), Colorado Springs, Colorado.

2. According to Haruo Yoshino in Dan King, *The Last Zero Fighter: First-hand Accounts from WWII Japanese Naval Pilots* (Rockwell: Pacific Press, 2012), 154–55.

3. According to Lt Yoshikazu Saito in Syd Jones, *Before and Beyond the Niihau Zero: The Unlikely Drama of Hawaii's Forbidden Island Prior to, during and after the Pearl Harbor Attack* (Merritt Island: Signum Ops, 2014), 61–63.

4. While Syd Jones determined that Nishikaichi would have had enough fuel to make it back to his carrier had he departed immediately after the attack on Bellows Field, the flyer's reasoning for not returning—instead flying over in the Hawaiian air space for nearly three hours—remains unclear. As Jones clarified, "The simplest explanation for Nishikaichi landing on Niihau [. . .] was that he initially overestimated the amount of fuel loss his airplane had suffered. By the time he realized his mistake [. . .], he had already burned thorugh the gasoline that could have taken him home." Syd Jones, *Before and Beyond the Niihau Zero*, 29–30.

5. Jones, *Before and Beyond the Niihau Zero*, 37.

6. "The Mizuha Report," December 14, 1941, from 1st Lt Jack H. Mizuha; Jones, *Before and Beyond the Niihau Zero*, 40–47.

7. "The Baldwin Report," December 16, 1941, from Lt C. B. Baldwin to the District Intelligence Officer; Jones, *Before and Beyond the Niihau Zero*, 48–54.

8. "Jap Aviator Stoned to Death by Woman," *San Bernardino Sun*, December 17, 1941.

9. George C. Larsen, *Pearl Harbor: A Memoir of Service*; as quoted in Jones, *Before and Beyond the Niihau Zero*, 56–58.

10. "He Got Mad and Japs Died," *Madera (California) Tribune*, December 17, 1941; "Strangest Tale of the War, Hawaiian Defends His Island," *Santa Cruz*

252 | Notes to pages 33–40

Evening News, December 17, 1941; "Hero of Niihau Has Letters Commending Him for Bravery," *Nippu Jiji (Honolulu)*, June 26, 1942.

11. "Regarded with Suspicion," *Nippu Jiji (Honolulu)*, March 26, 1942.

12. Message from US Secretary of State Cordell Hull to the Japanese Government, December 18, 1941, Records of the Judge Advocate General (Army) RG 153, Entry 132, Box 6, NARA; International Military Tribunal for the Far East, *Judgement*, Tokyo, November 1948, vol. 2, 1099.

13. Response from the Japanese Government to Hull, January 30, 1942, RG 153, Entry 132, Box 6, NARA.

14. Michel Paradis, *Last Mission to Tokyo: The Extraordinary Story of the Doolittle Raiders and Their Final Fight for* Justice (New York: Simon & Schuster, 2020), 194.

15. "Plan of the Enemy Air Raid Ends in Complete Failure," *Photo Weekly Magazine*, April 29, 1942, 12–13; see Paradis, *Last Mission to Tokyo*, 192–93; "Evil Enemy Strafe School Yard," *Asahi Shimbun*, April 19, 1942.

16. Extract from interrogation of Hideki Tojo, March 25, 1946, http://www .mansell.com/pow_resources/Formosa/IMTFE58-350_Tojo_Treatment_of_ POWs_1942-07_1946-03.pdf.

17. Telegram from the Minister of Switzerland (Harrison) to the US Secretary of State, November 5, 1942 (quoting an October 21, 1942, article from Nichi Nichi), in G. Bernard Noble and E. R. Perkins, eds., *Foreign Relations of the United States: Diplomatic Papers, 1942, General; The British Commonwealth; the Far East*, vol. 1 (Washington, DC: US Government Printing Office, 1960), Doc. 711; https://history.state.gov/historicaldocuments/frus1942v01/d711.

18. This crew consisted of: Capt Edward York, Lt Robert Emmens, Lt Nolan Herndon, S/Sgt Theodore Laban, and Sgt David Pohl.

19. Cpl Leland Faktor died after parachuting over a mountainous area in China, and Sgt William Dieter and Cpl Donald Fitzmaurice both drowned after their aircraft crashed in the sea. Lt Robert Meder survived the mission but was severely injured. Due to lack of proper medical care, disease, and malnutrition, Meder died in December 1943 while held captive in a Japanese prison. Throughout the rest of the war, twelve others died during combat: Lt Robert Clever, Lt Robert Gray, Lt Denver Truelove, Lt Donald Smith, Lt Richard Miller, Lt Kenneth Reddy, S/Sgt Edwin Bain, Sgt George Larkin, Lt Eugene McGurl, S/Sgt Omer Duquette, Sgt Melvin Gardner, and S/Sgt Paul Leonard.

20. Benshan Su, Report to Deputy Inspector of District Six, July 1943, XIangshan County Archives; "Fliers' Bodies Exhumed by Grave Team," *Shanghai Stars and Stripes*, March 28, 1946; see Paradis, *Last Mission to Tokyo*, 296.

21. Paradis, *Last Mission to Tokyo*, 101.

22. Philip R. Piccigallo, *The Japanese on Trial: Allied War Crimes Operations in the East, 1945–1951* (Austin: University of Texas Press, 1979), 68–72; *Law Reports of the Trials of War Criminals*, 15 vols. Selected and prepared by the UNWCC (London, 1947–1949), V. 5, Case No. 25, 2–3.

Notes to pages 40–43 | 253

23. The remaining five airmen were held on a starvation diet and eventually transferred to a prison in Nanking in April 1943. By December of that year, Meder died due to malnutrition and lack of medical care. Though physically and mentally battered and fragile, the remaining four airmen managed to survive the war.

24. *Thanatopsis* means "a consideration of death." Exhibit F, Letter from Lt William G. Farrow to his family, dated October 1942, US v. Shigeru Sawada et al., vol. 3, https://www.legal-tools.org/doc/abc3de/pdf.

25. *The Daily Illini*, April 23, 1943.

26. Quote from *(New York) Herald Tribune* in "Airmen from Tokyo Raid Captured?" *Morning Bulletin (Australia)*, October 24, 1942.

27. Quoted from *New York Times* in "Jap Threat to Airmen," *Townsville Daily Bulletin (Australia)*, October 23, 1942.

28. Quoted from *New York Times* in "Brother Barbarians: Germans Applaud Japanese Murders," *Kalgoorlie Miner (Australia)*, April 26, 1943.

29. "Japs Threat Torture for Yank Airmen," *Mandera (California) Tribune*, October 19, 1942; "Flyers' Execution Urged: Rome Newspapers Call for Death Penalty for Our Bombers," *New York Times*, April 30, 1943; "Aix Reprisals on Flyers are Demanded by Gayda," *New York Times*, May 4, 1943; "Nation's Anger Rises at Jap Murders," *Daily Illini* (Urbana-Champaign), April 23, 1943; "Angry Germans Lynch American Bombing Fliers," *(San Bernardino) Daily Sun*, October 22, 1943; "Death Facing Allied Airmen in Nazi Hands" *(Greencastle, IN) Daily Banner*, December 24, 1943; "Believed Executed by Japs," *Breckenridge (Texas) American*, April 23, 1943; "Jap Murders of US Airmen Horrifies United Nations; Americans Angry" *(Darwin, Australia)Army News*, April 23, 1943; "Churchill Vows R.A.F. to Help Avenge Murder," *San Bernardino Sun*, April 24, 1943; "Germany, Italy May Follow Jap Precedent in Executing Fliers," *San Bernardino Sun*, April 25, 1943; "Japanese Appeal to America to Stop Tokio Raids," *Queensland (Ipswich, Australia) Times*, April 30, 1943; "Tokyo Tells Yank Airmen Pay Penalty," *Mandera (California) Tribune*, July 15, 1944; "Mobs Enraged. Nazis Threatened Yank Airmen," *Brooklyn Daily Eagle*, October 21, 1943; "Flier Tells How Yanks Lynched," *Mexia (Texas) Weekly Harold*, October 22, 1943; "Citizens Menaced Hamburg Bombers," *New York Times*, October 22, 1943; "Goebbels Invites Attacks on Fliers," *New York Times*, May 28, 1944; "Urge Lynchings of Jewish Flyers," *Jewish Criterion (Pittsburgh)*, June 6, 1944; "Germany Admits Fliers' Lynchings," *New York Times*, June 1, 1944; "Prussian Killings Pressed by Nazis: Himmler Also Reported to Have Ordered Slaying of Allied Flyers Downed in Reich," *New York Times*, July 27, 1944.

30. Quote from *(New York) Herald Tribune* in "Punishment of Prisoners: Nazis Considering 'Severer' Steps," *Sydney Morning Herald*, October 23, 1942.

31. The largest bombing raid in World War II took place in February 1945 when over one thousand US bombers and hundreds of fighters attacked Berlin.

32. Overy, *Blood and Ruin*, 786.

254 | Notes to pages 43–52

33. For example, see "Records of Proceedings," US vs Yoshio Tachibana et al., August 15, 1946, Marianas Islands, Guam, https://www.legal-tools.org/doc/cd1a09/pdf; James Bradley, *Flyboys: A True Story of Courage* (New York: Basic Books, 2004); "Jap Cannibals to be Hanged," *Townsville (Australia) Daily Bulletin*, October 7, 1946.

34. Paradis, *Last Mission to Tokyo*, 123–24.

35. See, for example, Naruhiko Higashikuni, *The War Diary of a Member of the Royal Family* (Nihonshuhosha, 1957, 106); see Paradis, *Last Mission to Tokyo*, 192; Barak Kushner, *The Thought War: Japanese Imperial Propaganda* (Honolulu: University of Hawai'i Press, 2007), 166.

36. "Review of the Staff Judge Advocate," June 17, 1949, US v. Kajuro Aihara et al., October 11–December 29, 1948, Yokohama, Japan, https://www.legal-tools.org/doc/475ba3/pdf.

37 "Review of the Staff Judge Advocate," June 17, 1949, US v. Kajuro Aihara et al., October 11–December 29, 1948, Yokohama, Japan, https://www.legal-tools.org/doc/475ba3/pdf.

38. "Review of the Staff Judge Advocate," June 17, 1949, US v. Kajuro Aihara et al., October 11–December 29, 1948, Yokohama, Japan, https://www.legal-tools.org/doc/475ba3/pdf..

39. "Review of the Staff Judge Advocate," June 17, 1949, US v. Kajuro Aihara et al., October 11–December 29, 1948, Yokohama, Japan, https://www.legal-tools.org/doc/475ba3/pdf. .

40. "Review of the Staff Judge Advocate," June 17, 1949, US v. Kajuro Aihara et al., October 11–December 29, 1948, Yokohama, Japan, https://www.legal-tools.org/doc/475ba3/pdf..

41. Exhibit L, Direct Examination of Maj Takahashi Yanase, Review of the Staff Judge Advocate, June 17, 1949, Yokohama, US v. Kajuro Aihara, October 11–December 29, 1948.

42. "Review of the Staff Judge Advocate," June 17, 1949, US v. Kajuro Aihara et al., October 11–Decemebr 29, 1948, Yokohama, Japan, https://www.legal-tools.org/doc/475ba3/pdf.

43. "Review of the Staff Judge Advocate," June 17, 1949, US v. Kajuro Aihara et al., October 11–December 29, 1948, Yokohama, Japan, https://www.legal-tools.org/doc/475ba3/pdf.

44. "Review of the Staff Judge Advocate," June 17, 1949, US v. Kajuro Aihara et al., October 11–December 29, 1948, Yokohama, Japan, https://www.legal-tools.org/doc/475ba3/pdf.

45. "Review of the Staff Judge Advocate," June 17, 1949, US v. Kajuro Aihara et al., October 11–December 29, 1948, Yokohama, Japan, https://www.legal-tools.org/doc/475ba3/pdf (accessed January 21, 2021).

46. "Families of Slain US Fliers Differ on Verdict for Japs," Associated Press, April 16, 1946.

Notes to pages 52–56 | 255

47. "Edward Young, "Review of the Record of Trial by a Military Commission of Lt Gen Shigeru Sawada et al.," August 1946, Box 11, China War Crimes Files, Entry 180, Records of the Office of the Judge Advocate General (Army), RG 153, NARA.

48. Jacob DeShazer to Walton H. Walker, May 21, 1949, Box 1070, War Crimes Case Files, Entry 144, War Crimes Branch, Records of the Office of the Judge Advocate General (Army), RG 153, NARA.

49. Quote from the *New York Times* in "Punishment of Prisoners: Nazis Considering 'Severer' Steps," *Sidney Morning Herald*, October 23, 1942; "Brother Barbarians," *Kalgoorlie Miner (Australia)*, April 26, 1943.

50. "Prisoners Maltreated, Say Nazis," *Daily Telegraph (London)*, May 29, 1940.

51. Dennis Richards, *The Royal Air Force 1939–1945*. Volume I: *The Fight at Odds* (London: H.M. Stationery Office, 1954), 217.

52. Proceedings of a General Court Martial on October 10, 1940, against Brigadier Guy Percy Lumsden Drake-Brockman, The National Archives, Kew, WO 71/1048.

53. Testimony of Maj R.M. Millar, Proceedings of a General Court Martial on October 10, 1940, against Brigadier Guy Percy Lumsden Drake-Brockman, The National Archives, Kew, WO 71/1048.

54. Testimony of Maj R.M. Millar, Proceedings of a General Court Martial on October 10, 1940, against Brigadier Guy Percy Lumsden Drake-Brockman, The National Archives, Kew, WO 71/1048.

55. Closing arguments of the prosecution and defense, Proceedings of a General Court Martial on October 10, 1940, against Brigadier Guy Percy Lumsden Drake-Brockman, The National Archives, Kew, WO 71/1048.

56. Richard Overy, *The Bombers and the Bombed: Allied Air War Over Europe, 1940–1945* (London: Penguin Press, 2015).

57. Proceedings of a General Court Martial on October 10, 1940, against Brigadier Guy Percy Lumsden Drake-Brockman, The National Archives, Kew, WO 71/1048.

58. Adolf Hitler, Commando Order, October 18, 1942, RG 549, Entry A1 2238, Microfilm T1021, Reel 10, Frame No. 775-777, NARA, accessed February 10, 2021, https://catalog.archives.gov/id/40957462.

59. Letter from Wagner attached to the forwarded Hitler Decree from October 18, 1942, RG 549, Entry A1 2238, Microfilm T1021, Reel 10, Frame No. 774, NARA, accessed February 10, 2021, https://catalog.archives.gov/id/40957462.

60. Overy, *Blood and Ruins*, 769.

61. Heinrich Himmler memo from August 10, 1943, RG 549, Entry A1 2238, Microfilm T1021, Reel 10, Frame No. 771, NARA, accessed March 2, 2021, https://catalog.archives.gov/id/40957462.

62. Joseph Goebbels, "Ein Wort zum feindlichen Luftterror," *Völkischer Beobachter (Berlin)*, May 28, 1944.

256 | Notes to pages 56–59

63. Jürgen Förster, "From 'Blitzkrieg' to 'Total War': Germany's War in Europe," in *World at Total War: Global Conflict and the Politics of Destruction, 1937–1947*, ed. Roger Chickering, Stig Förster, and Bernd Greiner (Cambridge: Cambridge University Press, 2013), 89–108, here 91; For example, see Robert Gellately, *Backing Hitler: Consent and Coercion in Nazi Germany* (Oxford: Oxford University Press, 2001); Eric A. Johnson, *Nazi Terror: The Gestapo, Jews, and Ordinary Germans* (New York: Basic Books, 1999).

64. One Soviet collaborator was convicted and executed as well for treason. For more information, see Michael J. Bazyler and Frank M. Tuerkheimer, *Forgotten Trials of the Holocaust* (New York: NYU Press, 2014).

65. Telegram from the Minister of Sweden (Johnson) to the US Secretary of State, January 3, 1944, in *Foreign Relations of the United States: Diplomatic Papers, 1942, General; The British Commonwealth; The Far East*, vol. 1, ed. G. Bernard Noble and E. R. Perkins (Washington, DC: US Government Printing Office, 1960), Doc. 766, https://history.state.gov/historicaldocuments/frus1944 v01/d766.

66. Ambassador Ritter, "Draft of letter from the Foreign Office to Chief OKW concerning treatment of enemy Terror Flyers," to Chief of the High Command of the Armed Forces, Salzburg, June 20, 1944, *Trials of War Criminals before the Nuernberg Military Tribunals under Control Council Law* No. 10, Vol. III (Washington, DC: United States Government Printing Office, 1960), 175–77; "Behandlung der feindlichen Terrorflieger," from Deputy Leader of the Armed Forces Operations Staff (Stell v. Chef WFSt.), June 6, 1944, RG 549, Entry A1 2238, Microfilm T1021, Reel 10, Frame No. 760–763, NARA, https://catalog .archives.gov/id/40957462.

67. "Behandlung der feindl. Terrorflieger," letter from OKW to Oberbefehlshaber der Luftwaffe concerning Treatment of Enemy Terror Flyers, June 14, 1944, Trials of War Criminals before the Nuernberg Military Tribunals, 170–71. See also RG 549, Entry A1 2238, Microfilm T1021, Reel 10, Frame No. 758, NARA, https://catalog.archives.gov/id/40957462.

68. Bulletin from Senior SS and Political Führer West Göhrum, "Volksjustiz an plündernden Ausländern und abgesprungenen feindlichen Fliegern und Erschiessen dieser durch Ordnungspolizei," June 24, 1944, RG 549, Entry A1 2238, Microfilm, T1021, Reel 13, Frame No. 872–73, NARA, https://catalog.archives.gov /id/40957462.

69. Ritter, "Draft of Letter," *Trials of War Criminals before the Nuernberg Military Tribunals*, 175–77.

70. "Verhalten der Wehrmacht gegenüber abgesprungenen Terrorfliegern" from head of the SiPo and SD in Rhein/Westmark to the Gestapo, KriPo, and SD in Frankfurt a.M., Koblenz, Darmstadt, Saarbrücken, and Metz, October 6, 1944, RG 549, Entry A1 2238, Microfilm T1021, Reel 10, Frame No. 790, NARA, https:// catalog.archives.gov/id/40957462.

Notes to pages 60–70 | 257

71. Order by Lieutenant General Schmidt (Anti-Aircraft Artillery), transmitting order from Chief OKW of July 9, 1944, sent to Divisional Commanders, Commander of Anti-Aircraft Groups, Luftgau Forces, from December 11, 1944, *Trials of War Criminals before the Nuernberg Military Tribunals*, 179–80.

72. Testimony by August Kobus, Review of US v. Bernhard Stredele, Case No. 12-1155-1, June 25, 1951, Records of the Office of the Judge Advocate General (Army) NARA RG 153, Entry 143, Box 414.

73. Review and Recommendation for Case No. 12-1155, Deputy Theater Judge Advocate's Office, War Crimes Branch, February 6, 1946, Records of the Office of the Judge Advocate General (Army), RG 153, Entry 143, Box 414, NARA.

74. Testimony by August Kobus, Case No. 12-1155-1, Deputy Theater Judge Advocate's Office, War Crimes Branch, February 6, 1946, Records of the Office of the Judge Advocate General (Army), RG 153, Entry 143, Box 414, NARA.

75. Review and Recommendation for Case No. 12-1155, Deputy Theater Judge Advocate's Office, War Crimes Branch, February 6, 1946, Records of the Office of the Judge Advocate General (Army), RG 153, Entry 143, Box 414, NARA.

2. War Crimes Narratives: Pacific and Southeast Asia

1. Witness Statement by S/Sgt Anthony Tomczak, January 4, 1945, MACR 9964, https://catalog.archives.gov/id/91082712.

2. All four safely returned back to Allied control. Sgt Henry W. Wheaton (command gunner) was unable to bail out from the rear hatch due to a defective parachute.

3. Witness Statement by Maj Gen Kaburagi Masataka, #2805, December 29, 1945, in US v. Masataka Kaburagi et al., Shanghai, China, February 14, 1946, https://www.legal-tools.org/doc/0b3a09/pdf.

4. Report by 1st Lt Izumi, December 16, 1944, quoted in Witness Statement by Maj Gen Kaburagi Masataka, #2805, December 29, 1945, in US v. Masataka Kaburagi et al., February 14, 1946, https://www.legal-tools.org/doc/0b3a09/pdf.

5. US v. Masataka Kaburagi et al., February 14, 1946, https://www.legal-tools.org/doc/0b3a09/pdf.

6. Witness Statement by Col Fukumoto Kameji, #2801, December 22, 1945, in US v. Masataka Kaburagi et al., Shanghai, China, February 14, 1946, https://www.legal-tools.org/doc/0b3a09/pdf.

7. Statements made by Sung Wen Ching during direct examination at the postwar crime trial on February 11, 1946. US v. Masataka Kaburagi et al., Shanghai, China, vol. I, 52–55, https://www.legal-tools.org/doc/82a112/pdf.

8. Statement made by Chang Chia Yuan during the direct examination at the postwar crime trial on February 12, 1946. US v. Masataka Kaburagi et al., Shanghai, China, vol. 1, 60–65, https://www.legal-tools.org/doc/82a112/pdf.

258 | Notes to pages 70–77

9. Statement made by Sgt Maj Shozo Masui during direct examination at the postwar crime trial on February 23, 1946. US v. Masataka Kaburagi et al., Shanghai, China, vol. 4, 236–38, https://www.legal-tools.org/doc/f44173/pdf.

10. Statement made by Sgt Maj Shozo Masui during direct examination at the postwar crime trial on February 23, 1946. US v. Masataka Kaburagi et al., Shanghai, China, vol. 4, 236–38.

11. Report by 1st Lt Izumi, December 16, 1944, quoted in Witness Statement by Maj Gen Kaburagi Masataka, #2805, December 29, 1945. US v. Masataka Kaburagi et al., China, February 14, 1946, https://www.legal-tools.org/doc/0b3a 09/pdf.

12. Witness Statement by Maj Gen Kaburagi Masataka, #2805, December 29, 1945, in US v. Masataka Kaburagi et al., Shanghai, China, February 14, 1946, https://www.legal-tools.org/doc/0b3a09/pdf.

13. Statement made by Consul Shozo Masui during cross examination at the postwar trial on February 25, 1946. US v. Masataka Kaburagi et al., Shanghai, China, vol. 4, 358–59, https://www.legal-tools.org/doc/0b3a09/pdf.

14. Statement made by Consul Shozo Masui during cross examination at the postwar trial on February 25, 1946. US v. Masataka Kaburagi et al., Shanghai, China, vol. 4, 332, https://www.legal-tools.org/doc/f44173/pdf.

15. Statement made by Yasaburo Shirakawa during cross examination at the postwar trial on February 25, 1946. US v. Masataka Kaburagi et al., Shanghai, China, vol. 4, 333–37, here 336, https://www.legal-tools.org/doc/f44173/pdf.

16. Statement by 2nd Lt John Workman, MACR 12251, accessed December 4, 2020, https://catalog.archives.gov/id/91123908.

17. 24th War Graves Unit Report by Capt. G. A. Wickham, December 11, 1945, MACR 12251, accessed December 4, 2020, https://catalog.archives.gov/id/.

18. Witness statement by Lo Sioe Hong at postwar trial on October 14, 1945. US v. Sentaro Yamaguchi et al., vol. 1, September 5, 1946, Manila, Philippines, 69–71, https://www.legal-tools.org/doc/e4538a/pdf.

19. Witness statement by Sgt H. Brokenshire at postwar trial on October 14, 1945. US v. Sentaro Yamaguchi et al., vol. 1, September 5, 1946, 80, https://www .legal-tools.org/doc/e4538a/pdf.

20. Statement by Yamaguchi Sentaro at the postwar trial on October 25, 1945. US v. Sentaro Yamaguchi et al., vol. I, September 5, 1946, 88, https://www.legal -tools.org/doc/e4538a/pdf.

21. Review of the Staff Judge Advocate, US v. Otohiko Inoue et al., Yokohama, Japan, January 13, 1949, pages 52–53, https://www.online.uni-marburg.de/icwc /yokohama/Yokohama%20No.%20T258.pdf.

22. Review of the Staff Judge Advocate, US v. Otohiko Inoue et al., Yokohama, Japan, January 13, 1949.

23. Review of the Staff Judge Advocate, US v. Otohiko Inoue et al., Yokohama, Japan, January 13, 1949.

24. Review of the Staff Judge Advocate, US v. Otohiko Inoue et al., Yokohama, Japan, January 13, 1949.

Notes to pages 79–85 | 259

25. "The Deadliest Air Raid in History," accessed February 4, 2021, https://www.airspacemag.com/daily-planet/deadliest-air-raid-history-180954512/.

26. Richard Sams, "Inferno on the Omotesando: The Great Yamanote Air Raid," *The Asia-Pacific Journal* 13, Issue 21, No. 1, May 25, 2015, https://apjjf.org/-Richard-Sams/4321/article.pdf. Translated by Richard Sams from original: "Escaping by Bicycle," *The Great Tokyo Air Raids—Records of War Damages,* vol. 2 (Association for Recording Tokyo Air Raids, 1973). See also: "Paper City," https://www.japanairraids.org; "The Man Who Won't Let the World Forget the Firebombing of Tokyo," accessed March 10, 2021, https://www.nytimes.com/2020/03/09/magazine/the-man-who-wont-let-the-world-forget-the-firebombing-of-tokyo.html.

27. Statement by W/O Fujiyoshi Terazawa, October 2, 1945, US v. Toshio Tashiro et al., Yokohama, Japan, March–July 1948, https://www.online.uni-marburg.de/icwc/yokohama/Yokohama%20No.%20T078.pdf.

28. Statement by 2nd Lt Masao Koshikaw, October 2, 1945, US v. Toshio Tashiro et al., Yokohama, Japan, March–July 1948. See also Exhibit 8, page 10, US v. Toshio Tashiro et al., Yokohama, Japan, March–July 1948.

29. US v. Toshio Tashiro et al., Yokohama, Japan, March–July 1948, 1628, 1646–47.

30. Statement by Eihacki Abe, Exhibit 31, US v. Toshio Tashiro et al., Yokohama, Japan, March–July 1948, page 2.

31. Appendix to Report of Investigation Division, Legal Section by William R. Gill, February 18, 1947, US v. Toshio Tashiro et al., Yokohama, Japan, March–July 1948.

32. Those who died in the crash included: 1st Lt Samuel B. Hitt, Sgt Charles M. Santelli, Cpl James R. Smith, Cpl John W. Boyd, and Cpl Paul R. Sheehan.

33. Letter by 1st Lt Harmon Reeder Jr. to the Commanding General of the Army Air Forces, November 3, 1945, MACR 14503, https://catalog.archives.gov/id/91155163.

34. Report by S/Sgt Francis A. Tourat, 361st Quartermaster Graves Registration Company, US v. Masaaki Mabuchi and Jutaro Kikuchi, Yokohama, Japan, April 5–20, 1946; report by Capt Donald M. Eramwell, US v. Masaaki Mabuchi and Jutaro Kikuchi, Yokohama, Japan, April 5–20, 1946, https://www.online.uni-marburg.de/icwc/yokohama/Yokohama%20No.%20T026.pdf.

35. Statement by Minoru Moriyama, US v. Masaaki Mabuchi and Jutaro Kikuchi, Yokohama, Japan, April 5–20, 1946.

36. The identity of this flyer and whether he was a member of Emry's crew is undetermined.

37. Statement by Tadashi Toriyama, US v. Masaaki Mabuchi and Jutaro Kikuchi, Yokohama, Japan, April 5–20, 1946; statement by Masaaki Mabuchi, US vs Masaaki Mabuchi and Jutaro Kikuchi, Yokohama, Japan, April 5–20, 1946.

38. Statement by Masaaki Mabuchi, US v. Masaaki Mabuchi and Jutaro Kikuchi, Yokohama, Japan, April 5–20, 1946.

260 | Notes to pages 86–92

39. Only five airmen survived being shot down. This included: 1st Floyd F. Fielder, 2nd Lt George L. Sheridan, Sgt Abel P. Soto, Sgt Dennis E. Tyring, and 2nd Lt Harmon Reeder, Jr. Review of the Staff Judge Advocate, US v. Masaaki Mabuchi and Jutaro Kikuchi, Yokohama, Japan, April 5–20, 1946.

40. These include: 2nd Lt John S. Houghton, Cpl Seth Rigby, 2nd Lt Roland F. Nelson, Sgt William H. Osborn, Sgt Walter E. Walk, M/Sgt Erwin R. Griffin, Cpl Stanley Forystek, Cpl Elmer H. Bertsch, Jr., 2nd Lt Robert L. Wiilliams, Sgt Warren L. Olson, T/Sgt Harold E. Halldorson, Sgt Charles W. Snell, 2nd Lt Francis F. Jensen, 2nd Lt Theodore H. Fox, 2nd Lt George L. Sheridan, Sgt Kenneth Petterson, 2nd Lt Andrew J. Litz, S/Sgt Walter W. Dickerson, S/Sgt Thomas W. Peel, Capt Gordon P. Jordan, Sgt Lester C. Morris, Capt Vincent A. Gaudiani, 1st Lt Marvin S. Watkins, F/O Mark S. Kennard; Review of the Staff Judge Advocate, US v. Ranjo Fujino et al., Yokohama, Japan, May 24–October 13, 1948; Review of the Staff Judge Advocate, US v. Toyokazu Hikita et al., Yokohama, Japan, March 1–2, 1948.

41. Interview of Marvin S. Watkins, March 27, 1947, by Special Agent Johnathan H. Harrington, 109th CIC Detachment, Second Army, MACR 14363, https://catalog.archives.gov/id/91153540.

42. Letter from 1st Lt Marvin S. Watkins to Commanding General of the Army Air Forces, October 29, 1945, MACR 14363, https://catalog.archives.gov/id/91153540.

43. Thomas Easton, "A Quiet Honesty Records a World War II Atrocity," *Baltimore Sun*, May 28, 1995. http://mansell.com/pow_resources/camplists/fukuoka/fuk_01_fukuoka/fukuoka_01/Page05.htm#Vivisections.

44. Justin McCurry, "Japan Revisits Its Darkest Moments Where American POWs became Human Experiments," *Guardian*, August 2015, https://www.theguardian.com/world/2015/aug/13/japan-revisits-its-darkest-moments-where-american-pows-became-human-experiments.

45. Case 48-35-1, US v. Hiroshi Iwanami et al., JAG Case Files, Pacific-Army, November 1947. See also Sheldon H. Harris, "Japanese Biomedical Experimentation during the World War II Era," in Dave E. Lounsbury, ed., *Military Medical Ethics* 2 (Office of The Surgeon General, Department of the Army, US, 2003), 463–506, here 489–90; Roland CG. "Human Vivisection: The Intoxication of Limitless Power in Wartime," in Bob Moore and Kent Fedorowich, eds., *Prisoners of War and Their Captors in World War II* (Oxford: Berg, 1996, 149–55).

46. Japanese records (Exhibit 16 at the postwar trial) list the following men as being transferred to Tokyo: Lt Max E. Frellsen, Lt Norman W. Imel (beaten to death at Ofuna Naval Interrogation Center on March 10, 1945), Lt Donald C. Stanley, Ens Frederick D. Turnbull, Lt William Ziemer (died on August 8, 1945, due to physical exhaustion and malnutrition), Ens Sage N. Johnston, Lt William A. Davidson Jr., S 2/C Joseph Eugene, S 2/C Charles F. Buchhett, S 2/C Gordon G. Johnson, Ens Edwin J. Walasek, S 2/C William C. Upton, Lt Minos D. Miller, Jr., Lt William T. Ross, Jr., Ens John F. Bertrang, 1st Lt Michael C. Sherdon, Ens

Notes to pages 92–102 | 261

Kenneth F. Aston (died on July 23, 1945, due to physical exhaustion). US v. Harukei Isayama et al. Shanghai, China, August 10, 1946, vol. I, 141–43, https://www.legal-tools.org/doc/030cf4/pdf. Some of these men, in addition to other unnamed American POWs, experienced severe beatings and torture while they were held as POWs at the Ofuna Naval Interrogation Center, located near Yokohama. Their experiences are detailed in war crimes case #253, US v. Sueharu Kitamura, Yokohama, Japan, January–February 1948, https://www.online.uni-marburg.de/icwc/yokohama/Yokohama%20No.%20T253.pdf. For the Ofuna camp roster, see: NARA, RG 407, Records of the Adjutant General's Office, Philippine Archives Collection, Box 115, POW/Civilian Internees, POW Rosters Tokyo, "Diagnostic List of POWs held at the Ofuna Detachment of Tokyo Internment Camp," August 1945.

47. US v. Harukei Isayama et al. Shanghai, China, August 10, 1946, vol. 1.

48. Prosecution Exhibit 18, Statement made by Haruki Isayama, April 18, 1946, US v. Harukei Isayama et al. Shanghai, China, August 10, 1946, vol. 2, page 161–63, here 161, https://www.legal-tools.org/doc/8478c9/pdf; Army Secret Telegram No. 781, from Tokyo Vice-Minister of War, Deputy-Chief of Staff to Chief of the Judicial Dept. of the Formosa Army, May 28, 1945, US v. Harukei Isayama et al. Shanghai, China, August 10, 1946, vol. 3, 39, https://www.legal-tools.org/doc/296ef9/pdf.

49. US v. Harukei Isayama et al. Shanghai, China, August 10, 1946, vol. 1, 24, https://www.legal-tools.org/doc/030cf4/pdf.

50. Report by 2nd Lt Robert S. Scamara, June 25, 1945, MACR 14983, https://catalog.archives.gov/id/91160850.

51. Exhibit D, Statement by Chiyoshi Shimoda, Review of Staff Judge Advocate, January 26, 1949, US v. Seiji Nozaki et al., April 12–May 13, 1948, https://www.online.uni-marburg.de/icwc/yokohama/Yokohama%20No.%20T276.pdf.

52. Review of Staff Judge Advocate, January 26, 1949, US v. Seiji Nozaki et al., April 12–May 13, 1948.

53. Exhibit 27, 8–9; Exhibit 28, part 2, 7, Review of the Staff Judge Advocate, July 1, 1948, US v. Eitaro Uchiyama et al., July 18–August 28, 1947, https://www.online.uni-marburg.de/icwc/yokohama/Yokohama%20No.%20T123.pdf.

54. Review of the Staff Judge Advocate, July 1, 1948, US v. Eitaro Uchiyama et al., July 18–August 28, 1947.

55. Review of the Staff Judge Advocate, July 1, 1948, US v. Eitaro Uchiyama et al., July 18–August 28, 1947, https://www.online.uni-marburg.de/icwc/yokohama/Yokohama%20No.%20T123.pdf.

56. Exhibit 82, Statement by Lt Gen Eitaro Uchiyamam, US v. Eitaro Uchiyama et al., July 18–August 28, 1947.

57. Exhibit 85, Statement by Maj Gen Tsugio Nagatomo, Review of the Staff Judge Advocate, July 21, 1949, US v. Jiro Hamamoto, December 27, 1948–January 3, 1949, https://www.online.uni-marburg.de/icwc/yokohama/Yokohama%20No.%20T364.pdf.

262 | Notes to pages 102–7

58. The known victims included: 2nd Lt Harry W. Norton Jr., Ens Norman B. Bitzegaio, Sgt Lawrence W. Beecroft, Sgt James M. Fitzgerald, S/Sgt Erle P. Flanagan, Capt Richard H. Hamilton, Sgt Harvey B. Kennedy Jr., S/Sgt George C. Reed, Cpl Clarence E. Scritchfield, S/Sgt Logan M. Sparks, S/Sgt John R. Vincent, 1st Lt Harrison K. Wittee, and five unidentified flyers; Kempeitai officials poisoned two severely ill flyers (2nd Lt James R. Price and S/Sgt Russell W. Strong) held at the Kempeitai Headquarters on July 31, 1945, and three additional unidentified American prisoners on August 3, 1945.

59. The known victims included: 1st Lt Louis W. Lehnen, S/Sgt Robert L. Pellicot, and twelve unidentified American flyers.

60. The known victims included: 1st Lt Harold T. Cobb, 2nd Lt Joe S. McSpadden, Capt Jack K. Ort, 1st Lt Donald J. Schlitz, and one unidentified American flyer.

61. Statement by W/O Jiro Hamamoto, Review of the Staff Judge Advocate, July 21, 1949, US v. Jiro Hamamoto, December 27, 1948–January 3, 1949, https://www.online.uni-marburg.de/icwc/yokohama/Yokohama%20No.%20T364.pdf.

62. Exhibit 15, Statement by Tomekichi Hamada, Review of the Staff Judge Advocate, July 21, 1949, US v. Jiro Hamamoto, December 27, 1948–January 3, 1949, https://www.online.uni-marburg.de/icwc/yokohama/Yokohama%20No .%20T364.pdf.

63. Exhibit 15, Statement by Tomekichi Hamada, Review of the Staff Judge Advocate, July 21, 1949, US v. Jiro Hamamoto, December 27, 1948–January 3, 1949.

64. Review of the Staff Judge Advocate, June 17, 1949, US v. Kajuro Aihara et al., Yokohama, October 11–December 29, 1948, https://www.legal-tools.org/doc /475ba3/pdf.

3. War Crimes Narratives: Europe

1. For more information, see Kevin T Hall, *Terror Flyers: The Lynching of American Airmen in Nazi Germany* (Bloomington: University of Indiana Press, 2021).

2. United Nations War Crimes Commission Case No. 420, Records of the Office of the Judge Advocate General (Army) NARA RG 153, Entry 143, Box 523.

3. "Terror Raids," *Evening Post*, May 4, 1943.

4. Testimony of 1st Lt Richard B. Charlton, June 11, 1947, United Nations War Crimes Commission Case No. 420, Records of the Office of the Judge Advocate General (Army) NARA RG 153, Entry 143, Box 523,

5. Review of Record by Lt Gen John C. H. Lee, August 28, 1947, Record of Trial by US Military Commission of Ido Turchi, tried at Leghorn Italy June 3–5, 1947, https://www.legal-tools.org/doc/8f4cef/pdf/.

6. Escape and Evasion Report 797, 1st Lt Ivan E. Glaze, accessed June 7, 2021, https://catalog.archives.gov/id/5555437.

7. The crews consisted of: Sgt Vincent J. Reese from "Women's Home Companion" (42-39795) shot down on December 30, 1943, near Froidchapelle,

Belgium (MACR 1674); S/Sgt John J. Gemborski, T/Sgt Orian G. Owens, and T/Sgt Charlres A. Nichols from "Rationed Passion" (42-57879) shot down on January 11, 1944, near Rijssen, Holland (MACR 1931); 2nd Lt Robert J. Benninger, 2nd Lt George W. Eike, and Sgt John Pindroch from "Susan Ruth" (42-31499) shot down on February 8, 1944, near Macquenoise, Belgium (MACR 2493); 2nd Lt Billy H. Huish from "Skunkface" (42-29656) shot down on February 20, 1944, near Lens, Belgium (MACR 2460).

8. Steve Snyder, *Shot Down: The True Story of Pilot Howard Snyder and the Crew of the B-17 Susan Ruth* (Seal Beach, CA: Sea Breeze Publishing, 2015).

9. Herman Bodson, *Downed Allied Airmen and Evasion of Capture: The Role of Local Resistance Networks in World War II* (London: McFarland, 2001), 109–13; see also accessed June 7, 2021, http://aircrewremembered.com.

10. Review of Staff Judge Advocate, September 11, 1947, US v. Max Schmid, May 19, 1947, Dachau, Germany, accessed March 28, 2021, https://www.legal-tools .org/doc/446866/pdf.

11. "Picture of the Week," *Life Magazine*, May 22, 1944, 34–35.

12. Review of Staff Judge Advocate, September 11, 1947, US v. Max Schmid, May 19, 1947, Dachau, Germany.

13. 2nd Lt Daniel T. Loyd was a member of the 84th Fighter Squadron, 78th Fighter Group and based at Le Touquet, France.

14. MACR 5577, accessed January 23, 2021, https://catalog.archives.gov/id /90986268.

15. Witness statement by Cecile Marie Gruart, Exhibit 2, page 5, US v. Karl Kirchner et al., Dachau, Germany, March 8, 1948, https://www.legal-tools.org/doc /28b788/pdf.

16. Review of the Staff Judge Advocate, US v. Karl Kirchner et al., Dachau, Germany, March 8, 1948.

17. Review of the Staff Judge Advocate, US v. Karl Kirchner et al., Dachau, Germany, March 8, 1948.

18. Witness statement by Dr. Max Buerger, Exhibit 14, page 8, US v. Karl Kirchner et al., Dachau, Germany, March 8, 1948.

19. The aircraft was potentially a B-24 (41-28782). MACR 6042, accessed January 19, 2021, https://catalog.archives.gov/id/90994070.

20. For example, see Hall, *Terror Flyers*, 51, 137, 142–43.

21. Review of the Staff Judge Advocate, March 18, 1946, US v. Charlotte V. Battalo et al., Dachau, Germany, January 31, 1946, accessed March 6, 2021, https:// www.legal-tools.org/doc/c82d6d/pdf.

22. Witness statement by Charlotte V. Battalo, US v. Charlotte V. Battalo et al., Dachau, Germany, January 31, 1946.

23. Review of the Staff Judge Advocate, March 18, 1946, US v. Charlotte V. Battalo et al., Dachau, Germany, January 31, 1946.

24. MACR 8425, accessed January 17, 2021, https://catalog.archives.gov/id /91053762.

264 | Notes to pages 114–22

25. KU Report 895A, September 2, 1944, MACR 8425, https://catalog.archives.gov/id/91053762; https://www.aircrewremembered.com.

26. Review of Staff Judge Advocate, March 1, 1948, US v. Otto F. Isenmann et al., Dachau, Germany, May 28, 1947, https://www.legal-tools.org/doc/065426/pdf (accessed October 10, 2020).

27. Review of Staff Judge Advocate, March 1, 1948, US v. Otto F. Isenmann et al., Dachau, Germany, May 28, 1947.

28. Review of Staff Judge Advocate, March 1, 1948, US v. Otto F. Isenmann et al., Dachau, Germany, May 28, 1947.

29. Review of Staff Judge Advocate, March 1, 1948, US v. Otto F. Isenmann et al., Dachau, Germany, May 28, 1947.

30. MACR 8907, accessed January 10, 2021, https://catalog.archives.gov/id/91062647.

31. Review of the Staff Judge Advocate, August 6, 1947, US v. Christian Blum et al., Dachau, Germany, August 15–24, 1946, https://www.legal-tools.org/doc/e8010a/pdf.

32. Witness statement by Gottlob Hohloch, US v. Christian Blum et al., Dachau, Germany, August 15–24, 1946.

33. Witness statements by Gottlob Hohloch and Christian Blum, US v. Christian Blum et al., Dachau, Germany, August 15–24, 1946.

34. Review of the Staff Judge Advocate, August 6, 1947, US v. Christian Blum et al., Dachau, Germany, August 15–24, 1946.

35. KU Report 2969, Dulag Luft, October 5, 1944, MACR 8907, accessed January 10, 2021, https://catalog.archives.gov/id/91062647.

36. US v. Christian Blum et al., Dachau, Germany, August 15–24, 1946; see also Gert R. Ording's article "One Man's War- John Fuchs," accessed January 21, 2021, https://www.historynet.com/one-mans-war-john-fuchs.htm.

37. The bomber crew consisted of 1st Lt William F. Moore, 2nd Lt Edgar J. Powell, 1st Lt Franklin D. Coslett, 2nd Lt Edward Verbosky, Sgt James R. Anslow, T/Sgt Clinton L. Watts, S/Sgt Henry H. Allen, S/Sgt Walter T. Kilgore, S/Sgt Werner G. Braun, Maj Robert L. Salzarulo, and 1st Lt John L. Lewis Jr., MACR 4944, accessed February 2, 2021, https://catalog.archives.gov/id/90971570.

38. MACR 4449, accessed January 29, 2021, https://catalog.archives.gov/id/90960416.

39. Case NL 211, Adolf Glück prosecuted at Arnhem in March 1950, June 4, 2021, "Justiz und NS-Verbrechen," https://www.expostfacto.nl.

40. Eyewitness report by 1st Lt Sidney P. Upsher, December 9, 1944, MACR 10131, accessed January 18, 2021, https://catalog.archives.gov/id/91085163.

41. Review and Recommendations, October 14, 1945, US v. Franz Strasser, Dachau, Germany, August 24, 1945, https://www.legal-tools.org/doc/366a58/pdf.

42. KSU Report 2521, MACR 10131, accessed January 18, 2021, https://catalog.archives.gov/id/91085163.

Notes to pages 122–29 | 265

43. Review and Recommendations, October 14,1945, US v. Franz Strasser, Dachau, Germany, August 24, 1945.

44. Review and Recommendations, October 14, 1945, US v. Franz Strasser, Dachau, Germany, August 24, 1945; see also accessed January 22, 2021, http://www.leteckabadatelna.cz/havarie-a-sestrely/detail/523/.

45. The crew belonged to the 716th Bomb Squadron, 449th Bomb Group and included: 1st Lt William R. Farrington (Pilot), 2nd Lt John P. Knox (Copilot), 2nd Lt Warren F. Ames (Nav), 1st Lt Floyd B. Bremermann, Jr. (Bomb), T/Sgt Felix D. Kozekowski (Eng), S/Sgt Kenneth C. Rost (Asst. Eng), T/Sgt Donald P. Brown (Radio), S/Sgt James F. Bradley (Gunner), S/Sgt Hubert R. Burnette (Gunner), S/Sgt Preston J. Hill (Gunner).

46. Witness Report by Maj Howard T. Van De Car, March 2, 1945, Witness Report by 2nd Lt Frank H. Elser Jr., March 3, 1945, MACR 12745, https://catalog.archives.gov/id/91131058.

47. Despite the armistice signed between Hungary and the United States in January 1945, this voluntary Hungarian SS unit continued to fight for Nazi Germany.

48. Review of US v. Karolyi Ney et al., Salzburg, Austria, May 22–June 7, 1946, NARA RG 153, Entry 143, Box 516.

49. Review of US v. Karolyi Ney et al., Salzburg, Austria, May 22–June 7, 1946, NARA RG 153, Entry 143, Box 516.

50. Review of US v. Karolyi Ney et al., Salzburg, Austria, May 22–June 7, 1946, NARA RG 153, Entry 143, Box 516.

51. Witness Statement by 2nd Lt Carl E. Carey, April 1, 1945, MACR 13377, accessed June 6, 2021, https://catalog.archives.gov/id/91141360.

52. Another member of Manning's squadron, F/O William P. Armstrong, was also shot down during the dog fight; however, he was unable to bail out of his damaged aircraft (42-103971), known as "Little Li," and died in the crash. MACR 13376, accessed June 6, 2021, https://catalog.archives.gov/id/91141354.

53. Report of War Crimes Case No 5-157, NARA, RG 549/290/59/19/2-3, Box 13, Case 5-131. See also Hoffmann, *Fliegerlynchjustiz: Gewalt gegen abgeschossene alliierte Flugzeugbesatzungen 1943–1945* (Paderborn: Ferdinand Schöningh, 2015), 296.

54. According to Walter Waiss, the quote read: "Wir helfen uns selbst!" Walter Waiss, *Chronik Kampfgeschwader Nr. 27* Boelcke, Band VII (Aachen: Helios Verlag, 2010), 126; Hoffmann, *Fliegerlynchjustiz*, 296.

55. Report of War Crimes Case No. 5-157, NARA, RG 549/290/59/19/2-3, Box 13, Case 5-131. See also Hoffmann, *Fliegerlynchjustiz*, 296.

4. US Postwar Flyer Trials

Epigraph from closing comment by Lt Col Allan R. Browne at the US postwar trial that sought justice for the torture and execution of three US Navy

266 | Notes to pages 129–33

flyers (Lt Vernon L. Tebo, AM 1/C Warren H. Lloyd, and AM 1/C Robert Tuggle Jr.). Review of the Staff Judge Advocate, January 13, 1949, US v. Otohiko Inoue et al., Case #258, November 26, 1947–March 16, 1948, 111, 147, https://www.online.uni -marburg.de/icwc/yokohama/Yokohama%20No.%20T258.pdf.

1. A significant portion of this chapter was previously published in Kevin T Hall, "Downed American Flyers: Forgotten Casualties of Axis Atrocities in World War II," *Journal of Perpetrator Justice* 4, no. 1 (2021): 192–221.

2. Kevin T Hall, *Terror Flyers: The Lynching of American Airmen in Nazi Germany* (Bloomington: Indiana University Press, 2021); Georg Hoffmann, *Fliegerlynchjustz: Gewalt gegen abgeschossene alliierte Flugzeugbesatzungen, 1943–45* (Paderborn: Ferdinand Schönigh, 2015); Richard Overy, *The Bombers and the Bomber: Allied Air War over Europe, 1940–1945* (New York: Viking, 2013); Richard J. Evans, *The Third Reich at War* (New York: Penguin Press, 2009); James J. Wingartner, "Americans, Germans, and War Crimes: Converging Narratives from 'The Good War,'" *Journal of American History* 94, no. 4 (2008); Barbara Grimm, "Lynchmorde an alliierten Fliegern im Zweiten Weltkrieg," in *Deutschland im Luftkrieg: Geschichte und Erinnerung*, ed. Dietmar Süß (Munich: R. Oldenbourg, 2007); Klaus-Michael Mallmann, "Volksjustiz gegen anglo-amerikanische Mörder: Die Massaker an westalliierten Fliegern und Fallschirmspringern 1944–45," in *NS-Gewaltherrschaft: Beiträge zur historischen Forschung und juristischen Aufarbeitung*, ed. Alfred Gottwaldt, Norbert Kampe, and Peter Klein (Berlin: Hentricht, 2005); Ralf Blank, "Wartime Daily Life and the Air War on the Home Front," in *Germany and the Second World War*, ed. Jörg Echternkamp (Oxford: Oxford University Press, 2004).

3. See, for example, US v. Otohiko Inoue et al., Yokohama, Japan, January 13, 1949; US vs Kajuro Aihara et al., Yokohama, Japan, March 11–August 27, 1948; US v. Jiro Hamamoto, Yokohama, Japan, December 27, 1948–January 3, 1949; US v. Hiroshi Iwanami et al., JAG Case Files, Pacific-Army, November 1947; Sheldon H. Harris, "Japanese Biomedical Experimentation During the World War II Era," in Dave E. Lounsbury, ed., *Military Medical Ethics*, Volume 2 (Officer of The Surgeon General, Department of the Army, US, pages 463–506, here 489–90); Roland CG, "Human Vivisection: The Intoxication of Limitless Power in Wartime," in *Prisoners of War and Their Captors in World War II*, ed. Bob Moore and Kent Fedorowich (Oxford: Berg, 1996), 149–55.

4. Hall, *Terror Flyers,* 134–39.

5. Hall, 137.

6. Hall, 137–39.

7. The documents used in the analysis of flyers' trials held at Yokohama and throughout the Pacific (e.g., Guam, Singapore, Rangoon, Rabaul, Manila, Shanghai, Indonesia, and Marshall Islands) can be found here: "Yokohama–Philipps-Universität Marbug–ICWC, accessed December 17, 2020, https://www .unimarburg.de/icwc/forschung/2weltkrieg/yokohama?order=source&order _type=asc&offset=0&count=100&name=&id_trial; "The International Military

Notes to pages 133–39 | 267

Tribunal for the Far East," https://imtfe.law.virginia.edu; "International Criminal Court Database," accessed December 17, 2020, https://www.legal-tools.org.

8. Created by author. See Kevin T Hall, "Downed American Flyers: Forgotten Casualties of Axis Atrocities in World War II," *Journal of Perpetrator Justice* 4, no. 1 (2021): 208.

9. Joseph Goebbels, "Ein Wort zum feindlichen Luftterror," *Völkischer Beobachter* (Munich), May 28, 1944.

10. "Jews Head List of U.S. Fliers Facing Nazi Trials," *Jewish Criterion* (Pittsburgh), January 7, 1944.

11. Hall, *Terror Flyers*; Gregory A. Freeman, *The Last Mission of the Wham Bam Boys: Courage, Tragedy, and Justice in World War II* (New York: Palgrave Macmillan, 2011); Günter Neliba, *Lynchjustiz an amerikanischen Kriegsge-fangenen in der Opelstadt Rüsselsheim (1944): Rekonstruktion einer der ersten Kriegsverbrecher-Prozesse in Deutschland nach Prozessakten (1945–1947)* (Frankfurt: Brandes und Apsel, 2000); Augusto Nigro, *Wolfsangel: A German City on Trial 1945–48* (Washington, DC: Brasseys, 2000).

12. Joseph Goebbels, "Ein Wort zum feindlichen Luftterror," *Völkischer Beobachter* (Berlin), May 28, 1944.

13. Review and Recommendations for Case No. 12-1812, Record of U.S. Army Europe, War Crimes Case Files (Cases Tried), April 23, 1947, RG 549, Entry 290, Box 187, NARA; Hall, *Terror Flyers*, 165, 191.

14. Hall, *Terror Flyers*, 149–50; 166–67; 211–14.

15. Kevin T Hall, *Terror Flyers: The Lynching of American Airmen in Nazi Germany* (Bloomington: Indiana University Press, 2021); Kevin T Hall, "The Flyer Trials: Seeking Justice for Lynchjustiz Committed against American Airmen during World War II," *War in History* 27, no. 3 (2020), 486–516; Kevin T Hall, "Luftgangster over Germany: The Lynching of American Airmen in the Shadow of the Air War," *Journal Historische Sozialforschung/Historical Social Research* 43, no. 2 (June 2018): 277–312; Georg Hoffmann, *Fliegerlynchjustiz: Gewalt gegen abgeschossene alliierte Flugzeugbesatzungen, 1943–1945* (Paderborn: Schöningh, 2015); Richard Overy, *The Bombers and the Bombed: Allied Air War over Europe, 1940–1945* (New York: Viking, 2013); Bas von Benda-Beckmann, *A German Catastrophe? German Historians and the Allied Bombings, 1945–2010* (Amsterdam: Amsterdam University Press, 2010); Richard J. Evans, *The Third Reich at War* (New York: Penguin Press, 2009); James J. Weingartner, "Americans, Germans, and War Crimes: Converging Narratives from 'The Good War,'" *Journal of American History* 94, no. 4 (2008): 1, 164–83; Barbara Grimm, "Lynchmorde an alliierten Fliegern im Zweiten Weltkrieg," in *Deutschland im Luftkrieg: Geschichte und Erinnerung,* ed. Dietmar Süß (Munich: R. Oldenbourg, 2007), 71–84; Ralf Blank, "Wartime Daily Life and the Air War on the Home Front," in *Germany and the Second World War,* ed. Jörg Echternkamp (Oxford: Oxford University Press, 2008), 371–478. First published in German as *Das Deutsche Reich und der Zweite Weltkrieg* (Deutsche Verlags-Anstalt: Munich, 2004).

268 | Notes to pages 140–48

16. Niall Ferguson, "Prisoner Taking and Prisoner Killing in the Age of Total War: Towards a Political Economy of Military Defeat," *War in History* 11, no. 2 (2004): 148–92; Keith Lowe, *Savage Continent: Europe in the Aftermath of World War II* (London: Penguin Books, 2012), 122.

17. Barrett Tillman, *Whirlwind: The Air War against Japan, 1942–1945* (New York: Simon & Schuster, 2010); Edward Frederick Langley Russell, *The Knights of Bushido: A History of Japanese War Crimes during World War II* (Skyhorse Publishing, 2008); Timothy Long Francis, "'To Dispose of the Prisoners': The Japanese Executions of American Aircrew at Fukuoka, Japan during 1945," *Pacific Historical Review* 66, no. 4 (1997): 469–501.

Conclusion

1. Overy, *Blood and Ruins*, 664–65.

2. For more information on grass-roots perpetrators becoming killers, see Christopher R. Browning, *Ordinary Men: Reserve Police Battalion 101 and the Final Solution* (New York: Penguin, 2001).

3. MacMillan, *War*, 46.

4. Barak Kushner, *The Thought War: Japanese Imperial Propaganda* (Honolulu: University of Hawai'i Press, 2007), 111.

5. Kevin T Hall, *Terror Flyers: The Lynching of American Airmen in Nazi Germany* (Bloomington: Indiana University Press, 2021), 94–96.

6. For more information on German soldiers' obedience to authority and peer pressure, see Christopher Browning, *Ordinary Men: Reserve Police Battalion 101 and the Final Solution in Poland* (New York: Harper Perennial, 1992).

7. James Waller, *Becoming Evil: How Ordinary People Commit Genocide and Mass Killing* (Oxford: Oxford University Press, 2002), xvii.

8. For example, see Michel Paradis, *Last Mission to Tokyo: The Extraordinary Story of the Doolittle Raiders and Their Final Flight for Justice* (New York: Simon & Schuster, 2020); Margaret MacMillan, *War: How Conduct* Shaped Us (London: Profile Books Ltd), 2021.

9. Daniel Hedinger, *Die Achse: Berlin, Rom, Tokio, 1919–1946* (Munich: C.H. Beck, 2021), 414.

10. Hedinger, *Die Achse,* 363. See also Joseph Goebbels's diary, June 5, 1943, and April 1, 1944; Peter Herde, *Die Achsenmächte: Japan und die Sowjetunion, Japanische Quellen zum Zweiten Weltkrieg (1941–1945)* (Berlin: De Gruyter, 2018), 267.

11. Margaret McMillan, *War: How Conduct Shaped US* (London: Profile Books, 2021), 179.

12. McMillan, *War*, 69–74.

13. Isabel V. Hull, *A Scrap of Paper: Breaking and Making International Law during the Great War* (Ithaca: Cornell University Press, 2014), 278.

14. Hull, *A Scrap of Paper*, 291–92.

Notes to pages 148–50 | 269

15. Hedinger, *Die Achse,* 179, 418. The term was originally used in Rüdiger Hachtmann, *Das Wirtschaftsimperium der Deutschen Arbeitsfront, 1933–1945* (Göttingen: Wallstein Verlag, 2012), 488.

16. MacMillan, *War,* 203.

17. See for example Sarah Kovner, "A War of Words: Allied Captivity and Swiss Neutrality in the Pacific, 1941–45," *Diplomatic History* 41, no. 4 (2017): 719–46; Karl Hack and Kevin Blackburn, *Forgotten Casualties in Japanese-Occupied Asia* (New York: Routledge, 2008), 13–14.

18. Karl Hack and Kevin Blackburn, *Forgotten Casualties in Japanese-Occupied Asia* (New York: Routledge, 2008), 13–14.

19. Hedinger, *Die Achse,* 351, 354. See also Jochen Thies, *Architekt der Weltherrschaft: Die "Endziele" Hitlers* (Düsseldorf: Droste Verlag, 1980), 144.

20. Hedinger, *Die Achse,* 334–36.

21. Georg Hoffmann, *Fliegerlynchjustiz: Gewalt gegen abgeschossene alliierte Flugzeugbesatzungen, 1943–1945* (Paderborn: Shöningh, 2015), 189; Hall, *Terror Flyers,* 227.

22. "Entwicklung der Mannheimer Bevölkerung von 1600 bis 2019," accessed November 10, 2021, https://www.marchivum.de/de/stadtgeschichte/mannheim -wissen/bevoelkerungszahlen.

23. Lindbergh, *The Wartime Journals of Charles Lindbergh,* 943.

24. Hedinger, *Die Achse,* 361–62.

25. McMillan, *War,* 285; Carl von Clausewitz, *Vom Kriege* (Anaconda Verlag, 1834), 23.

Bibliography

Archival Documents

NATIONAL ARCHIVES AND RECORDS ADMINISTRATION (NARA)

"Allied flyers shot in their parachute over Denmark," October 17, 1944, Case No. 8-0, Records of the Office of the Judge Advocate General (Army), NARA RG 153, Entry 143, Box 119.

Deputy Theater Judge Advocate's Office (Europe), War Crimes Branch, Records of the Office of the Judge Advocate General (Army), RG 153; Entry 143; Box 155–510; National Archives at College Park, College Park, MD.

Deputy Theater Judge Advocate's Office (Far East), War Crimes Branch, Records of the Office of the Judge Advocate General (Army), RG 153; Entry 1021; Box 1–200; National Archives at College Park, College Park, MD.

"Escape and Evasion in China," Office of Naval Intelligence (ONI) Review, Headquarters US Naval Group China, Records of the Office of the Chief of Naval Operations, Naval Group China Papers, NARA, RG 38, Entry NHC-75, Box 37.

Escape and Evasion Reports, NARA, RG 498, Entry 133–34, Boxes 516–73.

Letter to Lt. Col. I. Davidson, AAG Liaison (British), War Crimes Branch, USFET, March 20, 1946, NARA, RG 153, Entry 143, Box 512.

Office of Strategic Services (OSS) Research & Analysis Report (R & A) No. 1113.65, June 24, 1944, Page 3, RG 153/Entry 143/Box 235/ Case 12-239-4. NARA, College Park, MD.

Records of the Judge Advocate General (Army) RG 153, Entry 132, Box 6, NARA; International Military Tribunal for the Far East, *Judgement*, Tokyo, November 1948, vol. 2, 1099.

AIR FORCE HISTORICAL RESEARCH AGENCY (MAXWELL AFB)

Escape Intelligence Bulletin Number 4. November 13, 1944. From the Fifteenth Air Force Headquarters. Maxwell AFB, Montgomery, Al.

Escape Intelligence Report—Escape Information Series A-13. "Late Information on Dulag Luft." June 21, 1944. Maxwell AFB, Montgomery, Al.

Escape Intelligence Bulletin. November 22, 1944. Fifteenth Air Force Headquarters. Maxwell AFB, Montgomery, Al.

272 | Bibliography

Special Escape Bulletin No. 16a. Fifteenth Air Force Headquarters. Maxwell AFB, Montgomery, Al.

THE NATIONAL ARCHIVES (LONDON)

Proceedings of a General Court Martial on October 10, 1940, against Brigadier Guy Percy Lumsden Drake-Brockman, National Archives, Kew, WO 71/1048.

ONLINE SOURCES

"Amerika als Zerrbild europäische Lebensordnung," Schulungs-Unterlage Nr. 19 (Der Reichsorganisationsleitung der NSDAP, Hauptschulungsamt, 1942), http://research.calvin.edu/german-propaganda-archive/hsa01.htm.

Army Air Forces Statistical Digest, World War II, Office of Statistical Control— December 1945, http://www.dtic.mil/dtic/tr/fulltext/u2/a542518.pdf.

Army Battle Casualties and Non-battle Deaths in World War II—Final Report: December 7, 1941—December 31, 1946, Statistical and Accounting Branch Office of the Adjutant General, 1950, https://archive.org/details/ArmyBattle CasualtiesAndNonbattleDeathsInWorldWarIiPt1Of4.

Bulletin No. 10, "Activities of Japanese Military Personnel Contrary to the Laws of War," April 29, 1944. http://www.mansell.com/pow_resources/camplists /other/rabaul/Beheading_of_airman_1943-03-29_ATIS_2533-2534.pdf.

"Convention Relative to the Treatment of Prisoners of War," Geneva, July 27, 1929, https://ihl-databases.icrc.org/ihl/INTRO/305.

"Demonstrates how B-29 Flyer was beheaded," March 17, 1946, Library of Congress, Prints and Photographs Division, NYWT&S Collection [LC-DIG-ppmsca-19024], https://www.loc.gov/item/2008677724/.

"Europe and Amerika: Fehlerquellen im Aufbau des amerikanischen Volkstums," Schulungs-Unterlage Nr. 18 (Der Reichsorganisationsleitung der NSDAP, Hauptschulungsamt, 1942), http://research.calvin.edu/german-propaganda -archive/hsa02.htm.

General William Mitchell, "Report on Inspection of United States Possessions in the Pacific and Java, Singapore, India, Siam, China and Japan," October 24, 1924, William Mitchell Papers, United States Air Force Academy Archives (USAFA), Colorado Springs, Colorado.

"Missing Air Crew Reports (MACRs), 1942–1947, NARA, RG 92, Records of the Office of the Quartermaster General, 1774–1985, https://catalog.archives.gov /id/305256.

"Recognizing and commending American airmen held as political prisoners at the Buchenwald concentration camp during World War II for their service, bravery, and fortitude." H.Con.Res.95 — 105th Congress (1997–1998), https:// www.congress.gov/bill/105th-congress/house-concurrent-resolution/95/text.

"Special Operations: AAF Aid to European Resistance Movements, 1943–1945," US Air Force Historical Study No. 121. Air Historical Office Headquarters, Army Air Forces, June 1947, 133–34.

Bibliography | 273

"The International Military Tribunal for the Far East," https://imtfe.law.virginia
.edu; "International Criminal Court Database," https://www.legal-tools.org.
*Trials of War Criminals Before the Nuremberg Military Tribunals under Control
Council Law No. 10, Volume XI* (United States Government Printing Office:
Washington, 1960), https://www.loc.gov/rr/frd/Military_Law/pdf/NT_war
-criminals_Vol-II.pdf.

"United Nations War Crimes Commission Archives," Human Rights after Hitler.
http://www.unwcc.org/unwcc-archives/.

US v. Charlotte V. Battalo et al., Dachau, Germany, January 31, 1946, https://www
.legal-tools.org/doc/c82d6d/pdf.

US v. Christian Blum et al., Dachau, Germany, August 15–24, 1946, https://www
.legal-tools.org/doc/e8010a/pdf.

US v. Franz Strasser, Dachau, Germany, August 24, 1945, https://www.legal-tools
.org/doc/366a58/pdf.

US v. Harukei Isayama et al., Shanghai, China, August 10, 1946, https://www.legal
-tools.org/doc/030cf4/pdf.

US v. Ido Turchi, Leghorn, Italy, June 3–5, 1947, https://www.legal-tools.org/doc
/8f4cef/pdf/.

US v. Kajuro Aihara et al., October 11–December 29, 1948, Yokohama, Japan.
https://www.legal-tools.org/doc/475ba3/pdf.

US v. Karl Kirchner et al., Dachau, Germany, March 8, 1948, https://www.legal
-tools.org/doc/28b788/pdf.

US v. Masataka Kaburagi et al., February 14, 1946, Shanghai, China, https://www
.legal-tools.org/doc/0b3a09/pdf.

US v. Max Schmid, May 19, 1947, Dachau, Germany, https://www.legal-tools.org
/doc/446866/pdf.

US v. Noboru Seki, August 18–22, 1947, https://www.legal-tools.org/doc/01e350
/pdf.

US v. Otto F. Isenmann et al., Dachau, Germany, May 28, 1947, https://www.legal
-tools.org/doc/065426/pdf.

US v. Shichisaburo Yajima, June 24, 1947, https://www.legal-tools.org/doc/0bd
5d8/pdf.

US v. Sentaro Yamaguchi et al., September 5, 1946, Manila, Philippines, https://
www.legal-tools.org/doc/e4538a/pdf.

US v. Shigeru Sawada et al., Vol. III, https://www.legal-tools.org/doc/abc3de
/pdf.

US v. Toyokazu Hikita et al., March 1–2, 1948, https://www.legal-tools.org/doc
/f0b9e9/pdf.

US v. Yoshio Tachibana et al., August 15, 1946, Marianas Islands, Guam, https://
www.legal-tools.org/doc/cd1a09/pdf.

"Yokohama—Philipps-Universität Marbug—ICWC," https://www.uni-marburg.de
/icwc/forschung/2weltkrieg/yokohama?order=source&order_type=asc&offset
=0&count=100&name=&id_trial.

274 | Bibliography

Secondary Literature

Abrahams, Ray. *Vigilant Citizens: Vigilantism and the State.* Malden: Polity Press, 1998.

Alpert, Michael. *Franco and the Condor Legion: The Spanish Civil War in the Air.* London: Bloomsbury, 2019.

Ambrose, Stephan. *The Wild Blue.* New York: Touchstone, 2001.

Ardery, Philip. *Bomber Pilot: A Memoir of World War II.* Lexington: University Press of Kentucky, 1996.

Arendt, Hannah. *Eichmann in Jerusalem: A Report on the Banality of Evil.* New York: Penguin Books, 2006.

———. *The Origins of Totalitarianism.* New York: Harcourt, 1973.

Arnold, Jörg, *The Allied Air War and Urban Memory: The Legacy of Strategic Bombing in Germany.* Cambridge: Cambridge University Press, 2016.

Ault, Brian, and William Brustein. "Joining the Nazi Party: Explaining the Political Geograpaphy of NSDAP Membership, 1925–1933." *American Behavioral Scientist* 41, no. 9 (1998): 1,304–23.

Bachrach, Susan, and Steven Luckert. *State of Deception: The Power of Nazi Propaganda.* US Holocaust Memorial Museum, 2009.

Bajohr, Frank, and Michael Weldt, eds. *Volksgemeinschaft: Neue Forschungen zur Gesellschaft des Nationalsozialismus.* Frankfurt: Fischer Verlag, 2009.

Baldoli, Claudia, Andrew Knapp, and Richard Overy, eds. *Bombing, States and Peoples in Western Europe, 1940–1945.* London: Continuum, 2011.

Baldoli, Claudia, and Andrew Knapp. *Forgotten Blitzes: France and Italy under Allied Air Attack, 1940–1945.* New York: Continuum, 2012.

Bandura, Albert. "Moral Disengagement in the Perpetration of Inhumanities." *Personality and Social Psychology Review* 3 (1999): 193–209.

———. "Selective Activation and Disengagement of Moral Control." *Journal of Social Values* 46, no. 1 (1990): 27–46.

———. "Social Cognitive Theory of Moral Thought and Action." In *Handbook of Moral Behavior and Development*, vol. 1, edited by W. M. Kurtines and J. L. Gewirtz. Hillsdale: Erlbaum, 1991.

Barber, Melanie. "Tales of the Unexpected: Glimpses of Friends in the Archives of Lambeth Palace." *Journal of the Friends Historical Society* 61, no. 2 (2007): 87–123.

Barclary, David E., and Elisabeth Glaser-Schmidt, eds. *Transantlantic Images and Perceptions: Germany and America since 1776.* New York: Cambridge University Press, 1997.

Bard, Mitchell G. *Forgotten Victims: The Abandonment of Americans in Hitler's Camps.* Oxford: Westview Press, 1994.

Barnett, Victoria J. *Bystanders: Conscience and Complicity during the Holocaust.* London: Praeger, 1999.

Bartov, Omer. *Germany's War and the Holocaust: Disputed Histories.* Ithaca and London: Cornell University Press, 2003.

Bibliography | 275

————. *The Holocaust: Origins, Implementation, Aftermath.* New York: Routledge, 2000.

Bazyler, Michael J., and Frank M. Tuerkheimer. *Forgotten Trials of the Holocaust.* New York: NYU Press, 2014.

Beck, Levitt Clinton, Jr. *Fighter Pilot.* Los Angeles: Wetzel Publishing Company, 1946.

Becker, P. *Dem Täter auf der Spur: Eine Geschichte der Kriminalistik.* Darmstadt: Wissenschaftliche Buchgesellschaft, 2005.

Beer, Edith H., and Susan Dworkin. *The Nazi Officer's Wife: How One Jewish Woman Survived the Holocaust.* New York: William Morrow, 2015.

Benz, Wolfgang, and Walter H. Pehle, eds. *Encyclopedia of German Resistance to the Nazi Movement.* New York: Continuum, 1997.

Berg, Manfred, and Simon Wendt, eds. *Globalizing Lynching History: Vigilantism and Extralegal Punishment from an International Perspective.* New York: Palgrove Macmillan, 2011.

Bergerson, Andrew Stuart. *Ordinary Germans in Extraordinary Times: The Nazi Revolution in Hildesheim.* Bloomington: Indiana University Press, 2004.

Bernstein, David. *Rehabilitating Lochner: Defending Individual Rights against Progressive Reform.* Chicago: University of Chicago Press, 2011.

Bialas, Wolfgang. *Moralische Ordnungen des Nationalsozialismus.* Göttingen: Vandenhoeck and Ruprecht, 2014.

Bialas, Wolfgang, and Lothar Fritze, eds. *Ideologie und Moral im Nationalsozialismus.* Göttingen: Vandenhoeck and Ruprecht, 2014.

Bird, Tom. *American POWs in World War II: Forgotten Men Tell Their Stories.* Westport, CT: Praeger, 1992.

Bishop, Patrick. *Fighter Boys: The Battle of Britain, 1940.* London: Penguin, 2004.

Blank, Ralf. "Wartime Daily Life and the Air War on the Home Front." In *Germany and the Second World War,* edited by Jörg Echternkamp, 371–478. Oxford: Clarendon Press, 2008.

Bloxham, Donald. "British War Crimes Trial Policy in Germany, 1945–1957: Implementation and Collapse." *Journal of British Studies* 42, no. 1 (January 2003): 91–118.

Boberach, Heinz, ed. *Meldungen aus dem Reich: Die geheimen Lageberichte des sicherheitsdienstes der SS 1938–1945,* no. 15. Herrsching: Pawlak, 1984.

Böhler, Jochen. "Die Wehrmacht im Vernichtungskrieg." In *Naziverbrechen: Täter, Taten, Bewältigungsversuche,* edited by Martin Cüppers, Jürgen Matthäus, and Andrej Angrick. Darmstadt: WBG, 2013.

Bodson, Herman. *Agent for the Resistance: A Belgian Saboteur in World War II.* College Station: Texas A&M University Press, 1994.

————. *Downed Allied Airmen and Evasion of Capture: The Role of Local Resistance Networks in World War II.* London: McFarland and Company, 2005.

Bradley, James. *Flyboys: A True Story of Courage.* New York: Back Bay Books, 2004.

276 | Bibliography

Brode, Patrick. *Casual Slaughters and Accidental Judgments: Canadian War Crimes Prosecutions, 1944–1948.* Toronto: University of Toronto Press, 1997.

Broszat, Martin. *The Hitler State.* New York: Routledge, 2013.

———. "Zur Struktur der NS-Massenbewegung." *Vierteljahrshefte für Zeitgeschichte* 1 (1983): 52–76.

Brown, Courtney. "The Nazi Vote: A National Ecological Stud." *American Political Science Review* 76, no. 2 (1982): 285–302.

Brown, Harold H., and Marsha S. Bordner. *Keep Your Airspeed Up: The Story of a Tuskegee Airman.* Tuscaloosa: University of Alabama Press, 2017.

Browning, Christopher. *Ordinary Men: Reserve Police Battalion 101 and the Final Solution in Poland.* New York: Harper Perennial, 1992.

Brundage, W. Fitzhugh. *Lynching in the New South: Georgia and Virginia, 1880–1930.* Chicago: University of Illinois Press, 1993.

Bryant, William Cullen. "Thanatopsis," *North America Review.* 1817.

Bunyak, Dawn Trimble. *The Last Mission: A World War II Prisoner in Germany.* Norman: University of Oklahoma Press, 2003.

Buscher, Frank M. *The US War Crimes Trial Program in Germany, 1946–1955.* New York: Greenwood Press, 1989.

Burgess, Colin. *Destination: Buchenwald.* Australia: Kangaroo Press, 1995.

Bytwerk, Randall L. *Bending Spines: The Propagandas of Nazi Germany and the German Democratic Republic.* East Lansing: Michigan State University Press, 2004.

Caine, Philip D. *Aircraft Down: Evading Capture in WWII Europe.* Washington, DC: Brassey's, 1997.

———. *Eagles of the RAF: The World War II Eagle Squadrons.* Washington, DC: National Defense University Press, 1991.

Carrigan, William D., and Christopher Waldrep, eds. *Swift to Wrath: Lynching in Global Historical Perspective.* Charlottesville: University of Virginia Press, 2013.

Casey, Donald E. *To Fight for My Country, Sir: Memoirs of a 19-Year-Old B-17 Navigator Shot Down in Nazi Germany and Imprisoned in the WWII "Great Escape" Prison Camp.* Chicago: Sterling Cooper, 2009.

Charlesworth, Lorie. "Forgotten Justice: Forgetting Law's History and Victims' Justice in British 'Minor' War Crime Trials in Germany 1945–48." *Amicus Curiae* 74 (2008): 2–10.

Chickering, Roger, Stig Förster, and Bernd Greiner, eds. *A World at Total War: Global Conflict and the Politics of Destruction, 1937–1945.* Cambridge: Cambridge University Press, 2005.

Chickering, Roger, and Stig Förster. *Great War, Total War: Combat and Mobilization on the Western Front.* Cambridge: Cambridge University Press, 2000.

Childers, Thomas, ed. *The Formation of the Nazi Constituency, 1919–1933.* New York: Routledge, 1986.

Childers, Thomas. *Wings of Morning.* New York: Addison-Wesley Publishing Company, 1995.

Bibliography | 277

Chorbajian, L., and G. Shirinian, eds. *Studies in Comparative Genocide*. New York: St. Martin's Press, 1999.

Clutton-Brock, Oliver. *Footprints on the Sands of Time: RAF Bomber Command Prisoners of War in Germany, 1939–1945*. London: Grub Street, 2003.

———. *RAF Evaders: The Comprehensive Story of Thousands of Escapers and Their Escape Lines, Western Europe, 1940–1945*. London: Grub Street, 2009.

Conrad, Robert Edgar. *Sandino: The Testimony of a Nicaraguan Patriot, 1921–1934*. Princeton: Princeton University Press, 1990.

Corum, James S. *The Luftwaffe: Creating the Operational Air War, 1918–1940*. Lawrence: University Press of Kansas, 1997.

Cooke, James J. *Billy Mitchell*. London: Lynne Riennner Publishing, 2002.

Counts, Major Laura C. "Were They Prepared? Escape and Evasion in Western Europe, 1942–1944." Thesis. Air Command and Staff College: Montgomery: 1986.

Crane, Conrad C. *Bombs, Cities and Civilians: American Airpower Strategy in World War II*. Lawrence: University Press of Kansas, 1993.

Crawley, Aidan. *Escape from Germany, 1939–1945: Methods of Escape Used by RAF Airmen During World War II*. London: The Stationery Office, 2001.

Creydt, Detlef. *Luftkrieg im Weserbergland*. Holzminden: Jörg Mitzkat, 2007.

Culberson, William C. *Vigilantism: Political History of Private Power in America*. New York: Greenwood Press, 1990.

Cull, Brian. *Buffaloes Over Singapore: RAF, RAAF, RNZAF and Dutch Brewster Fighters in Action over Malaya and the East Indies, 1941–1942*. Haverton: Casemate, 2003.

Dams, Carsten. *Staatsschutz in der Weimarer Republik, Die Überwachung und Bekämpfung der NSDAP durch die preußische politische Polizei von 1928–1932*. Marburg: Tectum Verlag, 2002.

Darling, Ian. *Amazing Airmen: Canadian Flyers in the Second World War*. Toronto: Dundurn Press, 2009.

Darlow, Steve. *Flightpath to Murder: Death of a Pilot Officer*. Somerset: Haynes Publishing, 2009.

Davies, Norman. *Europe at War, 1939–1945: No Simple Victory*. New York: Macmillan, 2006.

Dawes, Gavin. *Prisoners of the Japanese: POWs of World War II in the Pacific*. New York: William Morrow and Company, 1996.

Deutsch, Morton. "Psychological Roots of Moral Exclusion." *Journal of Social Issues* 46, no. 1 (1990): 21–25.

de Grazia, Victoria. *Irresistible Empire: America's Advance through Twentieth-Century Europe*. Cambridge: Harvard University Press, 2005.

de Mildt, Dick. *In the Name of the People: Perpetrators of Genocide in the Reflection of their Post-War Prosecution in West Germany: The "Euthanasia" and "Aktion Reinhard" Trial Cases*. The Hague: Martinus Nijhoff, 1996.

de Zayas, Alfred M. *The Wehrmacht Warcrimes Bureau, 1939–1945*. Rockport: Picton Press, 1989.

278 | Bibliography

Diggins, John P. *Mussolini and Fascism: The View from America*. Princeton: Princeton University Press, 1972.

Dittmann, Fred. *Mitteldeutschland im Luftkrieg 1944 und 1945*. Lutherstadt Eisleben: Henke, 2001.

Dorr, Robert F., and Thomas D. Jones. *Hell Hawks!: The Untold Story of the American Fliers Who Savaged Hitler's Wehrmacht*. Minneapolis: Zenith Press, 2008.

Douhet, Giulio. *The Command of the Air* (translated by Dino Ferrari). Washington, DC: US Government Printing Office, 1998.

Dower, John W. *War Without Mercy*. New York: Pantheon Books, 1997.

Drez, Ronald J. *Predicting Pearl Harbor: Billy Mitchell and the Path to War*. New York: Pelican Press, 2017.

Drooz, Daniel B. *American Prisoners of War in German Death, Concentration, and Slave Labor Camps*. Toronto: Edwin Mellen Press, 2004.

Dryden, Charles W. *A-Train: Memoirs of A Tuskegee Airman*. Tuscaloosa: University of Alabama Press, 1997.

Eiber, Ludwig, and Robert Sigel. *Dachauer Prozesse: NS-Verbrechen vor amerikanischen Militärgerichten in Dachau 1945-48*. Göttingen: Wallstein Verlag, 2007.

Eisner, Peter. *The Freedom Line*. New York: Harper Collins, 2004.

Ellwood, David. *The Shock of American: Europe and the Challenge of the Century*. New York: Oxford University Press, 2012.

Elster, Jon, ed. *Retribution and Reparation in the Transition to Democracy*. Cambridge: Cambridge University Press, 2006.

Emsley, Clive. *Soldier, Sailor, Beggerman, Thief: Crime and the British Armed Services since 1914*. Oxford: Oxford University Press, 2013.

Evans, Richard J. *Rituals of Retribution: Capital Punishment in Germany 1600-1987*. Oxford: Oxford University Press, 1996.

———. *The Third Reich at War*. New York: Penguin Press, 2009.

Fahrenwald, Ted. *Bailout over Normandy: A Flyboy's Adventures with the French Resistance and Other Escapades in Occupied France*. Philadelphia and Oxford: Casemate Publishers, 2012.

Falter, Jürgen W. "'Anfälligkeit' der Angestellten—'Immunität' der Arbeiter? Mythen über die Wähler der NSDAP." *Historical Social Research/Historische Sozialforschung*. Supplement, no. 25, Zur Soziographie des Nationalsozialismus. Studien zu den Wählern und Mitgliedern der NSDAP (2013): 90-110.

———. "Die 'Märzgefallenen' von 1933. Neue Forschungsergebnisse zum sozialen Wandel innerhalb der NSDAP-Mitgliedschaft während der Machtergreifungsphase." *Historical Social Research/Historische Sozialforschung*. Supplement, no. 25, Zur Soziographie des Nationalsozialismus. *Studien zu den Wählern und Mitgliedern der NSDAP* (2013): 280-302.

———. "The Young Membership of the NSDAP Between 1925 and 1933. A Demographic and Social Profile." *Historical Social Research/Historische*

Bibliography | 279

Sozialforschung. Supplement, No. 25, Zur Soziographie des Nationalsozialismus. *Studien zu den Wählern und Mitgliedern der NSDAP* (2013): 260–79.

———. "Wählerbewegungen zur NSDAP 1924–1933. Methodische Probleme—Empirisch abgesicherte Erkenntnisse—Offene Fragen." *Historical Social Research/Historische Sozialforschung.* Supplement, no. 25, Zur Soziographie des Nationalsozialismus. *Studien zu den Wählern und Mitgliedern der NSDAP* (2013): 49–89.

Fangemann, H., U. Reifner, and N. Steinborn. *Parteisoldaten: Die Hamburger Polizei im 3. Reich.* Hamburg: VSA Verlag, 1987.

Fatz, M. *Vom Staatsschutz zum Gestapo-Terror: Politische Polizei in Bayern in der Endphase der Weimarer Republik und der Anfangsphase der nationalsozialistischen Diktatur.* Würzburg: Echter Verlag, 1995.

Ferguson, Niall. *The Pity of War: Explaining World War I.* New York: Basic Books, 1998.

———. "Prisoner Taking and Prisoner Killing in the Age of Total War: Towards a Political Economy of Military Defeat." *War in History* 11, no. 2. (2004). 148–92.

Fischer, Klaus P. *Hitler and America.* Philadelphia: University of Pennsylvania Press, 2011.

Fitzgerald, David Scott, and David Cook-Martin. *Culling the Masses: The Democratic Origins of Racist Immigration Policy in the Americas.* Cambridge: Harvard University Press, 2014.

Flammer, Philip M. "Dulag Luft: The Third Reich's Prison Camp for Airmen." *Aerospace Historian* 19, no. 2 (1972): 58–65.

Fleisher, Michael L. "'Sungusungu': State-sponsored Village Vigilante Groups among the Kuria of Tanzania." *Journal of the Institutional African Institute* 70, no. 2 (2000): 209–28.

Flint, Colin. "Electoral Geography and the Social Construction of Space: The Example of the Nazi Party in Baden, 1924–1932." *GeoJournal* 51, no. 3 (2000): 145–56.

———. "Forming Electorates, Forging Spaces: The Nazi Party Vote and the Social Construction of Space." *American Behavioral Scientist* 41, no. 9 (1998): 1282–1300.

———. "A Timespace for Electoral Geography: Economic Restructuring, Political Agency and the Rise of the Nazi Party." *Political Geography* 20 (2001): 301–29.

Förster, Stig, and Jörg Nagler, eds. *On the Road to Total War: The American Civil War and the German Wars of Unification, 1861–1871.* Cambridge: Cambridge University Press, 1997.

Foot, Michael R. D., and J. M. Langley. *MI-9: Escape and Evasion, 1939–1945.* Boston: Little, Brown and Company, 1979.

Foy, David A. *For You the War Is Over: American Prisoners of War in Nazi Germany.* New York: Stein and Day, 1984.

280 | Bibliography

Francis, Timothy Long. "'To Dispose of the Prisoners': The Japanese Executions of American Aircrew at Fukuoka, Japan, during 1945." *Pacific Historical Review* 66, no. 4 (1997): 469–501.

Fredette, Raymond H. *The Sky on Fire: The First Battle of Britain, 1917–1918.* Tuscaloosa: University of Alabama Press, 2007.

Fredrickson, George. *Racism: A Short History.* Princeton: Princeton University Press, 2002.

Freeman, Gregory A. *The Last Mission of the Wham Bam Boys: Courage, Tragedy, and Justice in World War II.* New York: Palgrave MacMillan, 2011.

———. *The Forgotten 500: The Untold Story of the Men Who Risked All for the Greatest Rescue Mission in World War II.* New York: NAL Caliber, 2007.

Frei, Norbert. *Adenauer's Germany and the Nazi Past: The Politics of Amnesty and Integration.* New York: Columbia University Press, 2002.

Friedhoff, Herman. *Requiem for the Resistance: The Civilian Struggle against Nazism in Holland and Germany.* London: Bloomsbury, 1988.

Friedlander, Henry. *The Origins of Nazi Genocide: From Euthanasia to the Final Solution.* Chapel Hill: University of North Carolina Press, 1995.

Friedrich, Jörg. *The Fire: The Bombing of Germany, 1940–1945.* Translated by Allison Brown. New York: Columbia University Press, 2006.

Fry, Helen. *MI9: A History of the Secret Service for Escape and Evasion in World War Two.* New Haven: Yale University Press, 2020.

Funk, Albert. *Polizei und Rechtsstaat: Die Entwicklung des staatlichen Gewaltmonopols in Preußen 1848–1914.* Frankfurt/Main: Campus Verlag, 1986.

Galbreath, D. L., and Léon Jéquier. *Lehrbuch der Heraldik.* Frankfurt am Main: Krüger, 1977.

Garraty, John. "The New Deal, National Socialism, and the Great Depression." *American Historical Review* 78 (1973): 907–44.

Garrett, Stephen. *Ethics and Airpower in World War II: The British Bombing of German Cities.* London: Palgrave Macmillan, 1993.

Gatewood, Betty, and Jean Belkham. *Kriegie 7956: A World War II Bombardier's Pursuit of Freedom.* Shippensburg: Burd Street Press, 2001.

Gazit, Nir. "State-sponsored Vigilantism: Jewish Settlers' Violence in the Occupied Palestinian Territories." *Sociology* 49, no. 3 (2015): 438–54.

Geary, Dick. "Who Voted for the Nazis?" *History Today* 48 (November 10, 1998).

Geck, Stefan. *Dulag Luft/Auswertestelle West: Vernehmungslager der Luftwaffe für westalliierte Kriegsgefangene im Zweiten Weltkrieg.* Frankfurt am Main: Peter Lang, 2008.

Gellately, Robert. *Backing Hitler: Consent and Coercion in Nazi Germany.* Oxford: Oxford University Press, 2002.

———. *The Gestapo and German Society: Enforcing Racial Policy, 1933–1945.* Oxford: Clarendon Press, 1990.

Bibliography | 281

———. *Hitler's True Believers: How Ordinary People Became Nazis.* Oxford: Oxford University Press, 2020.

Goedde, Petra. *GIs and Germans: Culture, Gender, and Foreign Relations, 1945–1949.* New Haven: Yale University Press, 2003.

Goldhagen, Daniel. *Hitler's Willing Executioners: Ordinary Germans and the Holocaust.* New York: Vintage Books, 1997.

Goldstein, Daniel M. "Flexible Justice: Neoliberal Violence and 'Self-Help' Security in Bolivia." In *Global Vigilantes*, edited by D. Pratten and A. Sen, 239–66. London: Hurst, 2005.

Goll, Nicole-Melanie, and Georg Hoffmann. "'Terrorflieger': Deutungen und Wahrnehmungen des strategischen Luftkrieges der Alliierten in der nationalsozialistischen Propaganda am Beispiel der sogenannten Fliegerlynchjustiz." *Journal for Intelligence, Propaganda, and Security Studies* 1 (2011): 71–86.

Gorashko, Alexander. *Survival: An American Airman's Miracle Survival and POW Ordeal during WWII.* Self-published memoir, 2011.

Gotterbarm, Otmar. *Die Abgestürzten: Der Luftkrieg am 25. und 26. Februar 1944 über Augsburg und der Schwäbischen Alb.* Bad Schussenried: Gerhard Hess Verlag, 2013.

Graf, Christoph. *Politische Polizei zwischen Demokratie und Diktatur: Die Entwicklung der preußischen Politischen Polizei vom Staatsschutzorgan der Weimarer Republik zum Geheimen Staatspolizeiamt des Dritten Reiches.* Berlin: Colloquium Verlag, 1983.

Grimm, Barbara. "Lynchmorde an alliierten Fliegern im Zweiten Weltkrieg." In *Deutschland im Luftkrieg: Geschichte und Erinnerung*, edited by Dietmar Süß, 71–84. Munich: R. Oldenbourg Verlag, 2007.

Greene, Joshua M. *Justice at Dachau: The Trials of an American Prosecutor.* New York: Broadway Books, 2003.

Grill, Johnpeter Horst, and Robert L. Jenkins. "The Nazis and the American South in the 1930s: A Mirror Image?" *Journal of Southern History* 58, no. 4 (November 1992): 667–94.

Gross, Leonard. *The Last Jews in Berlin.* New York: Caroll and Graf: 1999.

Guillemin, Jeanne. *Hidden Atrocities: Japanese Germ Warfare and American Obstruction of Justice at the Tokyo Trial.* New York: Columbia University Press, 2017.

Günther, Lothar. *Missionen und Schicksale im Luftkrieg über Südwest-Thüringen 1944/45.* Untermaßfeld: Wehry-Verlag, 2015.

Hachtmann, Rüdiger. *Das Wirtschaftsimperium der Deutschen Arbeitsfront, 1933–1945.* Göttingen: Wallstein Verlag, 2012.

Hälbig, Eberhard, and Rainer Lämmerhirt. *Luftkrieg im Raum Eisenach, Gotha, Hainich, Werratal, Thüringer Wald: 1943–1945.* Bad Langensalza: Verlag Rockstuhl, 2012.

282 | Bibliography

Hack, Karl, and Kevin Blackburn, eds. *Forgotten Captives in Japanese Occupied Asia.* New York: Routledge, 2008.

Halbrainer, Heimo, and Martin F. Polaschek. *Kriegsverbrecherprozesse in Österreich: Eine Bestandsaufnahme.* Graz: Clio Verlag, 2003.

Hall, Kevin T. "Downed American Flyers: Forgotten Casualties of Axis Atrocities in World War II." *Journal of Perpetrator Justice* 4, no. 1 (2021): 192–221.

———. "The Flyer Trials: Seeking Justice for Lynchjustiz Committed against American Airmen during World War II." *War in History* 27, no. 3 (2020): 486–516.

———. "*Luftgangster* over Germany: The Lynching of American Airmen in the Shadow of the Air War." *Journal Historische Sozialforschung/Historical Social Research* 43, no. 2 (June 2018): 277–312.

———. *Terror Flyers: The Lynching of American Airmen in Nazi Germany.* Bloomington: Indiana University Press, 2021.

Hampe, Erich. *Der Zivile Luftschutz im Zweiten Weltkrieg.* Frankfurt am Main: Bernard and Gräfe Verlag für Wehrwesen, 1963.

Haney, Craig, Curtis Banks, and Philip Zimbardo. "Interpersonal Dynamics in a Simulated Prison." *International Journal of Criminology and Penology* 1 (1973): 69–97.

Hanley, Fiske, III. *Accused War Criminal: An American Kempei Tai Survivor.* New York: Brown Books, 2020.

Hassel, Katrin. *Kriegsverbrechen vor Gericht: Die Kriegsverbrecherprozesse vor Militärgerichten in der britischen Besatzungszone unter dem Royal Warrant vom 18. Juni 1945.* Baden Baden: Nomos, 2009.

Heberer, Patricia, and Jürgen Matthäus, eds. *Atrocities on Trial: Historical Perspectives on the Politics of Prosecuting War Crimes.* Lincoln: University of Nebraska Press, 2008.

Hedinger, Daniel. *Die Achse: Berlin, Rom, Tokio, 1919–1946.* Munich: C. H. Beck, 2021.

Herde, Peter. *Die Achsenmächte: Japan und die Sowjetunion, Japanische Quellen zum Zweiten Weltkrieg (1941–1945).* Berlin: De Gruyter, 2018.

Herf, Jeffrey. *The Jewish Enemy: Nazi Propaganda during World War II and the Holocaust.* Cambridge: Harvard University Press, 2006.

———. *Nazi Propaganda for the Arab World,* (New Haven: Yale University Press, 2010.

Hessel, Peter. *The Mystery of Frankenberg's Canadian Airman.* Toronto: James Lorimer & Company, 2005.

Hilberg Raul. *The Destruction of the European Jew.* New York: Holmes and Meier, 1985.

Hilton, Fern Overbey. *The Dachau Defendents: Life Stories from Testimony and Documents of the War Crimes Prosecutions.* North Carolina: McFarland, 2004.

Bibliography | 283

Hingston, Michael. *Into Enemy Arms: The Remarkable True Story of a German Girl's Struggle against Nazism, and Her Daring Escape with the Man She Loved*. London: Grub Street, 2006.

Hodges, Andrew Gerow, Jr., and Denise George. *Behind Nazi Lines: My Father's Heroic Quest to Save 149 World War II POWs*. New York: Penguin, 2015.

Hoffmann, Georg. *Fliegerlynchjustiz: Gewalt gegen abgeschossene alliierte Flugzeugbesatzungen 1943–1945*. Paderborn: Ferdinand Schoeningh: 2015.

———. "The Lynching of Airmen at Graz 1945: War Crimes Committed against Allied Airmen in the Context of Violence Control and Post-War-Trials." In *From the Industrial Revolution to World War II in Easter Central Europe*, edited by Marija Wakounig and Karl Ruzicic-Kessler, 207–25. Münster: LIT Verlag, 2011.

Horne, John, and Alan Kramer. *German Atrocities, 1914: A History of Denial*. New Haven: Yale University Press, 2001.

Hull, Isabel V. *A Scrap of Paper: Breaking and Making International Law during the Great War*. Ithaca: Cornell University Press, 2014.

Hurt, John J., and Steven E. Sidebotham, eds. *Odyssey of A Bombardier: The POW Log of Richard M. Mason*. Newark: University of Delaware Press, 2014.

Iredale, Will. *The Kamikaze Hunters: Fighting for the Pacific, 1945*. London: Macmillan, 2015.

Jackson, Daniel. *Fallen Tigers: The Fate of America's Missing Airmen in China During World War II*. Lexington: University Press of Kentucky, 2021.

Jefferson, Alexander, and Lewis H. Carlson. *Red Tail Captured, Red Tail Free: The Memoirs of a Tuskegee Airman and POW*. New York: Fordham University Press, 2005.

Johann, A. E. *Das Land ohne Herz: Eine Rise ins unbekannte Amerika*. Berlin: Deutscher Verlag, 1942.

Johnson, Eric A. *Nazi Terror: The Gestapo, Jews, and Ordinary Germans*. New York: Basic Books, 2000.

———. *Urbanization and Crime: Germany, 1871–1914*. Cambridge: Cambridge University Press, 1995.

Johnson, Eric A., and Eric H. Monkkonen, eds. *The Civilization of Crime: Violence in Town and Country Since the Middle Ages*. Urbana: University of Illinois Press, 1996.

Johnson, Eric A., and Karl-Heinz Reuband. *What We Knew: Terror, Mass Murder, and Everyday Life in Nazi Germany*. New York: Basic Books, 2005.

Johnston, Les. "What Is Vigilantism?" *British Journal of Criminology* 3, no. 2 (1996): 220–36.

Jones, Heather. *Violence against Prisoners of War in the First World War*. Cambridge: Cambridge University Press, 2011.

Jones, Syd. *Before and beyond the Niihau Zero: The Unlikely Drama of Hawaii's Forbidden Island Prior to, during and after the Pearl Harbor Attack*. Merritt Island: Signum Ops, 2014.

284 | Bibliography

Jost, Armin, and Stefan Reuter, eds. *Dillingen im Zweiten Weltkrieg: Eine Dokumentation der Dillinger Geschichtswerkstatt.* Dillingen, 2002.

Kakel, Carroll P. *The American West and the Nazi East: A Comparative and Interpretive Perspective.* New York: Palgrave Macmillan, 2011.

Kallis, Aristotle A. *Nazi Propaganda and the Second World War.* New York: Palgrave Macmillan, 2005.

Kater, Michael H. *The Nazi Party: A Social Profile of Members and Leaders, 1919– 1945.* Cambridge: Harvard University Press, 1983.

Katznelson, Ira. *When Affirmative Action Was White: An Untold History of Racial Inequality in Twentieth-Century America.* New York: Norton, 2005.

Kerr, E. Bartlett. *Surrender and Survival: The Experience of American POWs in the Pacific, 1941–45.* New York: William Morrow, 1985.

Kershaw, Ian. *The End: The Defiance and Destruction of Hitler's Germany, 1944– 1945.* New York: Penguin Books, 2012.

———. *Hitler: A Biography.* New York: W. W. Norton, 2010.

———. *Hitler, The Germans, and the Final Solution.* New Haven: Yale University Press, 2009.

———. *The "Hitler Myth": Image and Reality in the Third Reich.* Oxford: Oxford University Press, 2001.

———. *The Nazi Dictatorship: Problems & Perspectives of Interpretation.* Oxford: Oxford University Press, 2000.

King, Dan. *The Last Zero Fighter: Firsthand Accounts from WWII Japanese Naval Pilots.* Rockwell: Pacific Press, 2012.

Kirsch, Thomas G., and Tilo Grätz, eds. *Domesticating Vigilantism in Africa.* Rochester: James Currey, 2010.

Klee, Ernst, Willi Dressen, and Volker Riess. *"The Good Old Days:" The Holocaust as Seen by Its Perpetrators and Bystanders.* Translated by Deborah Burnstone. New York: Konecky & Konecky, 1991.

Kleiner, Sam. *The Flying Tigers: The Untold Story of the American Pilots Who Waged a Secret War against Japan.* New York: Viking, 2018.

Klemp, Stefan. *Freispruch für das "Mordbataillon": Die NS-Ordnungspolizei und die Nachkriegsjustiz.* Münster: Lit Verlag, 1998.

Knell, Hermann. *To Destroy a City: Strategic Bombing and Its Human Consequences in World War II.* Cambridge: De Capo Press, 2003.

Kochavi, Arieh J. *Prelude to Nuremberg: Allied War Crimes Policy and the Question of Punishment.* Chapel Hill: University of North Carolina Press, 1998.

Koller, Hans-Peter. *Der Fliegermord von Freienseen: Eine Dokumentation.* Anabas-Verlag: Giessen, 1995.

Koonz, Claudia. *Mothers in the Fatherland: Women, the Family and Nazi Politics* (New York: St. Martin's Press, 1987).

———. *The Nazi Conscience.* Cambridge: Harvard University Press, 2003.

Kovner, Sarah. *Prisoners of the Empire: Inside Japanese POW Camps.* Cambridge: Harvard University Press, 2020.

Bibliography | 285

———. "A War of Words: Allied Captivity and Swiss Neutrality in the Pacific, 1941–1945." *Diplomatic History* 41, no. 4 (2017): 719–46.

Kramer, Alan. *Dynamic of Destruction: Culture and Mass Killings in the First World War.* Oxford: Oxford University Press, 2007.

Krueger, Lloyd O. *Come Fly with Me: Experiences of an Airman in World War II.* New York: Excell, 2000.

Krug-Richter, B., and H. Reinke, eds. *Von rechten und unrechten Taten: Zur Kriminalitätsgeschichte Westfalens von der frühen Neuzeit bis zum 20. Jahrhundert.* Münster: Aschendorffsche Verlagsbuchhandlung (Westfälische Forschungen, vol. 54), 2004.

Kühl, Stefan. *The Nazi Connection: Eugenics, American Racism and German National Socialism.* New York and Oxford: Oxford University Press, 1994.

Kushner, Barak. *The Thought War: Japanese Imperial Propaganda.* Honolulu: University of Hawai'i Press, 2007.

LaGrandeur, Philip. *We Flew, We Fell, We Lived: Stories from RCAF Prisoners of War and Evaders, 1939–1945.* St. Catharines: Vanwell Publishing, 2006.

Leary, William M. *Fueling the Fires of Resistance: Army Air Forces Special Operations in the Balkans during World War II.* Air Force History and Museums Program, 2015.

Leitz, Christian, ed. *The Third Reich.* London: Blackwill, 1999.

Leonard, Thomas C. *Illiberal Reformers: Race, Eugenics, and American Economics in the Progressive Era.* Princeton: Princeton University Press, 2016.

Lichtenstein, Heiner. *Himmlers grüne Helfer: Die Schutz- und Ordnungspolizei im Dritten Reich.* Cologne: Bund-Verlag, 1990.

Linck, Stefan. *Der Ordnung verpflichtet. Deutsche Polizei, 1933–1949: Der Fall Flensburg.* Paderborn: Ferdinand Schöningh, 2000.

Lindbergh, Charles A. *The Wartime Journals of Charles Lindbergh.* New York: Harcourt Brace Jovanovich, 1970.

Lipset, Seymour Martin. *Political Man: The Social Bases of Politics.* New York: Anchor, 1963.

Longden, Sean. *To the Victor the Spoils: Soldiers' Lives From D-Day to VE-Day.* Gloucestershire: Arris Books, 2004.

Longerich, Peter. *"Davon haben wir nichts gewusst!"* Munich: Siedler Verlag, 2006.

Lounsbury, Dave E., ed. *Military Medical Ethics,* vol. 2. Office of the Surgeon General, Department of the Army, 2003.

Lovenheim, Barbara. *Survival in the Shadows: Seven Hidden Jews in Hitler's Berlin.* New York: Open Road, 2002.

Lowe, Keith. *Savage Continent: Europe in the Aftermath of World War II.* London: Penguin, 2013.

Lower, Wendy. *Hitler's Furies: German Women in the Nazi Killing Fields.* New York: Houghton Mifflin Harcourt Publishing, 2013.

Lulushi, Albert. *Donovan's Devils: OSS Commandos Behind Enemy Lines—Europe, World War II.* New York: Arcade Publishing, 2016.

286 | Bibliography

MacArthur, Brian. *Surviving the Sword: Prisoners of the Japanese, 1942–45*. London: Abacus, 2006.

Macaulay, Neill. *The Sandino Affair*. Durham: Duke University Press, 1985.

Macintyre, Ben. *Rogue Heroes: The History of the SAS, Britain's Secret Special Forces Unit That Sabotaged the Nazis and Changed the Nature of War*. New York: Crown, 2016.

MacKenzie, S. P. "The Treatment of Prisoners of War in World War II." *Journal of Modern History* 66, no. 3 (1994): 487–520.

MacMillan, Margaret. *War: How Conduct Shaped Us*. London: Profile Books Ltd, 2021.

Maga, Timothy. "'Away from Tokyo': The Pacific Islands War Crimes Trials, 1945–1949." *Journal of Pacific History* 36, no. 1: (2001): 37–50.

Makepeace, Clare. *Captives of War: British Prisoners of War in Europe in the Second World War*. Cambridge: Cambridge University Press, 2017.

Mallmann, Klaus-Michael. "Nationalsozialistische Gewaltverbrechen im Deutschen Reich." In *NS-Gewaltherrschaft: Beiträge Zur Historischen Forschung und Juristischen Aufarbeitung*, edited by Alfred Gottwaldt, Norbert Kampe, and Peter Klein, 202–14. Berlin: Hentrich, 2005.

Matteson, Thomas T. (Commander, USCG). "Report No. 128: An Analysis of the Circumstances Surrounding the Rescue and Evacuation of Allied Aircrew Men from Yugoslavia, 1941–1945." Air War College–Maxwell Air Force Base, Alabama: April 1977.

McFarland, Stephan L., and Wesley Phillips Newton. *To Command the Sky: Battle for Air Superiority over Germany, 1942–1944*. Washington, DC: Smithsonian Institution Press, 1991.

McLaughlin, J. Kemp. *The Mighty Eighth in WWII: A Memoir*. Lexington: University Press of Kentucky, 2006.

McManus, John C. *Deadly Sky: The American Combat Airmen in World War II*. New York: Nal Caliber, 2016.

Mears, Dwight S. "Interned or Imprisoned?: The Successes and Failures of International Law in the Treatment of American Internees in Switzerland, 1943–45." Dissertation, University of North Carolina at Chapel Hill, 2012.

Milgram, Stanley. *Obedience to Authority: An Experimental View*. London: Tavistock Publications, 1974.

Miller, Donald L. *Masters of the Air: America's Bomber Boys Who Fought the Air War against Nazi Germany*. New York: Simon & Schuster, 2006.

Miller, Scott. *Agent 110: An American Spymaster and the German Resistance in WWII*. New York: Simon and Schuster, 2017.

Mitchell, William. *Winged Defense: The Development and Possibilities of Modern Air Power—Economic and Military*. Tuscaloosa: University of Alabama Press, 2010.

Mommsen, Hans. "Der Nationalsozialismus: Kumulative Radikalisierung und Selbstzerstörung des Regimes." In *Meyers Enzyklopädisches Lexikon*, vol. 16. Mannheim: Inter Alia, 1976, 785–90.

Bibliography | 287

Moore, Bob, and Kent Fedorowich, eds. *Prisoners of War and Their Captors in World War II*. Oxford: Berg, 1996.

Morgan, Robert, and Ron Powers. *The Man Who Flew the Memphis Belle: Memoir of a WWII Bomber Pilot*. New York: Penguin Books, 2001.

Morris, Rob. *Untold Valor: Forgotten Stories of American Bomber Crews over Europe in World War II*. Washington, DC: Potomac Books, 2006.

Morrow, James D. *Order with Anarchy: The Laws of War as an International Institution*. Cambridge: Cambridge University Press, 2014.

Moser, Joseph F. *A Fighter Pilot in Buchenwald*. Bellingham: Edens Veil Media, 2009.

Mosse, George L. *Toward a Final Solution: A History of European Racism*. New York: Howard Fertig, 1997.

Moye, J. Todd. *Freedom Flyers: The Tuskegee Airmen of World War II*. Oxford: Oxford University Press, 2010.

Mrazek, Robert J. *To Kingdom Come: An Epic Saga of Survival in the Air War over Germany*. New York: Penguin Books, 2010.

Murray, Williamson, and Allan R. Millett, eds. *Military Innovation in the Interwar Period*. New York: Cambridge University Press, 2009.

Narayanaswami, Karthik. "Analysis of Nazi Propaganda: A Behavioral Study." https://blogs.harvard.edu/karthik/files/2011/04/HIST-1572-Analysis-of-Nazi -Propaganda-KNarayanaswami.pdf.

Neitzel, Sönke, and Harald Welzer. *Soldaten: Protokolle vom Kämpfen, Töten und Sterben*. Frankfurt am Main: Fischer Verlage, 2011.

Neliba, Günter. *Lynchjustiz an amerikanischen Kriegsgefangenen in der Opelstadt Rüsselsheim (1944): Rekonstruktion einer der ersten Kriegsverbrecher-Prozesse in Deutschland nach Prozessakten (1945–1947)*. Frankfurt: Brandes and Apsel, 2000.

Nielsen, Major General Andreas L. "The Collection and Evaluation of Intelligence for the German Air Force High Command: Karlsruhe Study." Montgomery, AL: Maxwell Air Force Base, 1955. K113.107-17168.

Niethammer, Lutz. *Die Mitläuferfabrik: Die Entnazifizierung am Beispiel Bayerns*. Berlin: J. H. W. Dietz Verlag, 1982.

Nigro, Augusto. *Wolfsangel: A German City on Trial, 1945–48*. Washington, DC: Brassey's Inc., 2000.

Noakes, Jeremy, ed. *Nazism, 1919–1945*. Vol. 4: *The German Home Front in World War II*. Exeter: University of Exeter Press, 1998.

Noble, Bernard, and E. R. Perkins, eds. *Foreign Relations of the United States: Diplomatic Papers, 1942, General; The British Commonwealth; the Far East*. Vol. 1. Washington, DC: US Government Printing Office, 1960.

Noggle, Anne. *A Dance with Death: Soviet Airwomen in World War II*. College Station: Texas A&M University Press, 1994.

Nolzen, Armin. "The NSDAP, the War, and German Society." In *Germany and the Second World War*, edited by Jörg Echternkamp, 111–206. Oxford: Clarendon Press, 2008.

288 | Bibliography

Nourse, Victoria. *In Reckless Hands:* Skinner v. Oklahoma *and the Near Triumph of American Eugenics.* New York: Norton, 2008.

Norwood, Stephan H. *The Third Reich in the Ivory Tower.* New York: Cambridge University Press, 2009.

O'Donnell, Patrick K. *Operatives, Spies, and Saboteurs: The Unknown Story of the Men and Women of World War II's OSS.* New York: Free Press, 2004.

O'Loughlin, John. "The Electoral Geography of Weimar Germany: Explanatory Spatial Data Analysis (ESPDA) of Protestant Support for the Nazi Party." *Society for Political Methodology* 10, no. 3 (2002): 217–43.

O'Loughlin, John, Colin Flint, and Luc Anselin. "The Geography of the Nazi Vote: Context, Confession, and Class in the Reichstag Election of 1930." *Annals of the Association of American Geographers* 84, no. 3 (1994): 351–80.

Olsen, Lynne, and Stanley Cloud. *A Question of Honor: The Kosciuszko Squadron: Forgotten Heroes of World War II.* New York: Vintage, 2003.

Ottis, Sherri Greene. *Silent Heroes: Downed Airmen and the French Underground.* Lexington: University of Kentucky Press, 2001.

Overy, Richard. *The Air War: 1939–1945.* Washington, DC: Potomac Books, 2005.

———. *Blood and Ruins: The Great Imperial War, 1931–1945.* London: Allen Lane, 2021.

———. *The Bombing and the Bombed: Allied Air War over Europe, 1940–1945.* New York: Viking, 2013.

Paradis, Michel. *Last Mission to Tokyo: The Extraordinary Story of the Doolittle Raiders and Their Final Flight for Justice.* New York: Simon and Schuster, 2020.

Pardo, Italo. *Morals of Legitimacy: Between Agency and the System.* New York: Berghahn, 2000.

Paris, John. *Pappy's War: A B-17 Gunner's World War II Memoir.* Bennington, VT: Merriam Press, 2005.

Paul, Gerhard, and Klaus-Michael Mallmann, eds. *Die Gestapo im Zweiten Weltkrieg: Heimatfront und "besetztes" Europa.* Darmstadt: Wissenschaftliche Buchgesellschaft, 2000.

Paul, Gerhard, and Klaus-Michael Mallmann, eds. *Die Gestapo: Mythos und Realität.* Darmstadt: Wissenschaftliche Buchgesellschaft, 1995.

Pawley, William D. *The Extraordinary Life of the Adventurer, Entrepreneur, and Diplomat Who Cofounded the Flying Tigers.* Washington, DC: Potomac Books, 2012.

Pendas, Devin O., Mark Roseman, and Richard F. Wetzell, eds. *Beyond the Racial State: Rethinking Nazi Germany.* Cambridge: Cambridge University Press, 2017.

Pennington, Reina. *Wings, Women, and War: Soviet Airwomen in World War II Combat.* Lawrence: University Press of Kansas, 2001.

Peukert, Detlev J. K. *Inside Nazi Germany: Conformity, Opposition, and Racism in Everyday Life.* New Haven and London: Yale University Press, 1987.

Bibliography | 289

Piccigallo, Philip R. *The Japanese on Trial: Allied War Crimes Operations in the East, 1945–1951*. Austin: University of Texas Press, 1979.

Pitchfork, Graham. *Shot Down and on the Run: The RCAF and Commonwealth Aircrews Who Got Home from behind Enemy Lines, 1940–1945*. Toronto: The Dundurn Group, 2003.

Pratten, David, and Atreyee Sen, eds. *Global Vigilantes: Anthropological Perspectives on Justice and Violence*. London: Hurst, 2007.

Proctor, Tammy M. *Civilians in a World at War, 1914–1918*. New York: New York University Press, 2010.

Redding, Tony. *Bombing Germany: The Final Phase: The Destruction of Pforzheim and the Closing Months of Bomber Command's War* (South Yorkshire: Pen & Sword Books, 2015).

Reifner, U., and B.-R. Sonnen, eds. *Strafjustiz und Polizei im Dritten Reich*. Frankfurt am Main: Campus Verlag, 1984.

Remarque, Erich. *All Quiet on the Western Front*. New York: Fawcett Books, 1987.

Reuter, Stefan. "'Operation No. 351'—Der 11. Mai 1944: Die Fliegende Festung des amerikanischen Piloten Marion Holbrook." In *Dillingen im Zweiten Weltkrieg: Eine Dokumentation der Dillinger Geschichtswerkstatt*. Dillingen, 2002.

Richard, Oscar G., III. *Kriegie: An American POW in Germany*. Baton Rouge: Louisiana State University Press, 2000.

Richards, Dennis, *The Royal Air Force 1939–1945*. Volume I: *The Fight at Odds*. London: H.M. Stationery Office, 1954.

Richey, Robert J. *My Brother Glenn: A Prisoner of the Gestapo during World War II*. Bloomington: Author House, 2011.

Riedel, Durwood. "The US War Crimes Tribunals at the Former Dachau Concentration Camp: Lessons for Today." *Berkeley Journal of International Law* 24, no. 2 (2006): 554–609.

Rochlitz, Imre, and Joseph Rochlitz. *Accident of Fate: A Personal Account, 1938–1945*. Waterloo: Wilfrid Laurier University Press, 2011.

Rodger, Daniel. *Atlantic Crossings: Social Politics in a Progressive Age*. Cambridge: Harvard University Press, 1998.

Rückerl, Adalbert. *The Investigation of Nazi Crimes, 1945–1978*. Translated by Derek Rutter. New York: Archon Books, 1980.

———. *NS-Verbrechen vor Gericht: Versuch einer Vergangenheitsbewältigung*. Heidelberg: C.F. Müller Juritischer Verlag, 1984.

Rumpf, Hans. *The Bombing of Germany*. Translated by Edward Fitzgerald. New York: Holt, Rinehart and Winston, 1962.

Russell, Edward Frederick Langley. *The Knights of Bushido: A History of Japanese War Crimes during World War II*. Skyhorse Publishing, 2008.

Saarpfalz-Blätter für Geschichte und Volkskunde. Sankt Ingbert: Westpfälzische Verlagsdrückerei,1999/3.

290 | Bibliography

Sagan, Günther. *Ostthüringen im Bombenkrieg, 1939–1945*. Fulda: Michael Imhof Verlag, 2013.

Sams, Richard. "Inferno on the Omotesando: The Great Yamanote Air Raid." *The Asia-Pacific Journal* 13 (21), no. 1, May 25, 2015. https://apjjf.org/-Richard -Sams/4321/article.pdf. Translated by Richard Sams from original: "Escaping by Bicycle." In *The Great Tokyo Air Raids—Records of War Damages*. Vol. 2 Association for Recording Tokyo Air Raids, 1973.

Samuel, Wolfgang W. E. *The War of Our Childhood: Memories of World War II*. Jackson: University Press of Mississippi, 2002.

Schaffer, Ronald. *Wings of Judgement: American Bombing in World War II*. Oxford: Oxford University Press, 1985.

Schivelbach, Wolfgang. *Three New Deals: Reflections on Roosevelt's America, Mussolini's Italy, and Hitler's Germany, 1933–1939*. Trans. Jefferson Chase. New York: Metropolitan, 2006.

Schmidt-Lux, Thomas. "Vigilantismus als politische Gewalt. Eine Typologie." *BEHEMOTH: A Journal of Civilization*, Verlag Walter de Gruyter, no. 6.1 (2013): 99–117.

Schmiechen-Ackermann, Detlef. *"Volksgemeinschaft": Mythos, wirkungsmächtige soziale Verheißung oder soziale Realität im "Dritten Reich"?* Paderborn: Ferdinand Schöningh Verlag, 2012.

Sebald, W. G. *On the Natural History of Destruction*. Translated by Anthea Bell. New York: Random House, 1999.

Seidler, Franz W. *Deutscher Volkssturm: Das letzte Aufgebot 1944/45*. München: Herbig Verlag, 1989.

Seidler, Franz W., and Alfred M. de Zayas, eds. *Kriegsverbrechen in Europa und im Nahen Osten im 20. Jahrhundert*. Hamburg: Verlag E. S. Mittler & Sohn GmbH, 2002.

Šelhaus, Edi. *Evasion and Repatriation: Slovene Partisans and Rescued American Airmen in World War II*. Manhatten: Sunflower University Press, 1993.

Sheridan, Jerome W. *Airmen in the Belgian Resistance: Gerald E. Sorensen and the Transatlantic Alliance*. Jefferson, NC: McFarland & Company Inc., 2014.

Siebenborn, Kerstin. *Der Volkssturm im Süden Hamburgs 1944/45*. Hamburg: Verlag Verein für Hamburgische Geschichte, 1988.

Siemens, Daniel. *Stormtroopers: A New History of Hitler's Brownshirts*. New Haven: Yale University Press, 2017.

Sigel, Robert. *Im Interesse der Gerechtigkeit: Die Dachauer Kriegsverbrecherprozesse 1945–1948*. Frankfurt: Campus Verlag, 1992.

Simmons, Kenneth W. *Kriegie*. New York: Thomas Nelson & Sons, 1960.

Simon, Marie Jalowicz. *Underground in Berlin: A Young Woman's Extraordinary Tale of Survival in the Heart of Nazi Germany*. New York: Bay Back Books, 2016.

Sirianni, Ralph E., and Patricia I. Brown. *POW#3959: Memoir of a World War II Airman Shot Down over Germany*. Jefferson, NC: McFarland and Company, Inc., 2006.

Bibliography | 291

Sollbach, Gerhard E. *Sie wollten die Heimat schützen.* Bochum: Project Verlag, 2010.

Sommers, Stan. *The European Story.* WI: American Ex-Prisoners of War, Inc., July 1980.

Snyder, Steve. *Shot Down: The True Story of Pilot Howard Snyder and the Crew of the B-17 Susan Ruth.* Sea Breeze Publishing, 2015.

Snyder, Timothy. *Bloodlands: Europe Between Hitler and Stalin.* New York: Basic Books, 2012.

Spencer, Otha Cleo. *Flying the Hump: Memories of an Air War.* College Station: Texas A&M University Press, 1992.

Spencer, Elaine Glovka. *Police and the Social Order in German Cities: The Düsseldorf District, 1848–1914.* DeKalb: Northern Illinois University Press, 1992.

Spurlock, Paul E. "The Yokohama War Crimes Trials: The Truth about a Misunderstood Subject." *American Bar Association Journal* 36, no. 5 (1950): 387–89, 436–37.

Stahl, Hans-Günther. *Der Luftkreig über dem Raum Hanau: 1939–1945.* Hanau: VDS Verlagsdruckerei Schmidt, 2015.

Stargardt, Nicholas. *The German War: A Nation Under Arms, 1939–1945.* New York: Basic Books, 2015.

Staub, Ervin. "Genocide and Mass Killings: Origins, Preventions, Healing and Reconciliation." *Political Psychology* 12, no. 2 (2000): 367–83.

———. *The Roots of Evil: The Origins of Genocide and Other Group Violence.* New York: Cambridge University Press, 1989.

Steber, Martina, and Bernhard Gotto, eds. *Visions of Community in Nazi Germany: Social Engineering and Private Lives.* Oxford: Oxford University Press, 2014.

Stelbrink, Wolfgang. *Die Kreisleiter der NSDAP in Westfalen und Lippe Versuch einer Kollektivbiographie.* Münster: Nordrhein-Westfälischen Staatsarchiv Münster, 2003.

Stout, Jay A. *Fighter Group: The 352nd "Blue-Nosed Bastards" in World War II.* Mechanicsburg, PA: Stackpole Books, 2018.

Strobl, Gerwin. *Bomben auf Oberdonau: Luftkrieg und Lynchmorde an alliierten Fliegern im "Heimatgau des Führers."* Linz: Oberösterreichisches Landesarchiv, 2014.

———. *The Germanic Isle: Nazi Perceptions of Britain.* Cambridge: Cambridge University Press, 2000.

Süß, Dietmar, and Winfried Süß. *Das 'Dritte Reich': Eine Einführung.* Munich: Pantheon Verlag, 2008.

Süß, Dietmar. *Tod aus der Luft.* München: Siedler Verlag, 2011.

Tanaka, Yuki. *Hidden Horrors: Japanese War Crimes in World War II.* Boulder: Westview Press, 1997.

Tanner, Stephan. *Refuge from the Reich: American Airmen and Switzerland During World War II.* New York: Sarpedon, 2000.

292 | Bibliography

Thies, Jochen. *Architekt der Weltherrschaft: Die "Endziele" Hitlers*. Düsseldorf: Droste Verlag, 1980.

Thurner, Paul W., Andre Klima, and Helmut Küchenhoff. "Agricultural Structure and the Rise of the Nazi Party Reconsidered." *Political Geography* 44 (2015): 50–63.

Thurston, Robert W. *Lynching: American Mob Murder in Global Perspective*. Farnham: Ashgate, 2011.

Tillman, Barrett. *Whirlwind: The Air War against Japan, 1942–1945*. New York: Simon & Schuster, 2010.

Todorov, Tzvetan. *Facing the Extreme: Moral Life in the Concentration Camp*. New York: Henry Holt, 1996.

Toliver, Raymond F. *The Interrogator: The Story of Hanns Joachim Scharff, Master Interrogator of the Luftwaffe*. New York: Schiffer Publishing, 1997.

Tooze, Adam. *The Deluge: The Great War, American, and the Remaking of the Global Order*. New York: Penguin, 2014.

Totani, Yuma. *Justice in Asia and the Pacific Region, 1945–1952: Allied War Crimes Prosecutions*. New York: Cambridge University Press, 2015.

Tremble, Lee, and Jeremy Dronfield. *Beyond the Call: The True Story of One World War II Pilot's Covert Mission to Rescue POWs on the Eastern Front*. New York: Penguin, 2015.

Tsang, Jo-Ann. "Moral Rationalization and the Integration of Situational Factors and Psychological Processes in Immoral Behavior." *Review of General Psychology* 6, no. 1 (2002): 34–35.

Tyas, Stephan. *SS-Major Horst Kopkow: From the Gestapo to British Intelligence*. London: Fonthill, 2017.

Ueberschär, Gerd R. *Der Nationalsozialismus vor Gericht*. Frankfurt am Main: Fischerverlag, 1999.

Ute, Stiepani. "Die Dachauer Prozesse und Ihre Bedeutung im Rahmen der Alliierten Strafverfolgung von NS-Verbrechen." In *Der Nationalsozialismus vor Gericht: Die Allliierten Prozesse gegen Kriegsverbrecher und Soldaten 1943–1952*, ed. Gerd R. Ueberschaer, 227–35. Frankfurt Am Main: Fischer Verlag, 1999.

von Benda-Beckmann, Bas. *A German Catastrophe? German Historians and the Allied Bombings, 1945–2010*. Amsterdam: Amsterdam University Press, 2010.

von Clausewitz, Carl. *Vom Kriege*. Anaconda Verlag, 1834.

von Wrochem, Oliver, ed. *Repressalien und Terror: "Vergeltungsaktionen" im deutsch besetzten Europa 1939–1945*. Paderborn, Ferdinand Schöningh, 2017.

Vourkoutiotis, Vasilis. *Prisoners of War and the German High Command: The British and American Experience*. New York: Palgrave Macmillan, 2003.

Wachsmann, Nichlaus. *Hitler's Prisons: Legal Terror in Nazi Germany*. New Haven: Yale University Press, 2004.

Wagner, Patrick. *Hitlers Kriminalisten: Die deutsche Kriminalpolizei und der Nationalsozialismus*. München: C. H. Beck, 2002.

Bibliography | 293

———. *Volksgemeinschaft ohne Verbrecher: Konzeptionen und Praxis der Kriminalpolizei in der Zeit der Weimarer Republik und des Nationalsozialismus.* Hamburg: Hans Christians Verlag, 1996.

Waiss, Walter. *Chronik Kampfgeschwader Nr. 27. Boelcke, Band VII.* Aachen: Helios Verlag, 2010.

Waller, James. *Becoming Evil: How Ordinary People Commit Genocide and Mass Killing.* Oxford: Oxford University Press, 2002.

Walzer, Michael, *Just and Unjust Wars.* New York: Basic Books, 1977.

Watt, George. *Escape from Hitler's Europe: An American Airman behind Enemy Lines.* Lexington: University Press of Kentucky, 1990.

Weber, Edwin Ernst, ed. *Opfer des Unrechts: Stigmatisierung, Verfolgung und Vernichtung von Gegnern durch die NS-Gewaltherrschaft an Fallbeispielen aus Oberschwaben.* Stuttgart: Jan Thorbeck Verlag, 2009.

Weinberg, Gerhard. *Hitler's Foreign Policy, 1933–1939: The Road to World War II.* New York: Enigma Books, 2010.

———. *A World at Arms: A Global History of World War II.* Cambridge: Cambridge University Press, 2005.

Weingartner, James J. "Americans, Germans, and War Crimes: Converging Narratives from 'the Good War.'" *Journal of American History* 94, no. 4 (2008): 1164–83.

Welch, David, ed. *Nazi Propaganda: The Power and the Limitations.* London: Routledge, 1983.

———. "Nazi Propaganda and the *Volksgemeinschaft*: Constructing a People's Community." *Journal of Contemporary History* 39, no. 2 (2004): 213–38.

———. *The Third Reich: Politics and Propaganda.* New York: Routledge, 1993.

———. *World War II Propaganda: Analyzing the Art of Persuasion during Wartime.* Santa Barbara: ABC-CLIO, 2017.

Welzer, Harald. *Täter: Wie aus ganz normalen Menschen Massenmörder warden.* Frankfurt am Main: Fischer Verlag, 2005.

Werle, Gerhard. *Justiz-Strafrecht und polizeiliche Verbrechensbekämpfung im Dritten Reich.* Berlin: de Gruyter, 1989.

Wernette, Dee R. "Explaining the Nazi Vote: The Findings and Limits of Ecological Analysis." Kean College of New Jersey, 1976. The Center for Research on Social Organizations, The University of Michigan, https://deepblue.lib.umich.edu /bitstream/handle/2027.42/50909/134.pdf?sequence=1.

Westricher Heimatblaetter Kusel. Landkreis Kusel: Heft 4/1995.

Wette, Wolfram, ed. *Zivilcourage. Empörte: Helfer und Retter aus Wehrmacht, Polizei und SS.* Frankfurt am Main: Fischer Taschenbuch Verlag, 2004.

Wetzell, Richard. *Inventing the Criminal: A History of German Criminology, 1880–1945.* Chapel Hill: University of North Carolina Press, 2000.

Whitlock, Flint. *Given Up for Dead.* New York: Basic Books, 2009.

Whitman, James Q. *Hitler's American Model: The United States and the Making of Nazi Race Law.* Princeton: Princeton University Press, 2017.

294 | Bibliography

———. "Of Corporation, Fascism, and the First New Deal." *American Journal of Comparative Law* 39 (1991): 747–78.

Whitmann, Rebecca. "Tainted Law: The West German Judiciary and the Prosecution of Nazi War Criminals." In *Atrocities on Trial: Historical Perspectives on the Politics of Prosecuting War Crimes*, ed. Patricia Heberer and Jürgen Matthäus, 211–30. Lincoln: University of Nebraska Press, 2008.

Widfeldt, Bo, and Rolph Wegmann. *Making for Sweden: The United States Army Air Force; the Story of Allied Airmen who Took Sanctuary in Neutral Sweden.* Walton-on-Thames (UK): Air Research Publications, 1998.

Wiesen, S. Johnathan. "American Lynching in the Nazi Imagination: Race and Extra-Legal Violence in 1930s Germany." *German History* 36, no. 1 (2017): 38–59.

Wildt, Michael. "'Volksgemeinschaft': Eine Antwort auf Ian Kershaw." Zeithistorische Forschungen/Studies in Contemporary History, online edition, 8: 2011. www.zeithistorische-forschungen.de/16126041-Wildt-2011.

Wilhelm, Friedrich. *Die Polizei im NS-Staat: Die Geschichte ihrer Organisation im Überblick.* Paderborn: Ferdinand Schöningh, 1997.

Williams, Kenneth Daniel. "The Saga of Murder Inc." World War II—Prisoners of War—Stalag Luft I. Accessed March 2021, http://www.merkki.com/images /murder%20inc%20german%20paper.jpg.

Wilson, Kevin. *Men of Air: The Doomed Youth of Bomber Command.* London: Phoenix Ebook, 2008.

Wingham, Tom. *Halifax Down!: On the Run from the Gestapo, 1944.* London: Grub Street, 2009.

Wolk, Bruce H. *Jewish Aviators in World War Two: Personal Narratives of American Men and Women.* Jefferson, NC: McFarland & Company, Inc., 2016.

Wood, Amy Louise. *Lynching and Spectacle: Witnessing Racial Violence in America, 1890–1940.* Chapel Hill: University of North Carolina Press, 2009.

Wyden, Peter. *Stella: One Woman's True Tale of Evil, Betrayal, and Survival in Hitler's Germany.* New York: Anchor Book, 1992.

Wylie, Neville. *Barbed Wire Diplomacy: Britain, Germany, and the Politics of Prisoners of War, 1939–1945.* Oxford: Oxford University Press, 2010.

Yavnai, Elisabeth M. "Military Justice: The US Army War Crimes Trials in Germany, 1944–47." Ph.D. Dissertation. University of London, 2007.

Zimbardo, Philip G. "The Psychology of Evil: A Situationist Perspective on Recruiting Good People to Engage in Anti-Social Acts." *Japanese Journal of Social Psychology* 11 (1995): 125–33.

Zimmer, Klaus. "Die Fliegende Festung "Solid Sender" des amerikanischen Piloten Merlin Chardi abgestuerzt am 25. Februar 1944 bei Alschbach." In *Saarpfalz: Blaetter fuer Geschichte und Volkskunde.* 1999/3.

Zimmer, Klaus, and Edward D. McKenzie. "Die Fliegende Festung bei Bubach im Ostertal abgestuerzt am 24. April 1944." In *Westricher Heimatblaetter Kusel.* Heft 4/1995.

Bibliography | 295

Zink, Harold. *The United States in Germany, 1944–55*. Princeton: D. Van Nostrand, 1957.

Newspapers

New York Times, "Color Line in Berlin," October 4, 1908.
New York Times, "Germany Protests Prager Lynching," June 13, 1918.
New York Times, "Bitter at Attacks on Germans Here," June 17, 1918.
New York Times, "President Demands that Lynchings End," July 27, 1918.
New York Times, "Germans Magnify Lynchings Here," September 9, 1918.
New York Times, "Lynchings Shock People of Berlin," January 20, 1919.
New York Times, "Germans Threaten Rhine Lynchings," February 8, 1923.
New York Times, "Fight for Doomed Negroes," June 1, 1931.
New York Times, "Ask Pardon for 8 Negroes," March 27, 1932.
New York Times, "Appeals in Germany in Scottsboro Case," May 11, 1932.
The Times (London), "Mr. Baldwin on Aerial Warfare—A Fear for the Future," November 11, 1932.
New York Times, "Hitlerism likened to Lynch Law Here," October 31, 1933.
New York Times, "British Gratified at Verdict on Fire," December 24, 1933.
New York Times, "All of Rebels Prisoners," July 26, 1934.
New York Times, "German Press Cites Race Hatred in US," August 30, 1935.
New York Times, "Methodists Find Liberty Ebbing," January 20, 1936.
New York Times, "Nazi Guards 'Lynch' Two for Attempting to Escape," December 11, 1939.
Daily Telegraph (London), "Prisoners Maltreated, Say Nazis," May 29, 1940.
Madera Tribune (California), "He Got Mad and Japs Died," December 17, 1941.
San Bernardino Sun, "Jap Aviator Stoned to Death by Woman," December 17, 1941.
Santa Cruz Evening News, "Strangest Tale of The War, Hawaiian Defends His Island," December 17, 1941.
Nippu Jiji (Honolulu), "Regarded with Suspicion," March 26, 1942.
Asahi Shimbun (Japan), "Evil Enemy Strafe School Yard," April 19, 1942.
Photo Weekly Magazine (Japan), "Plan of the Enemy Air Raid Ends in Complete Failure," April 29, 1942.
Nippu Jiji (Honolulu), "Hero of Niihau Has Letters Commending Him for Bravery." June 26, 1942.
Mandera Tribune, (California), "Japs Threat Torture for Yank Airmen," October 19, 1942.
Herald Tribune (New York), "Punishment of Prisoners: Nazis Considering 'Severer' Steps," October 23, 1942.
New York Times, "Jap Threat to Airmen," October 23, 1942.
New York Times, "Punishment of Prisoners: Nazis Considering 'Severer' Steps," October 23, 1942.

296 | Bibliography

Herald Tribune (New York), "Airmen from Tokyo Raid Captured?," October 24, 1942.

San Bernardino Sun, "Revenge Pledged for Executed Fliers: Barbaric Japs Murder Captive Tokyo Raiders," April 22, 1943.

Breckenridge American (Texas), "Believed Executed by Japs," April 23, 1943.

Madera Tribune (Texas), "Bombers to Blast Japan Near Future," April 23, 1943.

Army News (Australia), "Jap Murders of US Airmen Horrifies United Nations; Americans Angry," April 23, 1943.

Daily Illini (Urbana-Champaign), "Nation's Anger Rises at Jap Murders," April 23, 1943.

San Bernardino Sun, "Revenge Pledged for Executed Fliers," April 22, 1943.

Daily Illini, "World News at a Glance," April 23, 1943.

Daily Illini, "Nation's Anger Rises at Jap Murderers," April 23, 1943.

Daily Illini, "Public Aroused by Cold Blooded Executions of American Fliers," April 23, 1943.

Daily Illini, "Demands for Offensives against Japanese," April 23, 1943.

Breckenridge American (Texas), "Believed Executed by Japs," April 23, 1943.

Army News (Darwin, Australia), "Jap Murders of US Airmen Horrifies United Nations; Americans Angry," April 23, 1943.

San Bernardino Sun, "Churchill Vows RAF to Help Avenge Murder," April 24, 1943.

San Bernardino Sun, "German, Italy May Follow Jap Precedent in Executing Fliers," April 25, 1943.

Advocate (Burnie, Australia), "RAF Will Help to Avenge Murdered US Pilots," April 26, 1943.

New York Times, "Brother Barbarians: Germans Applaud Japanese Murders," April 26, 1943.

Examiner (Launceston, Australia), "Axis Barbarity May Extend," April 27, 1943.

New York Times, "Flyers' Execution Urged: Rome Newspapers Call for Death Penalty for Our Bombers," April 30, 1943.

Queensland Times (Ipswich, Australia), "Japanese Appeal to America to Stop Tokio Raids," April 30, 1943.

New York Times, "Flyers' Execution Urged: Rome Newspapers Call for Death Penalty for Our Bombers," April 30, 1943.

New York Times, "Aix Reprisals on Flyers Are Demanded by Gayda," May 4, 1943.

Evening Post, "Terror Raids," May 4, 1943.

Western Mail (Perth, Australia), "Allied Airmen Attacked Civilians in Italy," May 6, 1943.

Virginia Monocle, "US Flyers Executed," May 14, 1943.

San Bernardino Sun, "Natives Betray Allied Airmen, Nurses to Japs," May 16, 1943.

Brooklyn Daily Eagle, "Mobs Enraged Nazis Threatened Yank Airmen," October 21, 1943.

Daily Sun (San Bernardino), "Angry Germans Lynch American Bombing Fliers," October 22, 1943.

Bibliography | 297

New York Times, "Citizens Menaced Hamburg Bombers," October 22, 1943.

Mexia Weekly Herald (Texas), "Flier Tells How Yanks Lynched," October 22, 1943.

Daily Sun (San Bernardino), "Angry Germans Lynch American Bombing Fliers," October 22, 1943

Madera Tribune, "Germans Stone Yanks," October 28, 1943.

Völkischerbeobachter (Berlin), "USA—Luftgangster nennen sich selbst "'Mordverein,'" December 20, 1943.

New York Times, "Nazis Threaten Reprisal Trials on American and British Flyers," December 23, 1943.

Daily Banner (Greencastle, IN), "Death Facing Allied Airmen in Nazi Hands," December 24, 1943

The Daily Banner (Greencastle, Indiana), "Death Facing Allied Airmen in Nazi Hands," December 24, 1943.

The Jewish Criterion (Pittsburgh), "Jews Head List of US Fliers Facing Nazi Trials," January 7, 1944.

Das Schwarze Korps (Germany), "Die Gefahr des Amerikanismus," March 14, 1944.

The Jewish Criterion, "Goebbels Invites Attacks on Flyers," May 28, 1944.

The Times (London), "Goebbels on 'Murder' by Allied Airmen," May 28, 1944.

Goebbels, Joseph, "Ein Wort zum feindlichen Luftterror," *Völkischer Beobachter*, May 28, 1944.

The Palestine Post (Jerusalem), "Dr. Goebbels Incites to Murder," May 29, 1944.

Breckenridge American, "Five Yank Airmen Lynched by Nazis," May 30, 1944.

New York Times, "Flyers Reported Lynched in Reich," May 31, 1944.

Madera Tribune, "Huns Lynch Yank Airman," May 31, 1944.

New York Times, "Stimson Is Silent on Nazi 'Lynchings,'" June 2, 1944.

Army News (Darwin, Australia), "Nazis Wild Outburst on Airmen," June 4, 1944.

Jewish Criterion, "Urge Lynchings of Jewish Flyers," June 6, 1944.

Chicago Defender, "People and Places," June 10, 1944.

Mandera Tribune (California), "Tokyo Tells Yank Airmen Pay Penalty," July 15, 1944.

Mercury (Hobart, Australia), "Reprisals Urged Against Japs: Murder of Airmen Angers American Public," July 17, 1944.

New York Times, "Reprisal on Enemy Sought," July 20, 1944.

New York Times, "Nazis Rebuff Eden on Slain Captives," July 23, 1944.

New York Times, "Prussian Killings Pressed by Nazis: Himmler Also Reported to Have Ordered Slaying of Allied Flyers Downed in Reich," July 27, 1944.

Westdeutscher Beobachter (Eupen), "Feindlicher Luftterror schon seit 1914," August 24, 1944.

San Antonio Register, "Lynchers at Work in Tennessee and Japan," December 1, 1944.

Bakersfield Californian, "Thomas J. Walker," August 29, 1945.

Washington Star, "Execution of 3 Yank Flyers by Japs Revealed," September 26, 1945.

Montgomery Advertiser, "Joseph A. Cox," November 18, 1945.

298 | Bibliography

Galveston Daily News, "A Yank Flyer Learns How His Buddies Were Murdered," December 28, 1945.

Miami News, "He Murdered Two US Fliers," January 22, 1946.

Associated Press, "Families of Slain US Fliers Differ on Verdict for Japs," April 16, 1946.

Townsville Daily Bulletin (Australia), "Jap Cannibals to be Hanged," October 7, 1946.

Fort Worth Star Telegram, "Frank Pinto," January 7, 1949.

Thomas Easton, "A Quiet Honesty Records a World War II Atrocity," *Baltimore Sun*, May 28, 1995.

Thüringer Allgemeine, "Ums Überleben gekämpft: Buchenwald gedenkt alliierter Flieger," April 4, 2014.

Thüringer Allgemeine, "KZ-Gedenken in Weimar: Vier ehemalige Flieger mit dabei," April 10, 2014.

Thüringer Allgemeine, "69. Buchenwald-Gedenkfeier: Vier lebensbejahende Zeugnisse," April 14, 2014.

Thüringer Allgemeine (Erfurt, Germany), "Lost Airmen und Ex-Häftling des KZ Buchenwald erinnert sich," April 16, 2012.

Justin McCurry, "Japan Revisits Its Darkest Moments Where American POWs became Human Experiments," *Guardian*, August 2015.

Kessen, Hermann, "In 45 Tagen Gestapo-Haft den Freund nicht verraten," *Lingener Tagespost* (Lingen, Germany), November 2, 2015.

Magazines

Das Schwarze Korps, http://research.calvin.edu/german-propaganda-archive/index.htm.

Kladderadatsch, Berlin, January 1942–May 1944, http://digi.ub.uni-heidelberg.de/diglit/kla.

Life Magazine, "Picture of the Week," May 22, 1944.

Lustige Blätter, http://research.calvin.edu/german-propaganda-archive/index.htm.

Websites

"Accounts from End of WWII Reveal Divergent Fates of US B-29 Bomber Crews Crashing in Japan," https://mainichi.jp/english/articles/20200819/p2a/00m/0fe/019000c.

"Allied Aircraft and Airmen Lost over the Japanese Mainland," May 20, 2007, Toru Fukubayashi, http://www.powresearch.jp/en/archive/pilot/index.html.

"Boeing B-17 42-97739," http://www.leteckabadatelna.cz/havarie-a-sestrely/detail/523/.

"Capt. Chester E. Coggeshall Jr.," http://www.station131.co.uk/55th/Pilots/343rd%.20Pilots/Coggeshall%20Chester%20E.%20Jr.%20Capt.htm.

"*Children of Nippon*," April 1945; http://www.mansell.com/pow-index.html.

"Cleveland WWII Airman Receives Funeral in Willoughby," *News-Herald*, June 2, 2015, http://www.newsherald.com/article/hr/20150502/NEWS/150509896.

Bibliography | 299

"Crew Photo," https://www.cooksontributeb29.com/z-8-mission-to-albuquerque
.html.

"Das Netz der Gestapo," Haus der Geschichte, Baden-Württemberg, http://www
.geschichtsort-hotel-silber.de/das-netz-der-gestapo/europa/bds-fuer-die
-operationszonen-alpenvorland-und-adriatisches-kuestenland-in-triest/.

"Darwin Thomas Emry," https://www.findagrave.com/memorial/84122071/darwin
-thomas-emry.

David Allen, "Islanders to Honor Three World War II Aviators," *Stars and Stripes*,
April 15, 2005, https://www.stripes.com/news/islanders-to-honor-three-world
-war-ii-aviators-1.31938.

"The Deadliest Air Raid in History," https://www.airspacemag.com/daily-planet
/deadliest-air-raid-history-180954512/.

"Doolittle Raiders in China," https://www.fold3.com/image/29022815, NARA
RG 342, Series FH, Roll 3A02459-3A03299, Reference Number 3A02987
-A25759AC.

"Doolittle Raiders Outside Air Raid Shelter," https://www.fold3.com/image
/29022793, NARA RG 342, Series FH, Roll 3A02459-3A03299, Reference
Number 3A02984-C25758AC.

"Entwicklung der Mannheimer Bevölkerung von 1600 bis 2019," https://www
.marchivum.de/de/stadtgeschichte/mannheim-wissen/bevoelkerungszahlen.

"Extract from interrogation of Hideki Tojo," March 25, 1946, http://www.mansell
.com/pow_resources/Formosa/IMTFE58-350_Tojo_Treatment_of_POWs_1942
-07_1946-03.pdf.

"Farrington Crew," https://449th.com/farrington-crew/.

"Find a Grave," https://www.findagrave.com.

"Flight Lieutenant William Ellis Newton," Photograph 100644, https://www.awm
.gov.au/collection/P10676739.

"Four Doolittle Raiders," https://www.fold3.com/image/29022815, NARA
RG 342, Series FH, Roll 3A02459-3A03299, Reference Number 3A02987
-A25759AC.

"Frederick Allen Stearns," https://www.camptakodah.org/about/history/memorial
-lodge/lost-takodians-world-war-ii/frederick-allen-stearns/; http://macrj.net
/b24-42-94098/.

"Ghost Train," World War Two Escape and Evasion, http://www.conscript-heroes
.com/escapelines/EEIE-Articles/Art-17-Ghost-Train.htm.

"Hardlife Herald: Newsletter of the 358th Bombardment Group Association"
32, no., 3, September 2015, https://www.385thbga.com/wp-content/uploads
/Newsletter-9-15-2.pdf.

"The International Military Tribunal for the Far East," https://imtfe.law.virginia
.edu.

"Justiz und NS-Verbrechen," https://www.expostfacto.nl.

"Lt Col Doolittle," https://www.fold3.com/image/29022797, NARA, RG 342, Series
FH, Roll: 3A02459-3A03299, Reference Number 3A02985-B25758AC.

300 | Bibliography

"Major Cyrus E. Manierre, World War II—Prisoners of War—Stalag Luft I," http://www.merkki.com/manierrecyrus.htm.

"The Man Who Won't Let the World Forget the Firebombing of Tokyo," https://www.nytimes.com/2020/03/09/magazine/the-man-who-wont-let-the-world-forget-the-firebombing-of-tokyo.html.

"Memorial for B-29 #42-63549," http://macrj.net/b29-42-63549/.

"Memorial for Robert J. Aspinall's Crew," http://macrj.net/b29-44-69887/.

"Merlin R. Calvin," https://www.findagrave.com/memorial/56117066/merlin-r.-calvin.

"Mission to Albuquerque," https://www.cooksontributeb29.com/z-8-mission-to-albuquerque.html.

"Niihau Incident," https://en.wikipedia.org/wiki/Niihau_incident#/media/File:Nishikaichi's_Zero_BII-120.jpg.

"Niihau Incident—Benehakaka Kanahele—WWII, Medal for Merit," http://www.hawaiireporter.com/niihau-incident-benehakaka-ben-kanahele-wwii-medal-for-merit-purple-heart-1891-1962/.

"Paper City," https://www.japanairraids.org.

"Remains of Fallen WWII Airman Returned to Family for Burial," *Stars and Stripes,* August 23, 2012, https://www.stripes.com/news/ europe/germany/remains-of-fallen-wwii-airman-returned-to-family-for-burial-1.186673.

"Remains of Pilot Shot Down during WWII to be Buried in NY," CBS News, November 28, 2017, https://www.cbsnews.com/news/robert-mains-pilot-shot-down-wwii-remains-n-y-burial/.

"Robert J. Aspinall," https://www.findagrave.com/memorial/116133594/robert-james-aspinall.

"Robert G. Neal Crew," https://pacificwrecks.com/aircraft/b-25/44-31300/b25j-neal-pose.html.

"Robert Tuggle, Jr.," http://www.shipleybay.com/tuggle.htm.

"Robert Zercher en de bemanning van de Karen B," https://www.apeldoornendeoorlog.nl/achtergronden/robert-zercher-en-de-bemanning-van-de-karen-b.

Roger Freeman Collection, Imperial War Museum, http://www.americanairmuseum.com/.

"The Sandino Rebellion, 1927–1934: October 12, 1927, O'Shea, Engagement at Sapotillal," http://www.sandinorebellion.com/pcdocs/1927/PC271012-OShea.html.

"Stalag Luft I—Prison Camp Graphics," http://www.b24.net/powStoriesLuft1toons.htm.

"Survivors rescued at sea," https://www.fold3.com/image/55702041, NARA, RG 342, Series FH, Roll 3A45218-3A46062.

"The Taiwan POWs," http://www.powtaiwan.org/The%20Men/men_list.php.

"Tuskegee Airman 2LT Manning Remembrance Plaque," https://www.uswarmemorials.org/html/monument_details.php?SiteID=1358&MemID=1776.

"US Propaganda leaflet dropped over Taiwan," https://www.fold3.com/image
/29019486, NARA RG 342, Series FH, Roll 3A02459-3A03299, Reference
Number 3A02892A-27838AC.

"Vivisections at Kyushu Imperial University," http://mansell.com/pow_resources
/camplists/fukuoka/fuk_01_fukuoka/fukuoka_01/Page05.htm#Vivisections.

"Walter Peyton Manning," https://www.findagrave.com/memorial/56657981
/walter-peyton-manning.

"War for Civilians: 1945 Propaganda Leaflet," Pritzker Military Museum and
Library, https://www.pritzkermilitary.org/explore/museum/permanent
-current-upcoming-exhibits/allied-race-victory-air-land-and-sea-ca/warning
-civilians.

"World War II Accounting," https://www.dpaa.mil/Our-Missing/World-War-II/.

"WWII Army Aircrew Laid to Rest," Army News, October 26, 2011, https://www
.army.mil/ article/68064/wwii_army_ aircrew_laid_to_rest.

Index

Air-Ground Aid Section (AGAS)-China, 24

Alte Kämpfer, 27, 132,

Atomic weapons, 1, 9, 89

Australia, 18, 71–75

Austria, 9 60–62, 113, 122, 125–28, 139

Auswertestelle West (*See* Dulag Luft)

Baldwin, Stanley, 12

Balkans (*See* Operation Halyard)

Banana Wars, 10–12

Battle of Britain, 14, 27, 53, 147–49

Belgium, 12, 53, 106–111

Bell, Don, 25

Berchtesgaden, 60

Canada, 55

China, 10, 14–16, 24–25, 35–37, 43, 52, 63–69, 88, 148–49

Combined Bomber Offensive, 56

Czech Republic, 119–23

Dachau trials, 7, 26, 130–34

Doolittle Raid, 14–15, 27, 34–37, 40, 44, 52–55, 135, 147

Douhet, Guilio, 12

Dublon Island, 88

Dulag Luft, 4, 58, 117, 136

Emoto, 84–86

Enemy Airmen's Act, 39–40, 45, 58–59, 94, 99, 135–36

Escape lines, 23–26, 114, 116, 139

Formosa (*See* Taiwan)

France, 12, 23, 53, 111–15

Freilassing, 60–62

Fukuoka, 46–53, 86–88

Gauleiter, 114–15

Gendarmerie, 60, 64, 68–71, 115, 126, 132, 134

Geneva Conventions (1864), 10; (1929), 13–15, 22, 34, 56, 58; (1949), 21

Gestapo, 27, 35, 59, 107–8, 113–19, 127, 132, 146

Goebbels, Joseph, 56, 59, 139, 147

Gross-Gerau, 3–7

Guernica, 14, 148

Hague Conventions, 10–14, 56

Hankow, 63–71

Hell Ships, 9

Himmler, Heinrich, 56

Hirohito, 40

Hitler, Adolf, 19, 55

Hungary, 9, 123–25

Hull, Cordell, 34

Imperial Japanese Navy, 17, 29–30, 75, 133–34

Indonesia, 71–74, 129

International Military Tribunal, 129–30

Italy, 12–15, 27, 42, 104–5, 144, 147–49

Japan Demobilization Ministry, 100

Judge Advocate General, 52, 85, 106, 112, 129, 139

Kangaroo courts, 10, 14, 40–43, 56–58

Kempeitai, 1–3, 20, 35, 40–45, 52, 72–86, 92, 98–102, 133–34, 146

Kharkov, 56

Kobe, 34, 98–101

Korea, 64, 89, 141

Kreisleiter, 5, 60–61, 114–15, 119

Kyushu, 45, 86–89, 137

304 | Index

Lieber Code, 10
Lindbergh, Charles, 15–16, 143, 150
Luftwaffe, 14, 27, 53, 58–59, 109–11, 114, 117, 126–27, 133, 147
Lynching (Lynchjustiz), 4, 7, 9, 16, 21, 28, 56, 126, 130–32, 135

Manchuria, 64, 149
Medical Experiments, 87–89, 132, 137
Memorials, 6, 47–48, 77–78, 91, 128
Military Intelligence Service (MIS-X), 24
Missing Air Crew Reports (MACR), 27
Mitchell, Billy, 12, 29–30
Mussolini, Benito, 16, 105, 147

Nazi Party, 27, 56–59, 113–14, 127, 132–33, 139
Netherlands, The, 12, 53, 117–19
Niihau Island, 29–33
Nuremberg trials, 7–8, 129–30

Oberursel (See Dulag Luft)
Office of Naval Intelligence (ONI), 25
Office of Strategic Services (OSS), 23
Okinawa, 75–78
Okuna Naval Interrogation Center, 89
Omura, 63
Operation Halyard, 23
Ortsgruppenleiter, 60, 123, 126
Osaka, 98–102

Papua New Guinea, 16–18, 111
Pearl Harbor, 14, 21, 27–34, 41, 147
Propaganda (Axis), 7, 16, 22, 28, 35, 53, 56, 58, 67–70, 126, 135, 139, 143, 146; (US), 14, 34, 38–39

Resistance, 23, 55, 75, 108, 117
Roosevelt, Franklin Delano, 7, 41

Royal Air Force (RAF), 8–9, 53–54
Rüsselsheim, 4, 136

Schutzstaffeln (SS), 27, 58, 112–15, 124–25, 146
Sicherheitsdienst (SD), 27, 55–59, 117–19
Sino-American Cooperative Organization (SACO), 24
Sonderbehandlung, 58–59
Sonderkommando, 56
Soviet Union, 8, 14–15, 35, 56, 58, 149–50
Spanish Civil War, 10, 14, 16, 148
Special Operations Executive (SOE), 23
Strategic Bombing, 10, 12, 62, 148, 150
Sturmabteilungen (SA), 27
Sweden, 21
Switzerland, 34

Tachikawa, 1–3
Taiwan, 38, 89–96
Terajuku, 97–98
Tojo, Hideki, 35, 40
Tokyo, 45, 79–83
Treaty of Versailles, 148
Trenchard, Hugh, 12
Tuskegee Airmen, 125

US Graves Registration, 72, 82–85, 103
USS Benevolence, 86
USS Makassar Strait, 75

Vergeltungswaffen, 53

Wehrmacht, 56–59, 124, 127
Wever, Walter, 12
World War One, 9, 12–14, 21

Yawata, 145
Yokohama Trials, 7, 26, 82, 127–37

Kevin T Hall is a postdoctoral researcher at the Ruhr-Universität-Bochum in Germany. He specializes in modern Europe (primarily Germany), United States, and military history. He is the author of *Terror Flyers: The Lynching of American Airmen in Nazi Germany*.

World War II: The Global, Human, and Ethical Dimension
G. Kurt Piehler, *series editor*

Lawrence Cane, David E. Cane, Judy Barrett Litoff, and David C. Smith, eds.,
*Fighting Fascism in Europe: The World War II Letters of an American Veteran
of the Spanish Civil War*
Angelo M. Spinelli and Lewis H. Carlson, *Life behind Barbed Wire: The Secret
World War II Photographs of Prisoner of War Angelo M. Spinelli*
Don Whitehead and John B. Romeiser, *"Beachhead Don": Reporting the War from
the European Theater, 1942–1945*
Scott H. Bennett, ed., *Army GI, Pacifist CO: The World War II Letters of Frank and
Albert Dietrich*
Alexander Jefferson with Lewis H. Carlson, *Red Tail Captured, Red Tail Free:
Memoirs of a Tuskegee Airman and POW*
Jonathan G. Utley, *Going to War with Japan, 1937–1941*
Grant K. Goodman, *America's Japan: The First Year, 1945–1946*
Patricia Kollander with John O'Sullivan, *"I Must Be a Part of This War": One Man's
Fight against Hitler and Nazism*
Judy Barrett Litoff, *An American Heroine in the French Resistance: The Diary and
Memoir of Virginia d'Albert-Lake*
Thomas R. Christofferson and Michael S. Christofferson, *France during World
War II: From Defeat to Liberation*
Don Whitehead, *Combat Reporter: Don Whitehead's World War II Diary and
Memoirs*, edited by John B. Romeiser
James M. Gavin, *The General and His Daughter: The Wartime Letters of
General James M. Gavin to His Daughter Barbara*, edited by Barbara Gavin
Fauntleroy et al.
Carol Adele Kelly, ed., *Voices of My Comrades: America's Reserve Officers
Remember World War II*, foreword by Senators Ted Stevens and Daniel K.
Inouye
John J. Toffey IV, *Jack Toffey's War: A Son's Memoir*
Lt. General James V. Edmundson, *Letters to Lee: From Pearl Harbor to the War's
Final Mission*, edited by Dr. Celia Edmundson
John K. Stutterheim, *The Diary of Prisoner 17326: A Boy's Life in a Japanese Labor
Camp*, foreword by Mark Parillo
G. Kurt Piehler and Sidney Pash, eds., *The United States and the Second World War:
New Perspectives on Diplomacy, War, and the Home Front*
Susan E. Wiant, *Between the Bylines: A Father's Legacy*, Foreword by Walter
Cronkite
Deborah S. Cornelius, *Hungary in World War II: Caught in the Cauldron*
Gilya Gerda Schmidt, *Süssen Is Now Free of Jews: World War II, The Holocaust,
and Rural Judaism*

Emanuel Rota, *A Pact with Vichy: Angelo Tasca from Italian Socialism to French Collaboration*

Panteleymon Anastasakis, *The Church of Greece under Axis Occupation*

Louise DeSalvo, *Chasing Ghosts: A Memoir of a Father, Gone to War*

Alexander Jefferson with Lewis H. Carlson, *Red Tail Captured, Red Tail Free: Memoirs of a Tuskegee Airman and POW, Revised Edition*

Kent Puckett, *War Pictures: Cinema, Violence, and Style in Britain, 1939–1945*

Marisa Escolar, *Allied Encounters: The Gendered Redemption of World War II Italy*

Courtney A. Short, *The Most Vital Question: Race and Identity in the U.S. Occupation of Okinawa, 1945–1946*

James Cassidy, *NBC Goes to War: The Diary of Radio Correspondent James Cassidy from London to the Bulge*, edited by Michael S. Sweeney

Rebecca Schwartz Greene, *Breaking Point: The Ironic Evolution of Psychiatry in World War II*

Franco Baldasso, *Against Redemption: Democracy, Memory, and Literature in Post-Fascist Italy*

G. Kurt Piehler and Ingo Trauschweizer, eds., *Reporting World War II*

CPSIA information can be obtained
at www.ICGtesting.com
Printed in the USA
LVHW012015150723
752503LV00024B/635